GRACE
SALVATION & DISCIPLESHIP

**How to Understand
Some Difficult
Bible Passages**

Charles C. Bing

GRACE
THEOLOGY PRESS

Grace, Salvation, and Discipleship

Published by Grace Theology Press.

All Scripture quotations, unless noted otherwise, are from The Holy Bible, New King James Version © 1982. New King James Version, New Testament and New Testament with Psalms © 1980, 1979 by Thomas Nelson Inc.

Paperback ISBN 10: 996561412
Paperback ISBN 13: 978-0-9965614-1-9
eISBN 10: 996561420
eISBN 13: 978-0-9965614-2-6

Special Sales: Most Grace Theology Press titles are available in special quantity discounts. Custom imprinting or excerpting can also be done to fit special needs. Contact Grace Theology Press at info@gracetheology.org.

Printed in the United States of America

This book is based on a fundamental biblical distinction between justification and sanctification and between salvation and discipleship. Like myself, not everyone will agree with every solution to every biblical difficulty proposed in it. However, it provides helpful light on numerous biblical difficulties that other interpretations do not offer. I have added it to my short list of recommended books on biblical difficulties.

Norman L. Geisler, Ph.D.
Co-founder of Veritas Evangelical Seminary and
Southern Evangelical Seminary

Confusion reigns in many Christians and a number of scholars regarding the absolutely free nature of the good news of Jesus the Messiah. We are justified entirely by the grace of God expressed through Christ's work on the cross and appropriated through faith, but as Christians we are sanctified as we cooperate with the Holy Spirit as He seeks to mature us to conform to the image of Jesus. Charlie Bing, a friend and fellow traveler with me in trying to understand the Word of God better and to teach these truths to others, has produced a simple approach to separating the gospel, by which we become Christians, from discipleship, by which we become more like Christ. He has chosen A Truth and B Truth as labels for explanations regarding these differences. If the reader will carefully read through Charlie's book to discern the difference, he or she will be a step ahead of most in understanding the doctrine of God's grace that makes us redeemed and the grace that is working in us for living by the Holy Spirit.

H. Wayne House, Th.D., J.D.
Distinguished Professor of Theology, Law, and Culture
Faith Evangelical College and Seminary, Tacoma, WA

Difficult Bible passages are just that--difficult to interpret. Unfortunately, many popular interpretations end up neglecting the most important context. This has huge repercussions on our understanding of grace, salvation, and discipleship, as the title indicates. Not everyone will agree with all his interpretations, but Dr. Charles Bing tries to be faithful to the context. This book makes many of these difficult passages much easier to understand. I highly recommend it to Bible students everywhere.

Tony Evans, Th.D.
President, The Urban Alternative
Senior Pastor, Oak Cliff Bible Fellowship, Dallas

Dr. Charles Bing has performed a real service in helping believers see the distinction between justification by faith and commitment to Christ resulting in genuine discipleship. Because of the way many passages are interpreted in this book, many readers will not agree with all of Dr. Bing's explanations, in fact this is a concession the author makes himself. Nevertheless, believers need to be reminded of this important distinction.

Stanley D. Toussaint, Th.D.
Senior Professor Emeritus, Dallas Theological Seminary

Dedication

This book is dedicated to all the Bible teachers, students, and pastors I have met around the world who let God speak for Himself in His Word, make the extra effort to understand what He says, and ask the tough questions when they don't.

Contents

Acknowledgements

I WROTE THIS book in about five years and in a literal world of locations. I am deeply grateful to those who have allowed me to retreat to their "secret" places for solitude and writing: my good friends John O. and Lorraine Oliver, the silence of the New Mexican desert; Jim and Christy Caddock, the inspiration of the Oregon mountains; Peter and Carolyn Bennis, an unbeatable Texas room with a view; Gary and Janine McNally, the rustic north woods of upstate New York; and Dar and Chris Highlen, the opportunity to fish Florida between long periods of writing there. Parts of the book also came together in Ghana (West Africa), Burundi (East Africa), India, and the Philippines while ministering in those places.

No one who writes a book on so many Bible passages can claim sole credit for his or her views. Whatever I offer in this book is because I stand on the shoulders of insightful and godly Bible teachers who have influenced me in both the interpretation and practice of God's Word. I do not mention them by name because there are too many instructors, mentors, and colleagues to thank. But I sincerely thank you all.

I deeply appreciate the support and encouragement from the board of directors and friends of GraceLife Ministries who stand with me in spreading the message of God's grace around the world. I am also grateful to Grace Theology Press for the competent help of their staff and editors. But special thanks goes to David Anderson and Fred Chay who worked with me to make this book fair, clear, and biblically faithful. We all share a common love for God's Word and the gospel of His grace.

A special recognition goes to a great source of my inspiration, my mother, Beulah Bing. She tolerated a lot of this writing during my occasional visits with her in Virginia. At age 92 I am sure she will download the electronic version (when it is available) on her tablet device where she does her voluminous reading. At my side figuratively and prayerfully throughout this time while enduring my frequent absences is the love of my life, my wife for over 36 years, Karen.

Finally, and most importantly, I give thanks to the Alpha and Omega, my All in All, the Lord Jesus Christ, who saved me by His grace and gave me true life. To Him be the glory.

Foreword

THOSE OF US that were privileged to sit under the ministry of the inimitable Howard Hendricks walked out into the world with a smattering of his sayings tucked into our minds. One of them was: "Gentlemen, Satan never fogs in the area of the trivial; it is always in the area of the crucial. And there is no more crucial area than the relationship between faith and works." How true. Even one of the most quoted passages on salvation (Eph. 2:8-10) says we were not saved by works, but we were saved for works. Faith and works can't seem to get out of their own shadows. Another well-known passage (Jas. 2:14-26) appears to say that faith alone cannot save us; we must also have works. That one drives some Protestants like Luther into spiritual apoplexy since other passages like Romans 4:1-5 say we cannot be justified by works. Faith plus works is not a problem for the Catholic world since the Council of Trent declared that anyone saying works were not meritorious for entrance to heaven was anathema.[1] Many Protestants solved the riddle of faith plus works for entrance to heaven by simply saying that works are merely evidence of true, saving faith. Faith without works is a spurious faith, completely insufficient for salvation, they would charge.

Grace, Salvation, and Discipleship by Charlie Bing does a wonderful job of trying to unravel some of these Gordian knots of theological discussion. In doing so he employs a wonderful and, it appears to me, completely unique device previously unemployed by the pundits of historical theology: A Truth B Truth. By categorizing various passages as A Truth or B Truth, Dr. Bing helps us realize the difference between justification truth (A) and sanctification truth (B), our Position in heavenly places (A Truth) and our Condition on earth (B Truth), our Relationship with God (A Truth) and our

---

1   Council of Trent, Canon 24.

Fellowship with God (B Truth), eternal judgment (A truth) and temporal judgment (B Truth), God's gifts (A Truth) and God's rewards (B Truth), and so on.

Martin Luther was trying to do the same thing when he said, "*Simul iustus et peccator*": At the same time (*simul*) I am justified (*iustus*—A truth) and a sinner (*peccator*—B truth). In heaven I am seen as fully just or justified in my *position* in Christ (A Truth), but in my *condition* on earth (B Truth) I am still a sinner or sinful—both at the same time. A Truth B Truth. Luther was trying to sort out the categories. Yes, some passages are about the *way* (A Truth), but other passages are about the *walk* (B Truth). Dr. Bing helps us recognize these categories passage by passage.

An especially helpful aspect of this book is Dr. Bing's fair treatment of each passage in the sense that he looks at each through the lenses of A Truth and B Truth respectively. In other words, he takes a passage like Matthew 16:24-27 and interprets it through the eyes of A Truth and the eyes of B Truth. An A Truth perspective would say this passage is about how to go to heaven; a B Truth perspective would say this passage is about something dealing with the Christian life today that will affect future rewards tomorrow.

In some cases, a passage might have two or even three A Truth interpretations, each a viable option dealing with entrance to heaven or loss thereof. But sometimes there is also more than one B Truth interpretation. Dr. Bing presents the most popular options in each category (A Truth and B Truth). Then he explains why he prefers one of these options. And he does so without depreciating others that would select an option different from his favorite. Furthermore, he does not duck any difficult passage. In fact, he traverses the entire New Testament dealing with practically all the difficult passages and brings each into a clearer focus by refracting the verses through the lenses of A Truth B Truth.

Finally, Dr. Bing does what so many scholars fail to do. He "brings the cookies down to the lower shelf" (to close with another saying of Howard Hendricks). He also tells us how a clear distinction between A Truth and B Truth can help us in our ministries and our daily lives.

The reader will find *Grace, Salvation, and Discipleship* very helpful for understanding his or her Bible and thus understanding more clearly how to enter into and live the Christian life.

David Anderson, Ph.D.
President and Professor of Biblical Languages and Systematic Theology
Grace School of Theology, Woodlands, TX

Introduction

I MAY SEEM obsessed or arrogant, but I just can't get over the fact that most people don't seem to agree on the gospel and what it means to be a disciple of Jesus Christ. We might expect that of those who are not Christians, but many *Christians* don't agree with one another or hold differing views about these subjects. Many other Christians don't see any issues or don't care. To them I might appear both obsessed *and* arrogant. I guess I see the gospel and discipleship as two important things a person should understand clearly. Craig's email typifies the confusion many people encounter in trying to understand the gospel:

> Hey Dr. Bing, I love reading your articles/notes and I even purchased/ read your book *Simply by Grace*.... However, I am still very concerned with some passages in the Bible that seem contrary to the freeness of God's salvation and grace by faith ALONE. This troubles me so much that I have absolutely no assurance of my salvation nor do I even know how to get salvation if I were to discover I didn't have it. There are so many different versions of "how to get saved" out there that it leaves people confused like myself. Anyways, the problems I have with this free grace theology lie within the teaching and parables of Jesus found in Matthew, Mark, and Luke. (John's whole book basically supports the free grace position of salvation by grace through faith alone without any attachments.) However, in the 3 synoptic gospels ... we see something totally different. We see Jesus telling people how hard it is to get saved, enter the kingdom, and remain in the kingdom, etc. We see parables such as the 10 virgins where if we don't have lanterns lit, we are out of luck in entering the banquet feast. Many parables Jesus spoke about referred

to being obedient and doing good deeds in order to "get into the kingdom." Of course, this "getting into the kingdom/heaven" was mostly portrayed as being invited and entering a feast, wedding festival, etc.…. It seems that there are SEVERAL ways that achieving salvation is presented in the New Testament. The synoptic gospels portray Jesus' parables and teachings concerning obtaining salvation as experiencing and making lifestyle changes, good deeds, and obedience to His Lordship. John's gospel focuses on Jesus' deity and the idea that to be saved one must believe Jesus is God, etc. And then we have Paul who is different than both of them with this idea that to be saved you must believe in a resurrected Christ, and that belief alone (without any works) is what saves you due to God's grace. I am very very confused. On top of that, we have passages in 1 John that seem to show that if we sin then we are not saved, or if we hate our brother, we aren't saved.… Can you please help me? Craig

This book is an attempt to help Craig and others like him understand the Scriptures, the gospel, and discipleship. But in doing so, I hope to make a genuine contribution to something dear to all Christians and others who want to understand the Bible. It seems the main source of confusion about salvation and the gospel is the misinterpretation of New Testament passages that either speak about salvation or seem to speak about salvation. Too often a singular approach is used that lumps Bible passages indiscriminately together to produce a muddling jumble of sometimes contradicting conditions for how to be saved. I believe the Bible teaches clearly that we are saved by grace alone through faith alone in Jesus Christ alone. The tragedy of misinterpreting many Bible passages is that the gospel of grace is perverted while enriching truths about the Christian life in such passages are neglected. Let God speak in veiled form about the end times, but let Him be clear about our salvation!

I want to demonstrate a consistent approach to the Scriptures that equips people to discern the meaning of a passage for themselves. I don't want to call it a *method*. For lack of the perfect word, I call it an *approach*. But there are no secret formulas in this approach. I'm just advocating good principles of Bible study to yield the best interpretation. Neither are my interpretations unique. You will find others who have taught or written about them. What I hope to show is a consistent approach that you can use to see (or test) these interpretations.

My purpose is not to exhaust the exegesis or explanation of the selected Bible passages, but to show enough evidence to convince readers that there is another interpretive option than the one many assume. (I have more detailed explanations for many of these passages elsewhere.[2]) I am hoping to show a key but neglected distinction in the interpretations of what we might call difficult or "problem passages" about salvation and the Christian life. Also, I want to show the process used to get the most accurate interpretation. I purposely do not distract you with footnotes citing other commentators because I want you to see how the Bible interprets itself when context is emphasized.

Even some who are closest to me theologically will not agree with me on every interpretation. That's fine and expected—as long as they see the main distinction I am trying to make. If their interpretation helps keep the gospel of grace free and clear, then I applaud them. The interpretations I offer represent my convictions so far, and some are held more firmly than others, but I am always open to making them more consistent with the witness of Scripture. I'm sure good Bible students everywhere will be happy to suggest improvements that will make these interpretations better!

The reader should know that I am using the term *discipleship* to refer to issues of the Christian life. From the word that means *to become a learner (mathēteuō)*[3], a *disciple* is someone who is saved and in a learning or growing posture in relationship to Jesus Christ. There is a range of degrees of commitment covered by the biblical use of the term, from those who simply followed Jesus in the crowd to those who lived daily with Him, such as the Twelve. I am using the term to describe the Christian's life and responsibilities after salvation, that is, truth written to or for Christians.

I realize there are some who think that *disciple* is just a synonym for *Christian*. If you read through this book, you will see why I disagree. A Christian is someone who believes in Jesus Christ as the Son of God who

---

2   Bing, Charles C., "Does First John Tell Us How to Know We Are Saved?" in *21 Tough Questions about* Grace (Allen, TX: Bold Grace Ministries, 2015), pp. 203-213; Lordship *Salvation: A Biblical Evaluation and Response,* 2nd GraceLife Edition (Burleson, TX: Xulon Press, 2014); and the articles and *GraceNotes* at gracelife.org.

3   Throughout the book, the primary source for definitions of Greek words is Arndt, W.; Danker, F. W.; and Bauer, W. A., *A Greek-English Lexicon of the New Testament and Other Early Christians Literature* (Chicago: University of Chicago Press, 2000).

died for sins, rose again, and guarantees eternal salvation. (Sometimes I use shortcuts in my language to describe salvation or Christians such as "those who believe in Christ," but now you know what I mean). A disciple is someone committed to following Jesus Christ and learning from Him. Every Christian should be a committed and growing disciple, but not all are. The distinction is important, because when missed, it creates confusion about the gospel, loss of assurance, and crippling of both evangelistic and church ministries. Here is a simple comparison that shows the distinction I am making between a Christian and a disciple.

Christian	Disciple
Saved	Following
Has been justified	Is being sanctified
Spiritual birth	Spiritual growth
Free	Costly
Believes in Christ as Savior	Submits to Christ as Master
A Truth	**B Truth**

Understanding this distinction is crucial to understanding the Bible. Now here's what you need to know as you read this book: *I refer to the left column as A Truth and the right column as B Truth.* It's a simple way of making a very important distinction. I first heard this distinction expressed in a similar way by my friend, Dr. David Anderson, and have since used it in teaching around the world. Just as it made an impression on me, I invariably get an enthusiastic response from my audiences. So, I thank Dave for planting the seed.

I cannot discuss every word, phrase, and passage that touches on the distinction between salvation and discipleship, nor can I exhaust the exegesis of every passage I cover. My goal is to deal with the word or passage to the extent that we can clearly distinguish whether it is used in the context of salvation or discipleship, that is, whether it is A Truth or B Truth.

There's one more thing to note before we go on. Based on my understanding of the gospel and its essential tenet of salvation by grace alone through faith alone, I believe that those who have believed in Christ are eternally secure. It's as simple as this: If there is nothing one can do to earn salvation, then there is nothing one can do to lose salvation. That is what grace is all about. It is never earned or deserved, and it makes no conditions on its promise of eternal life to all who believe in Christ. Of course, I could also make a lengthy biblical argument as I have done elsewhere.[4] So this book will assume a position that salvation is secure. But I hope this does not discourage those who do not agree with me from reading this book. In fact, the A Truth B Truth approach will many times deal directly with passages that seem to say salvation can be lost. And if you think that eternal security encourages believers to sin, then you definitely need to read some of the interpretations in this book. Many of the passages I deal with involve the serious consequences for believers in disobedience.

---

4   See Appendix 1: Eternal Security.

1 Understanding the A Truth B Truth Distinction

Why Seeing Distinctions in the New Testament is Important

1

S MALL DISTINCTIONS CAN make a big difference. Consider the difference a letter can make: The letter "a" turns a *theist* into an *atheist*, and someone who is *moral* into someone who is not, or *amoral*. Writers know that a simple word can make a big difference. Mark Twain said, "The difference between the right word and the almost right word is the difference between lightning and a lightning bug."[5]

When it comes to understanding the Bible, some authors highlight crucial distinctions. Paul sees the difference between the plural and the singular use of a word to argue for the prophetic anticipation of Jesus Christ:

> *Now to Abraham and his Seed were the promises made. He does not say, "And to seeds," as of many, but as of one, 'And to your Seed,' who is Christ." (Gal. 3:16)*

The author of Hebrews bases his argument for the replacement of the Mosaic Covenant by the New Covenant with just one word:

> *In that He says, "A new covenant," He has made the first obsolete. Now what is becoming obsolete and growing old is ready to vanish away." (Hebrews 8:13)*

It is crucial to see the difference even a word makes, whether it is at the level of one word, one verse, an entire pericope (a set of passages), or a whole book.

---

5   Letter to George Bainton, October 15, 1888.

Confusion from assumptions without distinctions

Most of us have been around Christian influences so long, we are prone to careless assumptions. For example, perhaps you've heard a Christian say, "The Bible was written to tell us how to be saved." On its face, this seems an acceptable statement. But is it really accurate? Who is meant by "us"? If "us" is Christians, then we are already saved. It also assumes that the meaning of the word "saved" is saved from hell. But surely, the Bible was written to tell us Christians much more than that, and as we shall see, it uses the word "saved" in different ways.

Since we will be discussing many New Testament passages later, let's look at an Old Testament example to see that distinctions are important there also. Perhaps you have heard someone cite Ezekiel 18:4 as a warning against sinning and going to hell: "The soul that sins, it will die." But was Ezekiel speaking an evangelistic message to unbelievers, or might he have been speaking to believers—at least to God's people, the Jews? If he is speaking to unbelievers, is he stating that sinful acts will send them to hell? If he is speaking to God's people, what does he mean by the warning? In the context, is Ezekiel using "die" to describe eternal death, or physical death as a consequence of breaking the Mosaic Law? A proper interpretation of this passage demands observations that begin with the overall context and end with each word. In this example, the context shows God is warning individuals in Israel that they will be held accountable for their own sins - not for the sins of their fathers. Physical death was the penalty for the severe disobedience and idolatry mentioned in the context. So it is very confusing to use this of unbelievers or believers who sin today (as all do sin).

The Protestant Reformation began when a German Roman Catholic monk named Martin Luther discovered the distinction between forensic justification and progressive sanctification in the Epistle to the Romans. Again, distinctions are important.

It is unfortunate that a failure to notice valid distinctions in the Bible has resulted in distorted views of the gospel, loss of assurance, legalism, and the view that Christians can lose their salvation. It is very serious because an unclear or incorrect gospel message will keep people from eternal salvation. It is also tragic how Christians have divided over some of these issues. Consider the ongoing divide between Calvinists and Arminians, amillennialists and premillennialists, Covenant theologians and dispensationalists, Lordship Salvationists and Free Grace adherents.

Another regrettable consequence of failing to discern A Truth and B

Truth in Bible interpretation is that the rich fullness of scriptural teaching on the Christian life is neglected. Without A Truth B Truth distinctions, it is easy to ignore the many passages on Christian accountability, rewards, and intimate fellowship with God. The consequences are both temporal and eternal in nature.

My own observation of the distinction between A Truth and B Truth led me to a Free Grace view of the gospel and the Christian life.[6] People have asked me when I "converted" to the Free Grace position. I tell them there was no conversion, nor do I remember coming under the influence of anyone who radically changed my mind. From the time I became a Christian as a young man, I simply wanted to know what God says in His Word. I pursued that goal first on my own, then through Bible college and seminary. Left to speak for itself, the Bible just sorted itself out into certain truths and distinctions that made sense.

My goal is to go beyond theological constructs, traditional beliefs, historical assumptions, and straw man arguments, and with honesty before God see what the Scriptures say. I realize that identifying myself as Free Grace at the outset will prejudice some readers, revive certain falsehoods, or cause some to set the book down and not read it at all. There are many false notions about those who hold the Free Grace position. We are accused of being antinomian, promoting easy-believism, providing license to sin, and ignoring the lordship of Christ. All these accusations are wrong, as are the other canards and ad hominem attacks that seek to stigmatize the Free Grace position. So I ask that you read with prayerful discernment and an open mind, giving me the benefit of any doubt that I want to know what the Scriptures say, not prop up a theological system. If you are not persuaded by my approach and interpretations, at least you will have an informed and intelligent understanding of how someone from a Free Grace perspective approaches difficult Bible passages. I hope you will at least be persuaded that those of a Free Grace perspective try to deal honestly with the biblical text, and respectfully give them due credit for that.

Interpretations make a difference

We all have opinions about interpretations of Bible passages. I respect considered opinions much more than adopted opinions. Which honors

---

6   See Appendix 2: What Is Free Grace Theology?

God the most? In Acts 17:10-11 the Bereans were commended for taking what Paul taught them and doing their own personal investigation of the Scriptures to see if it was true. I respect that attitude toward God's Word.

One good test of biblical interpretation is cohesiveness. Is there consistency and lack of conflict or contradiction with other passages? We all seek a harmony of scriptural teaching. It should make us squirm when someone says that the Old Testament contradicts the New, Jesus contradicts Paul, Paul contradicts James, or the Synoptics (Matthew, Mark, and Luke) contradict John. Can we really live with that tension? Not me! A cannot equal non-A, or shall we say, A cannot equal B, especially in God's Word.

Most of all, we all strive for life change in ourselves and in others with whom we have influence. The Bible was not written to make us knowledgeable or clever, but to transform us into the image of Jesus Christ. For many of the passages I discuss in this book, one's perspective will make a difference in everyday Christian experience. I have talked or communicated with many people who are living their lives with daily fear and doubts about whether they have eternal life or not. They do not have assurance that they are going to heaven when they die.

This eventually leads to the whole issue of motivation, which I will discuss in Chapter 12. There are several motivations for living a godly life. Fear is one of them, but it does not deserve to be at the top of the list. Living for God out of love and gratitude would be more pleasing to God and satisfying for us. Any parent can identify with this. Would you rather have your child obey because he loves you and is grateful for you, or only because he fears your threatening consequences? And which child would be most happy and fulfilled, the one full of love and gratitude or the one full of fear? The answer is obvious, but so many Christians miss it and live in fear. The Christian life can be driven by performance that either leaves one proud of what has been done or not done, or leaves one wondering if enough has been done. Grace does away with fear and uncertainty. It puts the impetus on God's performance, not ours. The A Truth B Truth approach is essential to helping us stay consistent with God's free grace and a godly motivation.

It doesn't take much encouragement to stray toward a performance basis of measuring spirituality. Legalism is in our spiritual DNA. Note how often the Apostle Paul fought it in the New Testament in the early church (e.g. Acts 15, Romans, Galatians, Philippians, Colossians).

Differences in interpretation

I admit the difficulty of interpreting many Bible passages. To some degree, we are all skewed in our interpretations by theological presuppositions and influences. But many times, Christians simply perpetuate a theological, traditional, or popular interpretation of a passage even though it is not consistent with the context or other biblical truths.

In my decades of teaching from the Bible on salvation and discipleship issues, I have interacted with many different interpretations on many New Testament passages. I have come to expect certain questions, which prompted me to publish *GraceNotes* online as a resource.[7] In this book, I address many of the passages that raise questions. I present alternate interpretations that I disagree with, enabling you to see the important differences in how one approaches a problem passage. I do not try to explain the interpretations of others, but focus on explaining passages with good Bible study methods.

There are disagreements about some interpretations—sometimes passionate disagreements—but that is no cause to be unfair or mean-spirited. We are often too quick to label those with whom we disagree as "false teachers" or "heretics." The New Testament authors reserve the terms "false prophets" or "false teachers" for those who are maliciously undermining God's truth with blatant heresies. The New Testament only uses the term "false teachers" (*psuedodidaskaloi*) once where they are equated with the obviously unsaved "false prophets" who teach "heresies" (2 Pet. 2:1). I do not think the terms "false teacher" or "heretic" in the biblical sense are deserved by any sincere Christian who holds a well-intentioned but erroneous interpretation of a Bible passage. Otherwise, I think we would all be false teachers teaching heresy, because we all differ in our interpretations of passages. The prolific Bible teacher Apollos needed to be corrected by Priscilla and Aquila, associates of the Apostle Paul, but he was not previously considered a false teacher. He simply taught inaccurately and was open to correction (Acts 18:26). This does not mean that a sincere well-intentioned Christian teacher cannot be disastrously wrong and do severe damage to other Christians. This kind of teaching we want to correct, in the spirit of Priscilla and Aquila. *"And a servant of the Lord must not quarrel but be gentle to all, able to teach, patient, in humility correcting those who are in opposition, if God perhaps will grant them repentance, so that they may know the truth" (2 Tim. 2:24-25).*

---

7   GraceLife.org/GraceNotes.

In this book, I could cite other authors or Bible commentators who agree or disagree with my interpretation of almost every passage discussed. However, I have restrained myself from the tediousness of citing others. I want the reader to see that given the chance, with good observations of the context and content, these difficult Bible passages will generally interpret themselves. But the reader deserves to know that the various interpretations I mention are held by well-known and influential Bible teachers.[8] Let me be clear that I am not trying to attack or be abrasive and inflammatory. My goal is an open and honest investigation of the Bible and how to handle it.

Unless we know otherwise, we should assume good motives of all sincere Bible teachers. We all want to preach the gospel clearly and produce Christlike Christians. We all recognize the problem of worldliness and carnality in our churches, whatever label identifies them. I believe the solution is not to move toward legalism that dictates behavior, or to load the gospel with conditions to fulfill, but to move toward God's love and grace as motivations to live godly. The solution is not to require more outward performance, but to lavish God's love and grace to effect an inner change first. Performance-based religion gives comfort to some believers. It allows them to measure and pass judgment on the spirituality of others, usually in comparison to their own. But of course, everyone's ideas differ on the biblical

---

8   In my observation, the better-known authors and commentators who consistently fail to distinguish between A Truth and B Truth are from different theological backgrounds, but many are from either an Arminian or Reformed Calvinistic background. Examples include: Darrell Bock, James Montgomery Boice, F. F. Bruce, Ardel B. Caneday, D. A. Carson, Michael Deaver, Kenneth L. Gentry, Wayne Grudem, Michael Horton, Tim Keller, Andreas Kostenberger, John MacArthur, Jr., Scott McKnight, I. Howard Marshall, Leon Morris, Peter O'Brien, Grant Osborn, John Piper, Thomas R. Schreiner, Allen P. Stanley, John R. W. Stott, Robert Yarbrough, and Ben Witherington III.

Those who seem to consistently distinguish A Truth from B Truth include some who call themselves Reformed Calvinists, moderate Calvinists, or merely Biblicists. Examples include: David Anderson, Lewis Sperry Chafer, Thomas Constable, Joseph Dillow, Michael A. Eaton, Tony Evans, Zane C. Hodges, R. T. Kendall, G. H. Lang, R. Larry Moyer, Robert P. Lightner, Dwight Pentecost, Earl Radmacher, Charles C. Ryrie, Charles Swindoll, and Robert N. Wilkin.

Let me be absolutely clear that I speak in generalities. I do not disagree on all Bible interpretations of the first group, nor do I always agree with the second group. I am only saying that in general, one can count on these authors to show a pattern of either mixing A Truth and B Truth, or distinguishing the two.

standards of behavior that prove salvation or spirituality. Yet somehow the performance-based legalist always seems to arrange the rules so that he comes out ahead of the one being judged.

Toward a better understanding of Scripture

In my many years of answering questions about difficult or controversial Bible passages related to salvation (or thought to relate to salvation) and discipleship, I began to notice that most misunderstandings came mainly from the following errors: 1) Ignoring basic Bible study rules, especially those having to do with the plain sense of the language and the context; 2) Holding a theological bias, like assuming unsupported definitions for important words or resorting to careless proof-texting (i.e. citing Bible references authoritatively but not appropriately, as if the meaning should be taken for granted); 3) Tradition—holding a view that Christians have historically believed about this subject or Bible passage; 4) Parroting a respected teacher without a strong personal conviction based on firsthand study of the Bible's teaching.

Let's all admit that we are biased in our interpretation, but the final test is what the Scriptures say when interpreted properly. I am willing to modify my interpretations. But there are some biblical truths that are so overwhelmingly clear that I cannot easily become convinced otherwise. For example, I am convinced of the deity and humanity of Jesus Christ, and also the sufficiency of His death and resurrection on behalf of all people. I am convinced of the freeness of God's grace in salvation, that is, our salvation requires no human works, performance, or merit. Therefore, I am also convinced about the security of salvation. These things are just too clear.

We all should have one goal—to understand and accurately reflect what God has said. I assume this of others, and I would hope that others give me the same benefit of any doubt. At the same time, I encourage readers to verify my interpretations with their own study of the Scriptures. Since the Bereans were commended for verifying the apostle Paul's teaching with their own examination of the Scriptures (Acts 17:10-11), I strongly recommend the same for my interpretations.

We must give God's Word preeminence over any of our prejudices. Traditions die hard, and changing perspectives is not easy. Our commitment level has to outweigh our comfort level. In other words, we are committed to God and His truth more than any agenda, theology, tradition, teacher, pastor, or friend. Sacred cows make delicious hamburgers!

This book offers an approach to many New Testament passages on salvation and discipleship that will help distinguish between the two. I am eager to explain this because I have seen the enthusiasm of those who have heard it and grasped it. I will emphatically state that *learning to see the distinction between salvation and discipleship in the Bible is the one thing that most helps people understand the Bible, especially the New Testament, when it speaks on salvation or the responsibilities of the Christian life.* It has been a life-changing discovery for many.

Speaking of the distinction between salvation and discipleship, Charles C. Ryrie has said, "No distinction is more vital to theology, more basic to a correct understanding of the New Testament, or more relevant to every believer's life and witness."[9] I couldn't agree more or say it any better!

---

9   Charles C. Ryrie in Zane C. Hodges, *The Hungry Inherit: Winning the Wealth of the World to Come*, 3rd Edition (Dallas, TX: Redención Viva, 1997), p. 7.

The A Truth B Truth Distinction Explained

D ON'T PUT DIESEL fuel in a gasoline engine. Both are fuel, but they are distinctly different. Ignore the difference and disaster results. There are important distinctions in the Bible that can only be ignored with dire consequences.

A basic law of logic is called the Law of Non-contradiction. It states that contradictory statements cannot both be true in the same sense. For example, if the statement "A is B" is true, then the statement "A is not B" cannot be true. The statements are mutually exclusive. Two things or statements can be related, but have distinctions that give them identity and prevent them from being confused with another. For example, a man and woman are related in that both are human, but in the end, a man is not a woman. I think we all agree that this distinction is crucial!

In the same way, but with greater importance, it is necessary to make proper distinctions when interpreting the Bible. These distinctions are sometimes apparent. For example, Christians generally no longer follow the dietary regulations of Leviticus. Most recognize a difference between life under Moses and life under Jesus Christ, so we are free to eat pork, catfish, and shrimp—things that were forbidden under the Law of Moses. We know there is a difference between the Old Testament and the New Testament.

The A Truth B Truth principle is simply that all the passages of the Bible can properly be divided into those that concern people who are unsaved, or unbelievers, and those that concern people who are saved, or believers. Some passages may have a general application to both groups, but usually those are actually addressed to one or the other group. For example, the book of Proverbs contains wisdom for all people and even contains proverbs found in other ancient cultures, but the book was originally part of the Hebrew collection of Scriptures for God's chosen people, the Jews.

When the A Truth B Truth approach is applied to our interpretation of the Bible, we begin to see important distinctions. Below are some of those important distinctions. These distinctions arise from our discussion of key Bible passages in the rest of this book, so we will not treat the passages in detail here.

Salvation (A) is not Discipleship (B)

This distinction is the basis of this book. It is the difference between how we become a Christian and how we live as a Christian. The Bible addresses each issue distinctly.

Everyone who believes in Jesus Christ as Savior is a Christian, but not everyone who believes in Jesus Christ is a disciple. The two words mean different things. By definition, a Christian, or a believer, is someone who has believed in Jesus Christ as Savior. A disciple, by definition, is a learner or follower of Jesus Christ as Master. To believe in Jesus as Savior from sin is A Truth. To learn from and follow Jesus as Lord of one's life is B Truth.

This couldn't be clearer than in John 8:30-31 where Jesus tells those who have already believed in Him how they can become disciples—by abiding in His word:

As He spoke these words, many believed in Him. Then Jesus said to those who believed in Him, "If you abide in My word, you are My disciples indeed."

Abide does not mean *believe*. It means to *remain, continue in, adhere* closely to something, specifically here, to God's Word. Unless one argues that believe does not really mean believe here (in which case the burden of proof is on that person), then believing for eternal life is distinct from abiding in God's Word as disciples.

If we were to make abiding equivalent to believing, think of the implications for eternal salvation. No one could be saved unless he or she continues in God's Word, which implies progressive obedience. At what point would that person be able to say with certainty that he or she is sure of their salvation? Again, works encroach upon God's free grace, creating a false legalistic gospel and stealing the assurance of salvation.

Faith (A) is not Works (B)

Properly speaking, faith is a passive response to a proposition or a person. In other words, it does not involve any action by the one who believes. Faith is the persuasion or inner conviction that something is true and trustworthy. There is no action involved when I believe something is true. I believe the law of gravity, but I don't need to do anything to believe it. I may show evidence that I believe it when I try to jump over a fence, but even if I don't try, I still believe in gravity. Believing and jumping are distinctly different things. There is certainly a vital relationship between believing and obeying, but to be theologically precise, they are different things. That is why Paul says in Romans 4:5, "But to him who does not work but believes on Him who justifies, his faith is accounted for righteousness." He makes it as clear as possible that works and faith are distinct and different. He is not saying that when a person believes they will not have works. He expects them to have good works (Eph. 2:10).

Some claim that faith is the same as obedience. This is probably because the two ideas are associated closely in Scripture. For example, what has confused some is the phrase "obedience of faith" found in Romans 1:5 and 16:26. This is not saying that those who believe obey all things, but this speaks of one's response—believing in the gospel, which is an act of obedience. The gospel contains no list of things to do to be saved. In Romans, Paul argues strongly against that idea in the key chapters on justification, chapters 3 and 4, where he does not speak of obedience but faith. Of course, faith in Christ as Savior is expected to bring obedience to God's will. But the response of faith is distinct from the act of obedience. Faith and action are closely related in Hebrews 11 where we are given a long list of people of whom it is said "By faith…" followed by some action based on that faith. But the key here is seeing that though the action is related to faith and springs from it, it is distinct from faith itself. A Truth (faith) is related to B Truth (works), but A is not B.

Grace (A) is not Merit (B)

The nature of grace is that it is undeserved favor. Undeserved means that nothing can be done to earn or merit grace. We call this free grace or unconditional grace. Romans 11:6 could not be clearer: "And if by grace, then it is no longer works; otherwise grace is no longer grace. But if it is of works, it is no longer grace; otherwise work is no longer work." You see that the A Truth of grace is mutually exclusive of the B Truth of works. The presence of one negates the other. The moment one tries to earn grace, it ceases to be grace.

In relation to the gospel, there are some who speak of a *cheap grace* or a *costly grace*. If we understand the real nature of grace, neither can be true. It is not cheap or costly. The grace that saves us is absolutely free. *Cheap* implies not enough has been done to earn it or too little commitment is shown to deserve it. *Costly* implies the opposite—that a high price must be paid for grace through personal commitment, surrender, or obedience. But the moment we attach any price to grace, it ceases to be grace. The reason we have to use the redundant term *free grace* is for the sake of emphasis and clarity.

When it relates to our eternal salvation, grace must be kept absolutely unpolluted by personal works or merit. When works are introduced we have a false gospel, a legalistic gospel. Suddenly simple faith in Jesus Christ becomes a complex and subjective system of performance that can never give the believer assurance of salvation.

Justification (A) is not Sanctification (B)

Justification is the act of God that declares a sinner righteous in God's sight. It is a legal term that speaks of one's right standing in God's court of justice. On the other hand, sanctification (as it is usually used) refers to a process of growth. To sanctify something means to set it apart. When a person is sanctified, he is set apart to God first positionally when he is justified, then progressively as he grows in faith and in Christ. The latter is the most common understanding of sanctification and how it is used here.

Consider Romans 5:9-10:

> *Much more then, having now been justified by His blood, we shall be saved from wrath through Him. For if when we were enemies we were reconciled to God through the death of His Son, much more, having been reconciled, we shall be saved by His life.*

The salvation of justification is distinct from the salvation of sanctification. The former saves us from the penalty of sin once for all. The latter saves us from the power of sin in a lifetime process as Christ lives through us.

This simple chart helps us understand the distinctions.

Justification (A)	Sanctification (B)
One-time event	Lifetime process
Spiritual birth	Spiritual growth
Faith in Christ as Savior	Obedience to Christ as Lord
Placed into Christ	Transformed into Christlikeness
One condition	Many conditions
What God did for me	What God is doing through me
Christ died on the cross for me	I take up the cross for Christ
Saved from the penalty of sin	Saved from the power of sin

There are some who believe that justification happens in two stages, initial justification and final justification. In other words, a person can believe in Jesus Christ and be provisionally justified, but must prove their justification by persevering in faith and good works until the end of life in order to be finally justified. Sometimes language such as "already but not yet" is used to describe their view of two justifications. One is already justified upon belief, but not yet finally justified for eternity.

Though clever arguments have been offered in support, on the face of it this makes no sense. How can something *be,* yet *not be?* That violates the Law of Non-contradiction and the A Truth B Truth principle. If one is supposedly justified (A Truth), but does not prove it by persevering in faith and good works (B Truth sanctification), then that person was never justified at all. There was no justification "already" and there will be no "final" justification. Never does the Bible bifurcate justification into two events. It says that all who are justified will be glorified (Rom. 8:29).

The Bible distinguishes justification from sanctification with good reason. To confuse them is to inject the many principles of Christian growth into the one requirement for salvation—faith in Christ as Savior. It makes it impossible to know for certain that anyone is saved since sanctification is a lifetime process. It contradicts the unconditional gospel of grace with conditional requirements related to spiritual growth.

Spiritual Birth (A) is not Spiritual Growth (B)

The reality of spiritual birth and growth is another way of communicating the important distinction between justification and sanctification. Instead of legal terminology, life experience is the framework of understanding. Just as a person has a moment of physical birth and a lifetime of growth, so it is spiritually. One is born from above by God, then grows in relationship to God and in spiritual maturity. One results in the other, but they are distinct events, just as the event of a baby's birth is distinct from its subsequent growth.

The Bible presents the A Truth of spiritual birth as a new birth or being born again (literally, *from above*). In John 3:3, Jesus says, "Most assuredly, I say to you, unless one is born again, he cannot see the kingdom of God." Titus 3:5 calls this birth "the washing of regeneration and renewing of the Holy Spirit" and says it is "not by works of righteousness which we have done, but according to His mercy He saved us." Our works have no part in our new birth.

After spiritual birth, the Bible then presents the B Truth of a new life that must grow, which does involve works and obedience. It speaks of stages of spiritual development or progress. There are Christians who are "babes in Christ" (1 Cor. 3:1-2), those who have not grown enough to receive the "meat" of deeper truths (Heb. 5:11-13), and those who are mature (Heb. 5:14). First Peter 1:22-23 mentions them in reverse order showing that obedience and love is the result (not the cause) of spiritual birth: "Since you have purified your souls in obeying the truth through the Spirit in sincere love of the brethren, love one another fervently with a pure heart [B Truth], having been born again, not of corruptible seed but incorruptible [A Truth] . . ." Peter also tells those who have believed to "Grow in the grace and knowledge of our Lord and Savior, Jesus Christ" (2 Pet. 3:18).

The Gift (A) is not The Prize (B).

A gift is free, but a prize is awarded based on performance. Eternal salvation from hell is a gift from God, but temporal and eternal rewards are earned by our motives and conduct as Christians. Paul, already a Christian, says he presses forward with the goal of earning the "prize of the upward call of God in Christ Jesus" (Phil. 3:14). In the context of Philippians 3:11-14, that prize is a greater knowledge of Jesus Christ and the privilege of sharing in His experience of suffering and death.

In the last chapter of the Bible, Revelation 22, we find a nice juxtaposition of the gift and the prize. In verse 12, Jesus says "And behold, I am coming quickly, and my reward [prize] is with Me, to give to every one according to his work." Clearly the basis of the awarded prize is one's performance (B Truth). But John says a few verses later, "Whoever desires, let him take of the water of life freely" (v. 17; A Truth). Here John speaks of eternal life as a free gift of living water, just as he also does in his Gospel where we see Jesus' words to the unsaved woman at the well, "If you knew the gift of God, and who it is who says to you, 'Give Me a drink,' you would have asked Him, and He would have given you living water" (John 4:10). No conditions were attached to His offer of the gift to this woman. But in the same chapter when addressing His saved disciples, Jesus told them their labor would earn wages (John 4:36-38). The unsaved woman is given A Truth to offer her free salvation (the gift) while the saved disciples are given B Truth to offer them earned wages (the prize).

If we confuse the biblical teaching of salvation as a free gift with eternal rewards as a prize to be earned, we confuse the gospel by imposing works onto grace—an impossibility, as we have seen.

Relationship (A) is not Fellowship (B).

By relationship I mean an objective relationship, such as a son's biological relationship to his father. By fellowship I mean the quality of sharing between the two people in that relationship. Every son is related to his father, but not every son has a quality relationship with his father. A person can have a relationship with another person, but not necessarily fellowship. And fellowship can vary in the richness of its quality. We can compare the two concepts:

Relationship (A)	Fellowship (B)
Positional	Experiential
Established once for all	Maintained or lost
Secure	Conditional

Every person who believes in Jesus Christ as Savior has been established in an eternal relationship with God through birth into His family. That is an objective positional truth (A Truth). But not all believers share the same quality of fellowship in that relationship. That is a subjective truth (B Truth). Some Christians enjoy more intimacy with God than others. There are many reasons for this, such as sin in the believer's life, immaturity, lack of teaching, or lack of commitment. As we saw earlier, John 8:30-31 states that one condition of discipleship is a close adherence to God's Word. Those who obey God's Word enjoy a close fellowship with Him as followers. The intimacy available to obedient believers is described in John 14:21:

> *"He who has My commandments and keeps them, it is he who loves Me. And he who loves Me will be loved by My Father, and I will love him and manifest Myself to him."*

We will see later that fellowship with God is a theme in many Bible passages, especially in the Epistle of 1 John. It helps us understand some troublesome passages but also helps us see a richer side to our experience with God made possible by fulfilling certain conditions. In 1 John, John declares that his purpose for writing is to promote fellowship between the readers and the apostles, and so with God (1 John 1:3-4). If the purpose of the book is deeper fellowship, that should determine how we interpret its many "tests." We will discover that the purpose of John's Gospel is to help people establish a relationship with God (John 20:31), while the purpose of 1 John is to help people enjoy fellowship with God (1 John 1:3-4). John's Gospel has mostly A Truth with a little B Truth. John's first epistle has mostly B Truth with a little A Truth.

Too often, commentators and readers of the Bible confuse truths about relationship with God and fellowship with God. This results in a performance-based gospel, which is not really the gospel at all. Relationship cannot be earned; fellowship can. Relationship cannot be lost; fellowship can.

Believing in Christ for Salvation (A) is not Committing to Christ as Lord (B)

In Acts 16:31, the apostle Paul told a terrified Roman jailer how to be saved: "Believe in the Lord Jesus Christ and you will be saved." Was Paul telling the jailer that he needs to believe in (be persuaded that) Jesus Christ, who as the Lord (God), will save him, or that he needs to believe in (surrender to) Jesus as his own personal Lord and Master? The former preserves salvation by grace, the latter promotes salvation by merit (the merit of personal surrender or commitment). Both cannot be true.

The key to the question "What must I do to be saved?" is to understand that as Savior, Jesus saves; as Lord, He rules. By definition, salvation is knowing Jesus as Savior. It is because Jesus is the Lord that He can be our Savior. Because He is the Lord, those who are saved should serve Him. Jesus holds many positions: Savior, Lord, Master, Judge, Creator, High Priest, King, etc. But which aspect of Christ's person do we appeal to for salvation? The answer is obvious—Savior! Unsaved sinners need the help of a Savior; saved believers need to serve a Master.

The view called Lordship Salvation confuses the gospel by requiring that a person believe in Jesus as Savior and also commit to serve Him as Lord in order to be saved. By neglecting the distinction between justification truth (A Truth) and sanctification truth (B Truth), this view also negates unconditional grace by pre-empting it with human merit. In this view, grace is earned by making a promise or commitment, or by surrender. The tragic consequence is that grace ceases to be grace.

The simple gospel invitation stated clearly in verses like John 3:16, 5:24, and 6:47, is that whoever believes in Jesus Christ (as the Son of God who provides and guarantees eternal salvation) has eternal life. Three times the New Testament cites Genesis 15:6 to illustrate how Abraham received God's promise: "Abraham believed God, and it was accounted to him for righteousness." This is cited in contexts that specifically argue that works and keeping laws cannot save. Abraham did not have to make any promises or commitments to God. In fact, Abraham was sleeping when God made a covenant with him (Gen. 15:8-21).

Damnation (A) is not Discipline (B)

Those who are not born into God's family face God as the Judge who condemns them to the lake of fire eternally (2 Thess. 1:7-9; Rev. 20:11-15). But there is a great difference between how God deals with those who do not know Him and how He treats His own children. Like a good father, God disciplines His wayward children. Hebrews 12:5-11 argues that this is one way we know that He loves us. A good father does not disown his wayward child. The eternal condemnation of unbelievers by a just God falls under A Truth. The discipline of believers by a loving Father falls under B Truth.

Many times, passages that speak of God's discipline or chastisement are interpreted with eternal condemnation in mind. The warning passages of Hebrews are a good example of this. Since I will devote a chapter to Hebrews later, I will only say that in Hebrews, the author is clearly addressing believers (children of God). So the threat of eternal condemnation makes no sense unless you believe Christians can lose their salvation, which in my opinion creates bigger problems.[10] The severe language of these threats has caused many to be vexed over the message and interpretation of Hebrews. The only way some interpreters can deal with it is to bifurcate the book by claiming that some of Hebrews is written to believers and some to unbelievers. Yet the author makes no such explicit distinctions. Only when we understand that Hebrews has severe discipline in view, can we see the unity of its argument and purpose.

Grace (A) is not Law (B)

Can we eat bacon with our eggs? Not if we are still under the Old Testament Law of Moses which prohibited eating pork for the Jews. Thankfully (for us who like bacon), God declared to Peter that all food was now clean for the church (Acts 10: 9-16). Later, Paul wrote in Romans that "Christ is the end of the law for righteousness to everyone who believes" (Rom. 10:4), and that Christians "are not under law but under grace" (Rom. 6:14). In Galatians, Paul argued that the purpose of the law was to bring us to Jesus Christ so that we could be saved by grace through faith; therefore, we are no longer subject to the law (see the whole epistle, but especially 3:22-25).

Those who think we are still under law (whether the Mosaic Covenant or its moral stipulations) will have to make obedience to laws a condition for eternal salvation. But what does that do to grace? It nullifies it, of course. The Bible teaches that if someone wants to be saved by keeping the law, then they must keep it perfectly (Gal. 3:10; Jas. 2:10), which of course is impossible. This leads us to the need for grace. Grace offers blessings that are totally undeserved (A Truth). The Mosaic Law offers blessings that are earned by obedience (B Truth). Salvation by keeping the Law does not mix with salvation by God's free grace. That is the whole point of Paul's Epistle to the Galatians.

The Bible clearly states a difference between law and grace. We cannot confuse the two without tragically corrupting the gospel. The controversy

---

10   See Appendix 1: Eternal Security.

between law and grace became so intense in the early church that Paul took the problem to the church leaders for resolution (Acts 15). The issue there involved some believers who were insisting that Gentiles had to come under the law before they could be saved by faith in Jesus Christ. But the church leaders knew that giving in to that argument made works a basis for eternal salvation, which nullified grace, so they rightly rejected it (Acts 15:1, 7-11). The student of the Bible must recognize the difference between the demands of law keeping and the gift of grace.

Eternal wrath (A) is not Temporal wrath (B)

Wrath refers to the righteous anger of God. There is a tendency among many to reduce wrath to a single consequence, eternal condemnation in hell. There is little or no thought given to the possibility that God could be angry with Christians in a different way and with different consequences. For example, the anger a man has toward an escaped convict who tries to kill him is different from the anger he might have toward his disobedient son. This would certainly help us understand that the harsh warnings of Hebrews with its imagery of fiery punishment might actually apply to Christians, especially if fire is used figuratively and not literally.

A verse like Romans 1:18 states a universal truth. "God's wrath is being poured out (note the present tense) on all unrighteousness and ungodliness of men." It does not say His wrath is poured out on unsaved mankind only, but on *all* unrighteousness and ungodliness of men, which implies all men who exhibit unrighteousness and ungodliness. The simple principle is that sin, whether in an unbeliever or in a believer, merits God's righteous anger. The degree of God's anger and the way that anger is experienced differs between unbelievers and believers. God's anger with unbelievers results in their separation from Him in this life and eternal separation from Him in the lake of fire where the severity of that punishment is determined by their previous deeds (Rev. 20:12). God's anger toward believers takes the form of temporal discipline in this life and denial of rewards and blessings in eternity. Unless this is understood, there is no way to accurately interpret the warning passages in Hebrews written to believers. We will see God's discipline of believers mentioned in many other passages discussed later.

The distinction between A Truth (eternal wrath on unbelievers) and B Truth (temporal wrath on believers) is important, because if eternal condemnation is always imposed on our understanding of God's wrath or chastisement, and a believer's behavior is in view, then once again performance trumps grace and the gospel is corrupted. That believer, who was saved by grace, must preserve his salvation by his works lest he earn God's eternal condemnation. This is a contradiction of grace, grace that extends from our salvation in the past to our preservation in the future.

The Great White Throne Judgment (A) is not The Judgment Seat of Christ (B)

It is a great failure of many Bible interpreters to assume only one judgment at the end of the age, a judgment that separates believers from unbelievers. This causes major problems in harmonizing some Scriptures. For example, in John 5:24, Jesus says that anyone who believes in Him "shall not come into judgment," but in 2 Corinthians 5:10, Paul says of believers, "we must all appear before the judgment seat of Christ." Is there a contradiction?

Our application of A Truth and B Truth solves the problem. John 5:24 is A Truth relating to unbelievers who believe in Christ and receive eternal life. They will not have to face the final judgment of Revelation 20:11-15, a judgment of unbelievers after Christ's return to earth as King. However, 2 Corinthians 5:10 is B Truth speaking to believers about giving an account for how they used their lives, an event called the Judgment Seat of Christ, or *bema* (in Greek). Believers will not be judged for their faith in Christ as Savior (A Truth), but for their faithfulness in following Christ as Lord (B Truth).

This summary chart shows the distinctions we have discussed between A Truth and B Truth.

A Truth	B Truth
Salvation	Discipleship
Faith in Jesus Christ	Works for Jesus Christ
Grace for eternal salvation	Merit for eternal rewards
Justification	Sanctification
Spiritual birth	Spiritual growth
Gift given	Prize earned
Relationship established	Fellowship enjoyed

A Truth	B Truth
Believing in Christ for Salvation	Committing to Christ as Lord
Damnation for unbelief	Discipline for disobedience
Undeserved grace for salvation	Freedom from the Law
Eternal wrath	Temporal wrath
Great White Throne Judgment	Judgment Seat of Christ

After seeing how A Truth B Truth makes sense of so many Bible passages and concepts, I hope you understand why knowing this is crucial to Bible study. It gives us a solid paradigm to apply to many Bible passages that don't seem to harmonize with what the Bible clearly teaches about salvation by grace and the Christian life.

As I said previously, this distinction is one of the single most important concepts that serious Bible students can bring to their search for the correct interpretation of God's Word. Not only that, but the effect of this approach will radically change one's outlook on the Christian life. With a proper understanding of how to distinguish A Truth from B Truth, the believer can rest in the grace of God for assurance of salvation while living responsibly for a future evaluation and reward. Grace remains free while rewards are costly.

CHAPTER

A Truth B Truth in Bible Study

3

WHEN DETERMINING THE meaning of any Bible passage, there are certain rules of Bible study that lead to the best interpretation. This chapter will not review all the principles of Bible study and interpretation, all of which should be applied to any passage, but will remind us of some basics essential to discerning the difference between A Truth and B Truth.

All Bible study begins with observation. But do we know what we are looking for? Recently, a friend in Oregon took me fishing. As we stood on the high bank of the North Umpqua River, Evan pointed toward the swirling water and said, "There's a steelhead. There's another one. And over there are some Chinook salmon. I see one, two, three, four--looks like about twenty." Exasperated and embarrassed, I exclaimed, "I can't see *one!*" Then Evan taught me how to "see" these fish. They appear as a shadow or streak, but there are many such shapes in the river. The key is to stare at the shadow until you see it oscillate or waver, then you know it is a fish. And the Chinook are a darker streak than the steelhead. I began to see them, but I admit I have a long way to go in my powers of observing fish.

Too often we look at the Bible, but don't observe it. We assume we know what we see, but the best interpretation emerges only after keen and persistent observation. That begins with the context. When observed carefully, the Bible is its own best interpreter. If we use a simple approach to Bible study that begins with observation of the context and ends with comparisons to other Scriptures, we will be far along in our ability to interpret correctly.

It can be argued that the three most important rules of Bible study are: "Context, context, context." We cannot overemphasize context as the key to interpreting the Bible, especially difficult or problem passages. But there is more than one level of context. A remark attributed to Martin Luther describes his approach to Bible study this way:

I study my Bible as I gather apples. First, I shake the whole tree that the ripest might fall. Then I shake each limb, and when I have shaken each limb, I shake each branch and every twig. Then I look under every leaf. I shake the Bible as a whole, like shaking the whole tree. Then I shake every limb—study book after book. Then I shake every branch, giving attention to the chapters when they do not break the sense. Then I shake every twig, or a careful study of the paragraphs and sentences and words and their meanings.[11]

We will call these levels *circles of context*. What circles of context are the most helpful when interpreting a problem passage?

Check the contexts!

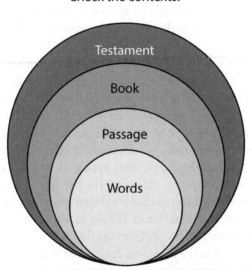

First, we observe the largest context.

Though the largest circle of context would be the cultural and historical background, let us begin with the Bible itself, in which case we observe whether the passage is in the Old Testament or New Testament. The Old

---

11   http://www.bibleexposition.net/2010/07/martin-luther-on-bible-study.html

Testament speaks primarily to or about the Jewish people as a nation under the Mosaic Covenant (also called the Law, or Old Covenant). The New Testament addresses issues concerning Israel during Jesus Christ's life as well as issues with the church and individual Christians. Though the New Covenant is not fulfilled until Israel is restored to God in their land, I believe that the church and Christians can enjoy some of the New Covenant's spiritual blessings. The Old Covenant emphasized blessings earned by obedience; the New Covenant emphasizes blessings to motivate obedience. Many consequences for disobedience in the Old Testament apply to the nation of Israel (sometimes other nations were judged for their sin also), not to individuals. Consequences for disobedience in the New Testament apply mostly to individual believers.

How does this affect the application of the A Truth B Truth approach? It is important to realize that God has an eternal relationship with Israel that will never be revoked, even in their disobedience. In other words, the nation of Israel will be saved and restored in the future though they are in disobedience now (Rom. 11:26). In the Old Testament era, there were *individuals* within the nation of Israel who were either saved or unsaved. Though God apparently saved everyone in the nation of Israel who applied the blood of the Passover lamb when they fled Egypt (Exodus 12), there arose later unsaved individuals within Israel (e.g., the evil kings of 1 Kings 16). We must determine whether Old Testament promises and judgments addressed the nation as a whole, or the individuals within it.

In the New Testament, however, God's salvation promises apply to the individual Christian. *It is more accurate to compare the salvation experience of the individual Christian with the experience of the whole nation of Israel,* because God's eternal promises made to Israel are inherited in the New Testament era by individuals through faith in Jesus Christ. In other words, in the Old Testament, an Israelite could be eternally lost even though God assured the nation it would be eternally saved. However, in the New Testament, the individual receives God's eternal promise through Jesus Christ directly, not through Israel or the church.

Someone might read an Old Testament story about disobedient Israelites, such as the sinful sons of Eli, Hophni and Phinehas, and conclude that they were not saved or lost their salvation because they abused their priestly duties and committed fornication with worshiping women (1 Samuel 2). Though they were Israelites and priests, 1 Samuel 2:12 says they "were corrupt [literally, 'sons of Belial']; they did not know the Lord" and God killed them (v. 34; 4:11). Reading this story, a person could conclude that a Christian can lose his or her salvation. The mistake often made is to fail to make distinctions between the Old and New Testaments as well as God's dealing with the nation of Israel and His dealing with individual Christians. It is clear enough in the New Testament that individual Christians cannot lose their salvation, so the comparison with the sons of Eli is misleading. The comparison should be with Israel who never lost her salvation and her special relationship to God.[12]

Observing the larger contexts of the Testaments and the change in dispensations (times in which God deals in a unique way suited to each period) is an indispensable background for interpreting specific Bible passages.

Second, we observe the book.

A lot of helpful information is also determined by considering the next circle of context, the book of the Bible where the passage occurs. These general observations about the book should include:

- The genre (type, kind) of literature
- The setting (time, culture, occasion, location)
- The purpose and audience
- The argument or theme of the book

Let's consider the importance of each of these observations.

The *genre* or *kind of literature* is important because it tells us whether the book should be approached as careful historical narrative, or interpreted as prophecy or poetry, which rely heavily on figures of speech. So when we read in Genesis 19 that God destroys Sodom and Gomorrah with fire, we assume this is literal fire because of the nature of the historical account. On the other hand, when God threatens to punish Israel with fire in a prophetic book using poetic language, it could be literal fire (Lam. 4:11; Amos 2:5), but sometimes it is obviously figurative for His fierce wrath (Lam. 2:3-4).

---

12 A growing number of Bible commentators believe that Israel did indeed lose her covenant relationship with God through disobedience and has been re-placed by the church as God's chosen people. Since this view departs from a plain literal sense of interpretation of God's promises to Israel and spiritualizes them in relation to the church, I reject it.

Fire does not necessarily speak of the fire of hell, but the fire of God's anger poured out in some other literal way. And note by the way that God is talking to Israel as a nation, not to individuals, and certainly not to New Testament Christian individuals. We will see later how important it is to interpret fire carefully when we examine it in an illustration in John 15:6 and Hebrews 6:8.

The *setting* is also important because to understand a passage, we must know when and where it was written in addition to other information we can learn about the history, culture, and occasion that produced the book. Was the book written before the church appeared, early in the history of the church, or later? Did the Apostle Paul write as a free man or from a prison cell? For example, if we know that Paul wrote from prison, that might influence our understanding of his use of the word "deliverance" (some versions, "salvation") in Philippians 1:19. Is he talking about deliverance or salvation as in eternal salvation (A Truth), or as in being saved or delivered from prison, or delivered from this life into the presence of the Lord (B Truth), or something else? The context of the book will help us decide.

Knowledge of the book's setting is crucial when interpreting Hebrews. To miss the clues about the setting is to guarantee an incorrect interpretation of the many difficult passages. In Hebrews, it is crucial to know whether the author is writing to believers, unbelievers, or both. In another example, knowing that Jesus spoke to the nation of Israel when He told His parables in Matthew, Mark, and Luke helps interpret them. The negative consequences of some of the parables might apply to Israel rather than to Christians.

The *purpose and audience* are related because the original author wrote to actual people about real and relevant issues. Were the readers already believers? What circumstances or problems did they face that prompted the book or letter? What was their spiritual condition—unsaved, saved but immature, or saved and growing? Here, we look for the author's purpose, which relates to the recipients' spiritual condition and is sometimes stated. In John 20:31, John says he wrote to bring people to faith in Jesus Christ. Therefore, it will be important to consider the stories, teachings, and words he chose to use for that purpose. There is no explicit purpose stated for the book of Romans, but it is clear that Paul was explaining to the readers the gospel and its implications for the Christian life as well as how the Jewish nation was included in God's plan. When interpreting difficult passages in First Corinthians, it is crucial to know that this epistle was written to address numerous problems in the church arising from *Christians* who were not acting right.

The *argument* of the book or letter is also crucial. By argument I do not mean that the author is argumentative, but that he has organized his material to persuade the reader toward a certain conclusion. Romans is a good example of this because we see a very calculated progression in thought as Paul takes the reader from sin (1:18-3:20) to salvation (3:21-4:25), sanctification (5:1-8:27), security (8:28-39), sovereignty (9:1-11:36), and service (12:1-15:13). The progression moves from A Truth to B Truth. In Romans, theology precedes practical exhortations. This is also very evident in Galatians, Ephesians, and Colossians. The exhortations in the latter parts of these books assume the salvation of the readers, an important observation for a proper interpretation. Note the general pattern in these Pauline epistles:

Theology – What God has done for us	Practice – What we can do for God
Romans 1-11	Romans 12-16
Galatians 1-4	Galatians 5-6
Ephesians 1-3	Ephesians 4-6
Colossians 1-2	Colossians 3-4

The Gospels have some clues about their purpose and argument. Matthew is apparently written to the Jews to prove that Jesus is their Messiah. Luke is written to a Gentile ruler to document the life of Christ. Many commentators believe that Mark gives a brief action-filled account of Jesus' life because it appealed to a pragmatic Roman audience. John argues his Gospel theologically to show that Jesus is the divine Messiah who offers eternal life to whoever believes in Him. Knowing that the purpose of Matthew is different from the purpose of Mark or John will help us understand why each chooses particular messages, stories, and words.

Third, we observe the passage.

At this stage, we want to ask a lot of questions to help in observation and yield an interpretation. Questions like these:

- How is this passage connected to the previous thought? Is there a connecting word like "and, but, therefore"?

- Do words or word order indicate any kind of emphasis?

- Are any of these words used in the surrounding context?

- What is the tone—argument, logic, emotion, sarcasm, irony, warning, compassion?

- Do we understand the subject and the verbs and their syntactical relationships?

- What modifying words are used and why?

- What words were chosen and why not others?

Matthew 24:13 is a greatly misunderstood passage in my opinion. If we were to use some of these questions on this passage, it would go like this:

- Who is Jesus talking to and why?

- Who is the subject "those"?

- What does the verb "endure" mean?

- How is the word "saved" used?

- What does "the end" refer to?

- What is the tone of the passage?

When these questions are asked and answered, you might find it hard to agree with those who take this passage to refer to the doctrine of Perseverance of the Saints, an A Truth (a person must persevere in faith and faithfulness to the end of his or her life in order to be saved). We observe Jesus is answering the disciples' question about His coming and the end of the age. He is talking about the Jewish people in the time of their Tribulation and their fate. This passage is discussed in more detail later.

Fourth, we observe words and phrases.

Have you heard this one? A bear goes into a bar, orders dinner, pulls out a gun and shoots up the place, then leaves. He does this daily causing one customer to ask the bartender about it. The bartender says, "Oh, that's a panda bear. He eats shoots and leaves." Obviously, the joke cleverly plays on the fact that "shoots and leaves" could be verbs or nouns. If commas were inserted--"eats, shoots, and leaves"—we would see these were intended as verbs. This joke illustrates an important premise of this book, that words (even punctuation—or lack of it) can be used in different ways, especially in the English language.

Words can have different meanings in different contexts. "Sit at the dining room table" uses the word table differently from the sentence "Study the table comparing per capita income of world nations." Bible students get into trouble when they rigidly apply one meaning to a word that may have different meanings, or at least different nuances. Again, context is key to determining how a word is used and its meaning.

I have already used the word *sanctification*, and said it usually refers to progressive Christian growth. But if we look carefully at some texts, we see that sanctification is used of the Christian's position obtained by his justification (1 Cor. 6:11; Heb. 10:10). That is why Christians are called "saints," or literally, "set apart ones." But sanctification is also used in the sense of a Christian's final and full separation from sin unto God when he is perfected or glorified at death or resurrection (1 Thess. 5:23). So the essential meaning is "to be set apart." The context determines if that is positional (past), progressive (present), or perfect (future).

Too often, the gospel is confused because words and phrases are not given the proper consideration of their meaning in context. Words or phrases like *salvation, repentance, faith, disciple, eternal life*, and *salvation of the soul* are crucial to a proper understanding of the gospel and the Christian life. Too often, they are assigned only to A Truth. In the next chapter, we will see how these particular words are used in the Bible.

One phrase we can use as an example is "delivered to Satan" (used of Alexander in 1 Tim. 1:20), or "deliver such a one to Satan" (used of the fornicator in 1 Cor. 5:5). If we simply assume that Paul is assigning Christians to hell, then we have a problem with Paul's other statements that assume eternal security for his Christian readers. Someone could say that Alexander and the fornicator were never saved to begin with, but there are problems in the contexts with that view. Alexander was a companion of Paul. It is hard to think he was not saved. And how could Paul assign an unsaved person to hell anyway, since he is already destined to go there? Likewise, in 1 Corinthians 5, the fornicator is a member of the Corinthian church. He is called a "brother" (1 Cor. 5:11). Furthermore, he later repents of his sin and is restored (2 Cor. 2:1-11). When Paul speaks of his repentance, he refers to it as a restoration, not salvation.

Based on our consideration of the contexts, delivering a person to Satan best applies to Christians as B Truth. There are a number of B Truth possibilities, and I will list them briefly without much explanation:

1. The term could speak of excommunication from church.

2. It could refer to taking the offender out from under the protection of the church's ministry and prayers and exposing him to Satan's harm (Satan desired to sift Peter like wheat, but Jesus prayed for him so that damage was limited; Luke 22: 31-32).

3. The term "for the destruction of the flesh" could speak of turning the sinner over to Satan for temporal (physical) discipline.

4. The term "flesh" could refer to sinful tendencies which would be destroyed by allowing Satan to chasten the fornicator in some way.

Which of these interpretations fits best? I tend to favor the second, but the important thing is that all four deal honestly with the context, which clearly shows:

1. Paul is writing to Christians about someone in the church who is in all likelihood a Christian.

2. Christians who sin should be disciplined by the church.

3. There are severe consequences that sinning Christians face in this life. In other words, there is no reason to automatically think Paul is sending someone to hell. There is no reason to assume this term is an A Truth and ignore the possibility of B Truth.

The definition of words and phrases are more influenced by theology and tradition than we care to admit. It is the responsibility of the student of God's Word to derive the best definition from context and usage.

Fifth, we observe figures of speech.

As with words, figures of speech need careful observation and interpretation. A figure of speech is a word, phrase, or clause used to convey meaning through some kind of comparison, similarity, or relationship. If we say, "Her words cut like a knife," we are picturing the harmful or painful nature of a woman's words with the pain that can be inflicted with a knife. Figures like these are usually obvious in everyday speech as well as in Bible study. In this example, we know the words themselves do not cut and produce blood. The point of correspondence is between the emotional pain in the heart and the physical pain in the flesh.

One example of a misunderstood figure of speech is the word "death" or "dead" and its use in a phrase like "dead in trespasses and sins." When some see the word "dead" or "death" in certain Bible passages, they assume the meaning of *eternal death*, also known as the "second death" (Rev. 20:14). Paul says in Romans 6:23 that "the wages of sin is death." He is writing to Christians; so would he be warning them about eternal death? That would not make sense unless Christians can lose their salvation and go to hell.

Another error is to assume that death means something never existed or has the qualities of non-existence. James 2:24 is commonly misunderstood when it says, "Faith without works is dead." Many assume that this refers to a faith that never existed. But that would be an odd way of stating non-existence. It actually states that there is faith, but goes on to describe it as "dead." Something that is dead is not what it once was. In James' usage, it is lifeless or useless. We say "The car battery is dead," meaning that the battery exists, but no longer has an electrical charge and is therefore useless. Death can be a figure of speech for something that is useless because it lacks vitality.

Another way that death can be misunderstood is to extend the figure of speech beyond its intended meaning. For example, in Ephesians 2:2, Paul describes the condition of the unsaved person as "dead in trespasses and sin." He speaks of spiritual separation from God in which unsaved people are hopeless and helpless to save themselves. But some impose their theology on this phrase to make it mean total inability to respond to any spiritual truth. And yet when Adam sinned and *died* (Gen. 2:17; 3:9-10), he responded to God's call in the Garden. In these examples, it fits well to understand death as a figure of speech portraying spiritual separation from God and helplessness. It is overreaching to interpret death as either non-existence or total inability to respond to spiritual truth.

Beginning with an assumption of either A Truth or B Truth without careful observation can influence how we interpret the use of the term *death* in Bible passages. There is nothing wrong with testing the interpretation as an A Truth relating to salvation. However, we must not let our theological tradition preclude the possibility of a B Truth interpretation. In the end, the text in its context must be allowed to determine the meaning. This meaning must be consistent with other passages and then tested theologically.

As we will see later in our discussion of John 15:6 (the fruitless branches are gathered and burned) and Hebrews 6:8 (the thorny ground is burned), the use of the imagery of burning has led many to interpret these passages as A Truth relating to salvation, forcing them to conclude that the readers either lost their salvation or were never saved to begin with. But is burning a figure of speech for the fire of hell, is it some other severe consequence for believers, or is it used in an illustration of uselessness (my preference)? Again, we will see that observing the context is key.

Sixth, we compare other Scriptures.

A basic principle of Bible study is the validation of an interpretation of a passage with the teaching of other passages in the Bible. We should let Scripture interpret Scripture.

Once more, we will use as an example James' statement that faith without works is dead, and that a man is not justified by faith only (Jas. 2:17, 24). Historically, commentators have recognized how that seems to contradict Paul's teaching of justification through faith alone (Rom. 3:28; 4:5; Gal. 2:16). Does James impugn the gospel of grace with works? Which is the clearer passage that should have priority consideration? Is it good enough to say that they are teaching different truths because they are writing from different perspectives? Obviously, the Bible could not contradict itself. Common sense would also tell us that this statement by James should give deference to Paul's clear arguments in Romans 3:21-4:25, Galatians chapters 2 and 3, and elsewhere. We will discuss these passages in James later.

The interpretation of a more difficult passage should always yield to the teaching of clearer passages. The Gospel of John is important when we interpret passages that seem to speak of the condition for salvation. John declares that His Gospel's purpose is to tell people how to have eternal life, and that is by believing in Jesus Christ (John 20:31). We can therefore assume that John would be clear about this, and indeed he uses *believe* almost one hundred times, most often as the condition for eternal salvation. So when we read a passage like 1 Timothy 6:18-19 that says good works and generosity lead to eternal life, we should become suspicious that Paul would contradict John. In light of John's clear teaching that faith is the only condition for obtaining eternal life, we wonder if we have understood Paul correctly. Who is Paul talking to, believers or unbelievers? What does it mean to "store up for themselves a good foundation for the time to come" and what does he mean by "that they may lay hold on eternal life"? This is certainly not John's language when he presents how to have eternal salvation. We will discuss the interpretation of 1 Timothy 6:18-19 later, but the point is, that the clear teaching of John should give us pause and inform our interpretation of it.

The same argument from John can also be used to clear up passages that people use to argue that baptism is necessary for salvation. Difficult passages like Acts 2:38 and 1 Peter 3:21 seem to say that baptism saves us. But shouldn't we weigh our interpretation against the explicit purpose, message, and word choice of John's Gospel and other Scripture? Nowhere does John say baptism brings eternal life, yet he wrote his book to tell people how to have eternal life (John 20:31). We also have the epistles to the Romans and the Galatians that argue that God's righteousness comes only by grace through faith in Jesus Christ. A correct understanding about these and other passages on baptism comes from interpreting unclear passages in light of clearer passages so that the Bible interprets itself.

Seventh, we test our interpretation theologically.

Theology synthesizes and organizes biblical teaching into coherent doctrines. For example, from biblical evidence we conclude that God is a trinity of Father, Son, and Holy Spirit even though the word *Trinity* is never used. The doctrine of the Trinity is so clear that when we encounter passages that say "The Lord our God is one" (Deut. 6:6) or "I and the Father are one" (John 10:30), we are able to evaluate them in a way that harmonizes with the idea of three persons of the Godhead separate but equal.

Many passages are construed to say that obedience, works, or commitment is necessary to be saved, and many passages are also construed to argue that Christians can lose their salvation. But the Bible's teachings are so clear that these passages cannot contradict the clear doctrines of salvation by grace through faith alone in Jesus Christ and the eternal security of the believer. When we encounter a difficult passage that seems to add performance to the clear teaching of salvation by grace through faith, we must look for the interpretation that is consistent with that doctrine. Likewise, if a passage seems to contradict the clear teaching on eternal security, we must consider an interpretation that adheres to the overwhelmingly clear doctrine of eternal security. Does the passage under study undermine the assurance consistent with our theology of grace and security? Then it must be interpreted with the clearer doctrines in mind.

We must be careful not to begin with our theology. Theology should come from our study of the Bible. Even so, it is difficult not to have our theology influence our understanding of the Scripture. In reality, we develop our interpretations through a cyclical process: We study the Scriptures, develop our theology, then test our theology with the Scriptures, and so on.

Eighth, we determine if our interpretation is A Truth or B Truth.

When faced with one of the difficult passages that seem to suggest a condition for salvation that does not agree with faith alone, it is helpful to test the passage to see if it can be understood in light of a particular B Truth. After doing our work of observation, we might keep these categories in mind as a possible help in interpretation. I have found that many passages mistaken for A Truth are better understood as one of these B Truths:

- It speaks of earning or losing rewards.
- It speaks of enjoying or being denied the full experience of the kingdom.
- It speaks of gaining or losing Jesus Christ's verbal blessing.
- It speaks of avoiding or deserving God's discipline.
- It speaks of deepening or injuring one's fellowship with God.
- It speaks of having confidence or regret at the Judgment Seat of Christ.
- It speaks of meeting a condition of discipleship.

As we discuss many difficult passages, you will notice that these are the main categories where these passages fall. Also, notice that each reflects a deeper aspect of discipleship and the Christian life that is lost if an A Truth interpretation is imposed on a respective passage.

A Truth B Truth Applied to
Important Words and Phrases

4

EVERY WORD IS important if it is God's Word. Small words can have big consequences. As the old proverb goes, "For want of a nail, the shoe was lost; for want of a shoe, the horse was lost; for want of a horse, the rider was lost; for want of a rider the message was lost; for want of a message, the battle was lost; for want of a battle, the kingdom was lost; and all for the want of a horseshoe nail." Words mean something, and they are the building blocks of sentences and ideas. Like any language, biblical words can have a range of meaning. Discovering the best meaning for every word will determine the quality of our final interpretation as a whole. There are some words and phrases used in salvation and discipleship passages that can change the meaning of the entire passage depending on how they are understood. Below are some of the most crucial terms often misused or misunderstood.

Gospel. The Greek word behind our English *gospel* is *euangelion*. It derives from two words, "good" and "message" or "good news." Most of the time, we tend to assume a meaning of good news about how to escape hell and get to heaven, which would be A Truth. Broadly defined as good news, *gospel* can refer to several aspects of good news. For example, in Luke 1:29, the good news is the announcement of the birth of John the Baptist, who will prepare people for the Messiah's coming. The term "gospel of the kingdom" (Matt. 4:23; 24:14; Mark 1:14) is the good news that the kingdom is near. In passages like 1 Corinthians 15:1-2, Galatians 1:8-11, Colossians 1:5-6, *gospel* clearly refers to the good news about Jesus Christ's person, work, and promise of eternal salvation (our justification). But in some passages, its meaning includes good news from justification to sanctification and on to glorification—God's complete deliverance. It seems that Romans 1:16 is such a use. Paul announces the theme of this book as the gospel, which is "the power of God unto salvation to all who believe." But the good news in Romans is more than good news about justification; it includes sanctification and glorification. That seems to imply that the word "salvation" in verse 16 refers not only to justification but also has significant B Truth meaning as well (see the discussion of *salvation* below).

When the term *gospel* is used, we can begin with the general definition of good news, but then we must ask and answer "good news about what?" The context answers that question and shows which meaning of *gospel* is being used.

Salvation. As we've just mentioned, the term *salvation* (from noun *sōteria*, verb *sōzō*) can be defined generally as *deliverance*, or *preservation*. Like the term *gospel*, we must ask, deliverance or preservation from what? Just as the English language has different uses for the word *salvation* or *saved*, so does the language of the Bible. It can refer to salvation from:

- physical death (Matt. 8:25; 14:30)
- trouble or unfortunate circumstances addressed in the context (Phil. 1:19; 1 Tim. 4:16)
- physical illness (Matt. 9:21)
- one's enemies (Ps. 7:1; 18:3)
- losing the fullness of God's life here and in eternity (Matt. 16:25-27)
- eternal condemnation (John 3:17; Eph. 2:5, 8)

When we say, as Ephesians 2:8-9 does, that we are *saved* by grace through faith alone without any kind of works, we are talking about initial justification (A Truth). However, in other passages we would contradict this clear teaching if we defined salvation the same way. James 2:14 is one example:

"What does it profit, my brethren, if someone says he has faith, but not have works? Can faith save him?"

What is James saying we are saved from? Hell is the traditional assumption. But it is not hell, as we will see from the context later.

We explained above how the word *gospel* is used in Romans as good news of salvation (Rom. 1:16). But that salvation is not only from eternal condemnation (justification), it includes salvation from the power of sin in us and God's wrath that is a consequence of sin, even in the believer (Rom. 1:18). Romans 5:9-10 says,

Much more then, having now been justified by His blood, we shall be saved from wrath through Him. For if when we were enemies we were reconciled to God through the death of His Son, much more, having been reconciled, we shall be saved by His life.

In this sense, it is B Truth salvation. Believers (indicated by "we") are delivered from present day consequences of sin (an aspect of God's wrath) by allowing the life of Christ to live through them. That is what Romans chapters 6-8 goes on to explain.

There are many uses of the word *salvation* or *saved* that either are not in the category of A Truth, or clearly in the category of B Truth. We will look at a number of examples later.

A – Eternal Salvation	B – Temporal Salvation
Received once in justification	Experienced many times
Used of unbelievers eternally delivered	Used of believers presently delivered
Deliverance from eternal hell	Deliverance from something undesirable

Eternal life. Most often we define this term as A Truth with the meaning that we have been saved from eternal death and hell so as to live forever in God's presence. Often, it is clearly used that way (e.g., John 5:24; John 6:47). However, in some passages it does not seem to fit the meaning of salvation from hell. In 1 Timothy 6:12 and 19, it is used with conditions of works or performance attached. In verse 12, Timothy is told to fight the good fight as a condition for him to "lay hold on eternal life," and in verse 19, those who are rich can "lay hold on eternal life" (the NKJV[13] supplies the word "eternal," but it is not in the Greek) by doing good works and being generous (v. 18). This would compromise the clear teaching of eternal salvation by God's unconditional grace received through faith alone.

---

13   Bible versions will be abbreviated as follows: NKJV, New King James Version; ESV, English Standard Version; HCSB, Holman Christian Standard Bible; NASB, New American Standard Bible; NET Bible (same); NIV, New International Version.

The problem is resolved if we do not restrict eternal life to only salvation from hell. The Bible uses it also in the sense of God's life. As such, it speaks not just of eternal duration, but also of a divine quality of life. Consider what John 17:3 teaches: "And this is life, that you might know God and the one whom He has sent." Clearly, eternal life here is God's life, or a relationship that we can have with God. This corroborates with Jesus' teaching in John 3 about the new birth. A new birth gives a new life. Literally, the phrase "born again" means "born from above," which denotes the reception of God's life. Eternal life should be seen not only as life with endless duration, but also as life with a divine quality.

A – Eternal Life Received	B – Eternal Life Enjoyed
New birth	Growth
Obtained in an instant	Enjoyed for a lifetime and eternity
Emphasis on quantity	Emphasis on quality
Received through faith	Enjoyed through faithfulness

A passage that is conveniently clear about this is John 10:10a. Jesus said,

A thief comes to steal and rob. I have come that you might have life, and have it abundantly.

To obtain Jesus' gift of life is to live eternally in heaven or the kingdom of God (A Truth), but it is also to enjoy His life abundantly in our present earthly experience (B Truth).

Death. There are several things that must be understood about the Bible's use of the word *death*. First, it never means cessation, as people often tend to think of it. When someone dies, he does not cease to exist, but has life removed from him. It is better to think of death in terms of separation. Death is used in a number of ways in the Bible (see the chart below). For example, Genesis 2:17 shows death as a separation from God. When God warned Adam and Eve not to eat of the forbidden tree, He said, "in the day that you eat of it you will surely die." Adam and Eve ate from the tree, but they did not fall over and die physically. However, they died spiritually in that they were now separated from God by their sin. One day they would die physically, and without redemption, they would be separated from God forever in a second death.

There is another use of death that is often misunderstood. It refers to the experience of separation in the believer's fellowship with God. In this sense, death describes a *deadening* of fellowship. By fellowship, I mean the intimacy a believer can enjoy with God when he is walking in truth and righteousness (upright behavior). There is an experience of deeper love, joy, and peace when a believer is living obediently. When a believer lives disobediently, this experience is deadened—he reverts to a similar feeling of separation from God as when he was an unbeliever. This seems to be the meaning of death in Romans 6:16, which is addressed to Christians in a sanctification context: "Do you not know that to whom you present yourselves to obey, you are that one's slaves whom you obey, whether of sin leading to death, or of obedience leading to righteousness." This passage is written to Christians as a motivation to obey God. The principle is clearly stated in Romans 6:23: "The wages of sin is death." Sin pays out a deadening experience in the believer's fellowship with God if he is not living the divine life God gives him.

Death is best understood in the Bible as some kind of separation. This chart explains the separation in different kinds of death.

Kind of Death	Separation of	Examples
Physical	Body from spirit	John 19:33; Acts 12:23
Spiritual	Unbeliever from God spiritually	Gen. 2:17; Rom. 5:12; Eph. 2:2
Experiential	Believer from God in fellowship	Rom. 6:16, 21, 23
Second	Unbeliever from God eternally	Rev. 20:14-15
Uselessness	Something from its vitality	Heb. 11:12; Jas. 2:20, 26
Positional	Believer's new man from sin and the law	Rom. 6:11
Powerlessness	Believer from Christ's victorious life and Spirit	Rom. 7:9-11, 24; 8:2, 6, 13

A failure to notice the meaning and different uses of death have caused some to interpret it in various passages as A Truth related to salvation when it should be interpreted as B Truth related to Christians.

Salvation of the soul. The use of this term is found in a number of passages, some of which will be discussed in detail later. But it is helpful for now to see that the term, though used popularly as an expression of A Truth, has deep B Truth significance and apparently *only* B Truth significance. Literally, the phrase can be translated as "preservation of the life." We have already seen how the word *salvation* can be used to mean *deliverance* or *preservation*. Now we should note that *soul* translates the Greek word *psychē*, which means a person's essential life and sometimes, physical life. We use the word *life* in this way today. We talk about someone having a meaningful life, or a wasted life, or losing his life by death. We see T-shirts that say "Soccer is life" or "Tennis is life" (usually followed by the phrase "Everything else is details").

Someone I know referred to the suicide of his Christian daughter as an example of a soul that was saved, but a life that was lost (he meant *wasted*.). Obviously, he was using popular terminology to say that she was a Christian, but never fully lived God's purpose for her life, or never experienced God's life to the fullest. This seems to be the sense of how losing the life is used in Matthew 10:39; 16:25-26; Mark 8:35-37; and Luke 9:24-25.

It may surprise you that the phrase "save the soul" probably never has A Truth meaning. It appears not only in the passages mentioned above, but also in 1 Peter 1:9, and James 1:21; 5:20. In each of these passages, we can easily establish a B Truth context, as you will see later in the book.

Faith. The word *faith* means to be persuaded or convinced that something is true. It is the noun form of the verb *believe* (both from the same Greek word—the noun *pistos* or verb *pisteuō*). When one is convinced of the gospel, this brings eternal salvation (A Truth; Eph. 2:8-9). However, faith is often used in the sense of B Truth. Probably, both A and B uses are seen in Paul's statement of his theme for Romans in 1:17—"For in it is the righteousness of God revealed, from faith to faith." Evidently, this speaks of the broad effect of salvation that Paul covers in Romans, from initial faith for justification to faith for a victorious life. Nothing could be clearer than Paul's teaching that we are justified through faith. Three times he cites the Old Testament example of Abraham who "believed God and it was accounted to him for righteousness" (Rom. 4:4; Gal. 3:6; Jas. 2:23).

That we are justified through faith is clear, but having been justified, we also access God's grace for Christian living through faith (Rom. 5:2). Paul alludes to this in his statement in Romans 1:17 where he adds a quote from Habakkuk 2:4 which says, "the just shall live by faith." Habakkuk was addressing the faithful remnant in Israel and telling them how to face a looming invasion by having faith that God is working in and through that event.

A – Faith for Eternal Salvation	B – Faith for Christian Living
One time	Continual
In Jesus Christ as Savior	In Jesus Christ as power, provision
Justification issue	Sanctification issue
In order to be declared righteous positionally	In order to become righteous experientially

Paul also uses the term in the sense of B Truth when he says, "I have been crucified with Christ, and it is not I who live, but Christ lives in me, and the life I now live in the flesh I live by faith in the Son of God who loved me and gave himself for me" (Gal. 2:20). Paul is saying to the Galatians that they must live a life of faith and not revert to the legalism of living under the law. Yet when he discusses how they were justified, he clearly uses *faith/believe* in its A Truth sense. In Galatians 2:16 he says, "For we know that no flesh is justified in His sight by works of the law but through faith in Jesus Christ."

Faith is the key principle by which we are to relate to God, whether it is in receiving His grace for salvation or receiving His grace for Christian living. For "without faith it is impossible to please God" (Heb. 11:6).

Repentance. This word remains one of the most troublesome words for Bible interpreters who try to remain faithful to the context where it is used. Some interesting observations can be made. First, it is derived from two Greek words, *meta* which means *after* and *noeō*, which means *to think*. So we get an essential meaning of *after thought* or *change of mind*. In the New Testament, the word *mind* is used of the inner person, sometimes interchangeably with the word *heart* (cf. Rom. 1:28; 7:23, 25; Eph. 4:17, 23; Col. 2:18). It refers to the seat of decision-making, the unseen part of us that makes us who we are; therefore, it is also accurate to translate the word repentance as a *change of heart*.

Unfortunately, we have no other single word that translates *metanoia* except *repentance*. Some linguists have called this an unfortunate circumstance of our language. Part of the reason is because the English word *repentance* is derived from the Latin *poenatentia*, or the doing of deeds of contrition or penance. This concept is a part of Roman Catholicism. As a result, many people view repentance as a sorrowful forsaking and abandoning of sin, or in other words, an outward action. Outward actions may (and usually do) result from an inner change of heart, but they may not or it may not be apparent when they do. We must keep the inward aspect of repentance distinct from the outward exhibit of conduct. Repentance is the root, but conduct may or may not be the fruit. Obviously, an inner change should result in an outward change—that would be natural and expected, but it is not automatic. Otherwise, John the Baptist would not have exhorted the Pharisees to "bear fruits worthy of repentance" (Matt. 3:8/Luke 3:8). In other words, if they repent, it would be consistent (but not automatic) to also show it.

The word *repent* or *repentance* is very flexible. It can be used for unbelievers or believers. It is ill-advisable to speak of repentance without understanding its particular context. Furthermore, there are different objects of repentance—in other words, that which is to be repented of. The Bible speaks of repentance as a change of heart about one's sins (2 Cor. 12:21), the identity of Jesus Christ (Acts 2:38), trust in pagan idols (Acts 17:30), God (Acts 20:21), false doctrine (2 Tim. 2:25), and dead works (Heb. 6:1), to name some. Sometimes, repentance is a change of heart that leads to salvation (A Truth; Matt. 9:13; Luke 24:47; Acts 11:18), and sometimes it is a change of heart that leads to deeper sanctification (B Truth; 2 Cor. 12:21; 2 Tim. 2:25).

Unfortunately, repentance is frequently used indiscriminately as A Truth relating to salvation. While I believe that in the New Testament it is sometimes used to describe the change of heart indicated by saving faith— for whenever one believes in Jesus Christ as Savior, he has changed his mind or heart about something—(e.g. Luke 5:32; 24:47; Acts 11:18; 17:30, 34; 2 Pet. 3:9), many times it is used as B Truth either applied to Israel as those disobedient under the Mosaic Covenant (Matt. 4:17; 11:20-21; 12:41; Luke 10:13; 11:32; 13:3, 5; Mark 1:15) or to believers for their sanctification (2 Cor. 12:21; 2 Tim. 2:25; Rev. 2:5, 16, 21, 22; 3:3, 19).

Disciple. This is another word that is best understood in context. A disciple is a learner, someone who is learning to become like his teacher. The New

Testament contains references to disciples of Moses, disciples of the Pharisees, and more commonly, disciples of Jesus Christ. So the word *disciple* does not automatically refer to someone who is eternally saved. In John 6:66, some are called disciples who had followed Jesus out of curiosity, but refused to follow Him further. Jesus said that some of them did not believe (John 6:64).

Some have failed to distinguish between those who believe in Jesus Christ (A Truth) and those who are committed disciples of Jesus Christ (B Truth). They claim that every Christian is a disciple and the conditions for discipleship are conditions for eternal salvation. But this can hardly be the case when we see a passage like John 8:30-31. Here, Jesus addresses those who have believed in Him for eternal life (v. 30) yet He gives them a condition for being a committed disciple: "Then Jesus said to those who believed in Him, 'If you abide in My word, you are my disciples indeed'" (v. 31). To *abide* means to *continue in*, not *believe in*. A believer becomes a committed disciple if he follows and keeps God's Word. Not every believer does that.

Admittedly, in Acts, the term *disciples* seems to refer to Christians as a whole without distinction (Acts 6:1-2, 7; 14:20, 22, 28; 15:10; 19:10). But that is not surprising, because in the early church of Acts, Christians are generally pictured as those who are eagerly growing and following God's Word. Those who were not are exceptions and are singled out for attention (like Ananias and Sapphira in chapter 5 and Simon the sorcerer in chapter 8). In the Epistles, the word *disciple* is not found. Instead we find the concept of discipleship in the apostle Paul's exhortations to "imitate" or "follow" him as he follows Jesus Christ (1 Cor. 4:16; 11:1; Phil. 3:17; 1 Thess. 1:6; 2 Thess. 3:7, 9).

The distinction between the A Truth condition for salvation (believe) and the B Truth conditions for discipleship is crucial. If we wrongly interpret the conditions for discipleship as conditions for salvation, we add to God's free grace and thus obliterate it. Consider the tragic consequences of simple unconditional grace if these conditions of discipleship are made conditions of salvation:

- Deny yourself (say no to your desires in order to say yes to God's will). Luke 9:23

- Take up your cross daily (be willing to suffer for Christ). Luke 9:23

- Follow Christ (adopt His purpose for your life). Luke 9:23

- Hate your father, mother, wife, children (meaning love God more than them). Luke 14:26

- Abide in God's Word (continue to adhere to and obey God's Word). John 8:31

- Love others. John 13:35

- Bear fruit. John 15:8

A – Salvation	B – Discipleship
One condition of believing in Christ as Savior	Many conditions of commitment to Christ as Lord
Jesus Christ as Savior	Jesus Christ as Master
A justification issue	A sanctification issue
Absolutely free	Very costly
An instantaneous event	A lifetime process

The tragedy of interpreting B Truth about discipleship as A Truth for salvation results in a false gospel based on performance, or in other words, works. It cancels grace. It therefore also cancels any possible assurance of salvation, since salvation is made dependent on one's commitment and faithfulness instead of God's promise. Our commitment always varies; God's promise never changes.

Judgment. It is common to hear of only one judgment at the end of life or at the end of the age. Many people believe they will endure this judgment to see if their works make them worthy of heaven or hell. However, this thinking overlooks a major teaching of the Scripture, especially the New Testament. All people will face judgment, but there are different judgments—one for unbelievers and one for believers. If we fail to distinguish these different judgments, we will have problems keeping the gospel clear. There is an A Truth judgment and a B Truth judgment.

Unfortunately, many Christians assume only one judgment, the one at the end of the millennial kingdom called the Great White Throne Judgment (Rev. 20:11-15). This is a judgment of all those who have not believed in Jesus Christ as their Savior. The unbeliever's works are examined and the book of life checked to confirm that their name is not in it. No believers are judged at the Great White Throne. Too often, the many passages that mention a coming judgment are interpreted as this judgment for unbelievers, when sometimes the judgment mentioned is clearly referring to those who are already believers.

What many miss is that the New Testament speaks of another judgment known as the Judgment Seat of Christ. This judgment is for believers only. The purpose of this judgment is not to determine whether someone is saved or not, but to determine whether a saved person is worthy of reward. It is clear that this judgment is for Christians only when the Apostle Paul writes, "For we shall all stand before the judgment seat of Christ" and "So then each of us shall give and account of himself to God" (Rom. 14:10; 12). First, Paul is writing to Christians and includes himself among those who face this judgment. Second, he states the purpose is to give an account of our life to God, not to see if we are saved. Then in 1 Corinthians 3:11-15, he describes how some will be rewarded at that judgment while some will have their worthless works burned up, or in other words, receive no reward. That he only speaks of a loss of reward (not a loss of salvation) is clear from verse 15: "if anyone's works are burned, he will suffer loss; but he himself will be saved, yet so as through fire." The fire speaks of God's discerning judgment, not hell fire. A Christian can be saved from hell, but enter heaven without reward.

Believers have had the judgment of their salvation already decided. In John 5:24 Jesus says, "Most assuredly, I say to you, he who hears My word and believes in Him who sent Me has everlasting life, and shall not come into judgment, but has passed from death into life." In Romans 8:33-34, the Apostle Paul argues that Christians do not face condemnation because of Christ:

> *Who shall bring a charge against God's elect? It is God who justifies. Who is he who condemns? It is Christ who died, and furthermore is also risen, who is even at the right hand of God, who also makes intercession for us.*

Clearly, the Christian does not face a judgment for salvation, because that judgment was settled when he believed in Jesus Christ who paid the price for sin on the cross and rose from the dead to show God's acceptance of His sacrifice. Now Jesus lives at the right hand of God to intercede for us in the face of any accusation or attempt to condemn. Our salvation is settled and secure.

A – Great White Throne Judgment	B – Judgment Seat of Christ
For unbelievers	For believers
At the end of the kingdom era	Before or during the kingdom era
Based on lack of faith in Christ	Based on faithfulness to Christ
Results in eternity in the lake of fire	Results in eternal rewards gained or denied

The often-overlooked B Truth is that Christians are judged for their works and their faithfulness at the Judgment Seat of Christ. If this judgment is confused with the A Truth of the Great White Throne Judgment, where the unbeliever's works are also judged, then works encroach upon the gospel of grace. It is important to keep the two judgments clear!

Fire or burning. There is a natural inclination among many who read the Bible to associate the mention of fire or burning with the eternal hell fire that burns unbelievers in the lake of fire. The eternal fire of God's judgment *is* mentioned in Jesus' story of the rich man and Lazarus (Luke 16:19-31) and in the passage on the Great White Throne Judgment (Rev. 20:11-15).

However, there are many uses of fire and the imagery of burning that have believers in view. This does not mean that the believer can lose salvation and is eternally punished by fire. It refers to God's disciplinary fire. It is a basic scriptural principle that God disciplines His children when they go astray, because He loves them.

> *My son, do not despise the chastening of the Lord, Nor be discouraged when you are rebuked by Him; For whom the Lord loves He chastens, And scourges every son whom He receives. Hebrews 12:5-7*

Fire is used to describe God's disciplinary burning of the believer's unworthy works (1 Cor. 3:14-15). It is also used in an analogy that shows fruitless believers are like sticks and thorns that are burned because they are not useful (John 15:6). The book of Hebrews mentions fire as God's discipline upon the readers who were believers turning back to Judaism. Actually, it does not say they will be burned, but fire imagery is used in several places. In Hebrews 6:7-8, it is used in an analogy very similar to that used in 1 Corinthians 3 and John 15. It seems to refer to disciplinary action on useless or unfaithful believers. In Hebrews 10:27, it only speaks of "fiery indignation," which is like saying "hot anger." But in the context, that anger is toward His people (Heb. 10:30). The final reference in Hebrews 12:29 simply states, "For our God is a consuming fire." But the author writes as a believer about the character of God. God can be a fiery Judge toward believers who disobey. How that fire is demonstrated is not specified or described, but it nowhere speaks about the eternal fire of hell.

A – Hell Fire	B –Disciplinary Fire
Eternal	Temporal
For unbelievers only	For believers or unbelievers
Burns the unbeliever	Burns the believer's unworthy works

If we assume that all references to fire and burning are A Truth, meaning eternal damnation, then we would have to conclude that Christians can lose their salvation since some of the New Testament passages that mention fire and burning are addressed to Christians. Furthermore, we would have to conclude that works are the basis of salvation or the loss of it, which is contrary to the gospel of grace. That is why it is important to understand there is a biblical B Truth category of God's discipline of believers. Believers are never burned, but their works are, or they can be chastised by a fiery angry God.

Accursed or disqualified. Another assumption made too quickly by many Bible readers is that the mention of a curse or of disqualification is a sentence to hell. Again, the problem presented by that view is that since these terms are sometimes used of believers, we would have to conclude salvation is lost. But we will see that these terms are not necessarily A Truth and do not demand eternal condemnation.

The word *accursed* is usually a translation of *anathema*, which means "under God's curse." The Apostle Paul uses it in Galatians 1:8-9 for those who preach a false gospel. The NIV interprets the phrase as the threat of hell: "let him be eternally condemned." Paul is writing to Christians, but he could be addressing either the unbelieving false teachers in Galatia, or the believers who have adopted and propagated their teaching. If eternal security is assumed, then if it is used of believers, it cannot mean they lose their salvation. Paul even includes himself and angels in his hypothetical example of someone who could teach a false gospel. This curse also seems to be used of Christians in 1 Corinthians 16:22 who do not love the Lord Jesus. How God's curse is experienced is not specified in these passages, but it certainly implies a severely unpleasant consequence.

Similarly, the word *disqualified* (*adokimos*) does not necessarily mean someone is sentenced to hell. The word simply expresses the idea of disapproval, that is, disapproval in regards to an award. The Apostle Paul uses it in 1 Corinthians 9:27 to refer to a fate that could possibly be his if he does not discipline his body. He is not saying he will lose salvation, but rather be disqualified from a reward. The context uses an athletic metaphor of a runner and a fighter who must discipline their bodies or else lose the award for winning.

Christians do not stand in danger of an eternal curse, because that curse was placed upon Jesus Christ on the cross (Rom. 8:34; Gal. 3:13; Col. 2:14). Neither can they be disqualified from eternal life. The B Truth understanding of the words *accursed* and *disqualified* hold serious truths about losing the blessing of God or losing His rewards.

Knowing God. The word *know* can be used as A Truth or B Truth. It is used by Jesus as A Truth in the sense that He knows those who do or do not belong to Him (see Matt. 7:23 and John 10:27).

However, it is often used for someone who comes into a relationship with God and has the privilege of knowing God intimately. John 17:3 describes having eternal life as knowing God and Jesus Christ. Salvation establishes the relationship with God that offers intimacy. Intimate knowledge of God is not available to the unbelieving world; it is the kind of intimacy enjoyed by Jesus with His Father (John 17:25). The Apostle Paul was already saved, but desired a greater intimacy with God, thus his desire "to know Him" (Phil. 3:10).

Another B Truth use of knowing God is in 1 John. The term is used there to describe the intimacy of fellowship with God, which is the theme of the epistle (1 John 1:3-4). Knowing God in an intimate way is demonstrated by those who keep His commandments (1 John 2:3-5).

If knowing God is assigned to A Truth only, then these examples teach that Paul was seeking to be saved, and those who do not keep God's commandments cannot be Christians. Knowing that some uses of *know* can be interpreted as B Truth avoids the pitfalls that destroy the Gospel of God's free grace.

2

A Truth B Truth Applied to Bible Passages

HE PURPOSE OF this section is to show how the A Truth B Truth approach helps us interpret Bible passages that are often misinterpreted and misunderstood. No doubt you will recognize many of them as passages you had to struggle with or help other people understand. In fact, most of these come from my own long experience of answering my and others' questions about passages that didn't seem to "fit" my or their understanding about salvation or the Christian life.

The list is not exhaustive. There will always be other passages that raise questions. But these are most of the passages that mislead people about the nature of salvation and its distinction from Christian life issues. I hope that two things are accomplished here. First, you see that using the A Truth B Truth approach yields a good and biblically consistent interpretation. Second, that you see how to apply the A Truth B Truth approach to other "problem" passages you encounter in your Bible study or teaching.

I focus on the New Testament because that is where much of the confusion is and where we find so clearly the discussions about eternal salvation and the Christian life. Also, the Old Testament was not written to the church specifically, but to the nation of Israel. I do see a distinction between Israel and the church. I understand that the church began in Acts 2:1-4 (cf. Acts 11:15 and 1 Cor. 12:13).

The passages are organized mostly by groupings of similar books in the New Testament and their sequential order in a particular book. I could have organized the passages by topic (passages that look like they teach we can lose salvation, passages that speak of rewards, passages that speak of judgment, etc.), and that has its merits, but I realized that if I did that, I would have to constantly re-establish the context of a passage or re-explain terms. It would have resulted in a lot of redundancy. One benefit of this sequential treatment is that there will be some continuity with the overall context. Another benefit is that the discussion of a particular passage will be easy to find, and thus make the book more useful as a reference tool.

The Gospels of Matthew, Mark, Luke

5

THESE FIRST THREE books of the New Testament are called the Synoptic Gospels. *Synoptic* means *to see things together,* and it is used of Matthew, Mark, and Luke because they share much of the same material about the life of Jesus Christ. Since there is overlap or repetition of stories, sayings, parables, etc., I will address passages that appear in multiple Gospels in one discussion, sometimes organized by topic.

It is essential to remember that the Gospels convey events and messages from the life of Jesus Christ, who was usually addressing Jewish people or crowds about Jewish issues under the Old Mosaic Covenant. Some of Jesus and John the Baptist's teachings would apply then, but not now, because we are no longer under the Mosaic Law. Knowing this historical, cultural, and theological context will help interpretation. In addition to that original setting, the authors of the three Gospels also had different audiences in mind as they wrote, which is one reason accounts may be described or conveyed differently.

Passages from the Sermon on the Mount

A number of passages in the Sermon on the Mount are misunderstood when the A Truth B Truth approach is ignored. When we look at the Sermon, we observe that it came at a time when Jesus had not yet formally presented Himself as Israel's King, so Israel had not yet rejected Him. He came to teach the nation about the nature of the kingdom of God. A key to understanding the Sermon is knowing the background controversy with the scribes and Pharisees (leaders of Israel), and their errant view of how to be right with God. Throughout His ministry, Jesus criticized these Jewish leaders for their hypocritical religion. Their actions were fastidious, but their hearts were evil

(Matt. 23:1-28; Mark 7:1-9). Jesus' message to Israel was that the standard of righteousness for the kingdom is more than what the Scribes and Pharisees had to offer: "For I say to you, that unless your righteousness exceeds the righteousness of the scribes and Pharisees, you will by no means enter the kingdom of heaven" (Matt. 5:20). The Sermon on the Mount expounds kingdom righteousness for Israelites as a guide for present conduct, but it also prepares them for the only One who could uphold such a standard, Jesus Christ.

There are obvious reasons that the Sermon is not a presentation of the saving gospel. First, the primary audience is addressed as believers. They are "persecuted for righteousness' sake," are "the salt of the earth," and "the light of the world" (Matt. 5:10-12; 13-14). Jesus instructs them in how to pray, give, and fast (Matt. 6:16-18). They have a Father in heaven (Matt. 6:9; 7:11). He does not explain the gospel to them. Second, if this were an evangelistic message, then it would be a works gospel, indeed a works gospel that required one to exceed the ethical righteousness of the Jewish leaders (Matt. 5:20) and match the perfection of God the Father (Matt. 5:48). Third, we see a great difference from John's Gospel that *was* written with an evangelistic purpose (John 20:31). John shows Jesus presenting the gospel as a free gift early in His ministry (John 3:1-21; 4:1-26) before John the Baptist was imprisoned (John 3:23-24; 4:1). By the time of Jesus' public ministry, John was in prison (Matt. 4:12-17; Mark 1:14-15; Luke 3:20), and the disciples had heard Jesus' presentation of the gospel as a free gift. It is inconceivable that they would then understand the Sermon on the Mount as an ethical system that earns salvation.

That said, we observe that in addition to the disciples in the forefront of the audience, there is also a multitude present (Matt. 5:1). Though not a presentation of the gospel to the unsaved, the Sermon has a pre-evangelistic aspect. While explaining the righteous conduct appropriate for those disciples who anticipate the coming kingdom, those who are not yet saved and not yet disciples would see a high standard that should cause them to confront their shortcomings and long for God's kingdom righteousness. Near the end of the Sermon, Jesus confronts the hearers with a choice between the narrow way that leads to life and the broad way that leads to destruction (Matt. 7:13-14). He also challenges the audience to build their lives on the solid foundation of His teachings instead of the unstable sand (Matt. 7:24-27). Such choices appeal to disciples to lead a righteous life, as well as to the unsaved to find and live in the narrow way that leads to a stable life.

With this context in mind, we can examine some of the sections of the sermon where A Truth and B Truth are often confused.

The Beatitudes. Matthew 5:3-12 (cf. Mark 1:16-20)

3   *"Blessed are the poor in spirit,*
       For theirs is the kingdom of heaven.

4   *Blessed are those who mourn,*
       For they shall be comforted.

5   *Blessed are the meek,*
       For they shall inherit the earth.

6   *Blessed are those who hunger and thirst for righteousness,*
       For they shall be filled.

7   *Blessed are the merciful,*
       For they shall obtain mercy.

8   *Blessed are the pure in heart,*
       For they shall see God.

9   *Blessed are the peacemakers,*
       For they shall be called sons of God.

10   *Blessed are those who are persecuted for righteousness' sake,*
       For theirs is the kingdom of heaven.

11   *Blessed are you when they revile and persecute you, and say all kinds of evil against you falsely for My sake.* [12] *Rejoice and be exceedingly glad, for great is your reward in heaven, for so they persecuted the prophets who were before you."*

A Truth Interpretation: These virtues describe the traits one must have to be a Christian.

B Truth Interpretation: These virtues describe the traits that are characteristic of kingdom righteousness.

The first part of the Sermon on the Mount is popularly called The Beatitudes (from the idea of happy, blessed, fortunate), which is named from the supreme blessings pronounced in each statement. Each of these eight virtues has a corresponding consequence. Some have taken the beatitudes as a list of virtues required for salvation with each consequence describing some aspect of salvation (A Truth).

Understanding the context helps us discern whether this is A Truth or B Truth. Jesus was speaking first to His disciples (the antecedent nearest to "them" in verse 2 is "His disciples in verse 1, unless "them" refers to both the multitudes and His disciples). We might say that Jesus spoke to all who came and heard, but His disciples were on the front row (Matt. 4:25-5:2). If we understand that He is contrasting these kingdom virtues with the hypocritical righteous posing of Israel's religious teachers, we understand the Beatitudes are B Truth because they describe a lifestyle consistent with God's kingdom. They are not a presentation of the gospel. In fact, in light of the coming kingdom, they assume the state of someone who is eternally saved, someone who wants to live in anticipation of the kingdom.

The word "blessed" (from *makarios*) does not mean *saved*. It denotes the joyful and happy state of those who live out the virtues listed. They are blessed because the future kingdom holds special blessings for them. Note that the consequences are future, except the first and last (Matt. 5:3, 10). If this were an evangelistic appeal, *all* the blessings would be stated in the present or perfect tense (past action with continuing results). The present tense used in verses 3 and 10 assures "the poor in spirit" and "those who are persecuted for righteousness' sake" that "theirs is the kingdom of heaven." This phrase, along with verses 11-12, seem to be an assurance that persecution cannot cause the humble and persevering believer to forfeit the security of a kingdom destiny that they presently possess which will also yield future rewards for enduring persecution.

As we anticipate the kingdom, we should appropriate the virtues of the Beatitudes as our own because they are kingdom virtues. As we do so, we can enjoy the blessing of a present assurance of our kingdom destiny and a promise of our future kingdom reward.

Pluck out your eye. Matthew 5:29-30

> ²⁹ *"If your right eye causes you to sin, pluck it out and cast it from you; for it is more profitable for you that one of your members perish, than for your whole body to be cast into hell.* ³⁰ *And if your right hand causes you to sin, cut it off and cast it from you; for it is more profitable for you that one of your members perish, than for your whole body to be cast into hell."*

A Truth Interpretation: A person who does not do what is necessary to stop sinning will be thrown into hell.

B Truth Interpretation: It is better to be a believer who suffers loss in order to stop sinning than to be a whole unbeliever thrown into hell.

We remember that Jesus is addressing His disciples with the multitude listening in. He is not telling His disciples that if they continue to sin they will lose their salvation. He is certainly not suggesting if people stop sinning they will avoid hell. He is telling his disciples that kingdom conduct demands a radical effort to avoid a serious sin like the sin of adultery that He mentions (vv. 27-28). Of course, plucking out the eye and cutting off the hand are metaphors for a radical commitment to not sin. While the disciple will have to suffer severely in order to deny his sinful desires, he is better off than an unsaved person who sins with abandon, makes no effort to avoid sin, and remains a whole person (with all his body parts), but is thrown into hell. While cutting off body parts is symbolic, the reality behind the metaphor can involve things like suffering a financial loss to avoid sin, suffering a severed relationship, or suffering a relocation to avoid a temptation. The loss is real and may be painful, but it is nothing compared to those who refuse to deal with their sin and end up in hell.

Mark 9:43-48 uses the same metaphors (but includes cutting off a foot) and the same consequences. In this context, Jesus is teaching his disciples a lesson about greatness in the anticipated kingdom (Mark 9:33-35). Greatness is found in those disciples who value, accept, and serve those who are younger, weaker, and less committed to Christ (the children of Mark 9:36-37 and the one who is not following Christ as a committed disciple, vv. 38-41). Together, these are the "little ones" or the young and immature believers of verse 42. It is a serious offense to the Lord to cause one of these to sin, and therefore wreck their fragile faith, as is shown by the reference to hanging a millstone around the offender's neck and throwing him into the sea.

In verse 43, there is a dramatic shift from talking about someone who causes a little one to sin to directly addressing the disciples' potential to sin. This is probably because a disciple who sins can lead a less mature believer to sin also. As disciples, suffering a temporary loss (if we continue with the metaphor, all body parts would be restored in eternity) and entering life is a better fate than an unbeliever who suffers no loss as he indulges in sin and goes to hell with all his body parts, a whole person (vv. 43-48). Disciples shouldn't grieve about losses in this life when they sacrifice desires for the sake of others, because enduring such a brief loss is nothing compared to the fate of an unbeliever. Worse, the sin of an indulgent unbeliever may cause a little one to sin, bringing the severe punishment represented by the millstone and watery fate.

As followers of Christ, we have a kingdom responsibility to take drastic measures to avoid sin. Sin misrepresents the Lord, despises His grace, and can cause less mature believers to sin, injuring their walk with the Lord. The Lord takes sin seriously, and so should we.

Forgive to be forgiven. Matthew 6:14-15 (cf. Mark 11:25-26)

[14] *"For if you forgive men their trespasses, your heavenly Father will also forgive you. [15] But if you do not forgive men their trespasses, neither will your Father forgive your trespasses."*

A Truth Interpretation: If a person does not forgive others who sin against him, he cannot be saved, or will lose his salvation.

B Truth Interpretation: If a believer does not forgive others who sin against him, he will suffer in the quality of his fellowship with God.

The statement in Matthew is clear in its teaching: If someone does not forgive others, then God will not forgive him. If this forgiveness from God refers to the forgiveness that we receive at the time of salvation (Eph. 1:7; Col. 2:13-14), then it makes salvation conditioned on our willingness to forgive others. As an A Truth statement, it would speak of the positional aspect of our salvation: In God's eyes we are forgiven once and for all and forever based on the payment for our sins by Jesus Christ dying on the cross.

But there is another kind of forgiveness. In fact, the context demands it because here, Jesus is teaching His followers to pray (Matt. 6:5-13). This forgiveness is not positional forgiveness, but fellowship forgiveness because it tells those who already know God how to maintain a close walk with Him. Jesus taught this truth to Peter and the disciples in the Upper Room. When He attempted to wash Peter's feet, Peter refused Him. Jesus then explained, "He who is bathed needs only to wash his feet, but is completely clean; and you are clean, but not all of you." So for those who are saved, there is a daily need to confess sins and claim a new experience of fellowship forgiveness based on Christ's past provision (His death on the cross) and our present position (a child of God). First John 1:9 shows that confessing sin and receiving God's forgiveness is necessary for walking in the light and maintaining fellowship with God (1 John 1:3-8).

In the realm of B Truth, forgiveness is very important to Christians not only to maintain fellowship with God, but harmony with other people. Thus, we are exhorted to forgive others just as Jesus Christ forgave us (Eph. 4:32; Col. 3:13). If we harbor unforgiveness toward others, we will not enjoy the intimacy God desires to have with us. If we harbor unforgiveness toward others, not only do we disobey God's command to forgive, but the barrier of our hardened heart keeps us from enjoying God's full fellowship.

Understanding this truth about fellowship forgiveness keeps us from imposing a condition on the gospel other than faith alone. The gospel invitation is not, "Believe and forgive others," but simply "Believe."

Fruit and false prophets. Matthew 7:15-20

[15] *"Beware of false prophets, who come to you in sheep's clothing, but inwardly they are ravenous wolves.* [16] *You will know them by their fruits. Do men gather grapes from thorn bushes or figs from thistles?* [17] *Even so, every good tree bears good fruit, but a bad tree bears bad fruit.* [18] *A good tree cannot bear bad fruit, nor can a bad tree bear good fruit.* [19] *Every tree that does not bear good fruit is cut down and thrown into the fire.* [20] *Therefore by their fruits you will know them."*

A Truth Interpretation: A person proves he is unsaved by having bad fruit and no good fruit, which refers to his conduct.

B Truth Interpretation: A false prophet evidences he is not genuine by having bad fruit, or no good fruit, which may refer to his teaching.

It is common to see this passage interpreted as A Truth: If a person does not bear good fruit, then that person is not saved. Visible fruit is necessary for salvation to be proven genuine, it is said.

Of course there are problems with that position at the outset: What is good fruit, how is it measured, who measures it, and how much fruit is necessary to prove salvation? You see that these questions cannot be answered easily and objectively. Something that looks like good fruit could come from a selfish or nefarious motive. How could anyone definitely know? Any two people will probably not agree on a definition of what comprises good fruit and how much is necessary to prove someone's salvation.

Careful observation helps us understand this passage. It is explaining how to identify false prophets, not professing Christians in general. What is discerned is not their salvation, but whether they represent God as a true prophet. The test is not whether they have any fruits, but whether they have bad fruits (v. 17). Evidently, false prophets have fruits that look good because they are able to outwardly present themselves as sheep (v. 15), but the bad nature of their fruit eventually betrays them (v. 16). Since fruits can refer to either words (Matt. 12:33-37) or deeds (Matt. 3:8; 13:23; John 15:2-8), it is best to see words primarily in view here. The ultimate test of a prophet is not how he acts, but what he teaches. That was the test in the Old Testament with which the Jews were familiar (Deut. 13:1-6; 18:20-22). In other New Testament passages, both words and works combine to identify false prophets (2 Pet. 2:1-3, 10, 12-15; Jude 4, 8-11, 16).

Making good works a test of salvation contradicts the gospel of grace. While we acknowledge that salvation should result in good works and that God both desires and commands them, they cannot be the ultimate test of salvation because there is no objective standard for what comprises good works, what motivates them, and how many are needed. Works can reflect the true nature of a person, but cannot ultimately determine whether that person is saved or not. In this passage, words and works are best understood as a test for false prophets. Works in general are relevant to the realm of B Truth, which concerns believers since God's purpose (not guarantee) is for all believers to do good works (Eph. 2:10). As Christians, we should do good works, but make sure they are from good motives and good teaching.

False professors. Matthew 7:21-23

> [21] *"Not everyone who says to Me, 'Lord, Lord,' shall enter the kingdom of heaven, but he who does the will of My Father in heaven.* [22] *Many will say to Me in that day, 'Lord, Lord, have we not prophesied in Your name, cast out demons in Your name, and done many wonders in Your name?'* [23] *And then I will declare to them, 'I never knew you; depart from Me, you who practice lawlessness!'"*

A Truth Interpretation: Many who profess to be Christians are not really saved because they are practicing sin.

Second A Truth Interpretation: Many who profess to be Christians are not really saved, because they do not know Jesus as Savior.

This passage is often used to argue that not all who profess to know Jesus Christ as Savior are truly saved because they do not have corroborating good works. Works, therefore, are necessary evidence of salvation. While it is certainly true that not all *professors* of salvation are *possessors* of salvation, it does not follow from this passage that works are the determinative test. If anything, works in this passage actually show the opposite—that they cannot prove one's salvation.

If we are mindful of the context, we see that this passage relates to the discussion of false prophets in 7:15-20 (see v. 22—they "prophesied"). While 7:21-23 would surely include the false prophets, Jesus seems to broaden the application to "everyone" (v. 21) who makes spiritual claims. He focuses first on professing believers who are false *prophets*, then on unbelievers who are false *professors*. Like the false prophets, they have the outward appearance of true sheep. But these also have miraculous deeds and some correct theology, acknowledging that Jesus is Lord. But ultimately, Jesus Christ rejects them with the verdict that he *never* knew them. They are not genuine believers.

Jesus' criterion for rejecting these professors of salvation is that they are not doing "the will of My Father in heaven." The will of the Father could not simply be good works because they had those. If they could achieve kingdom righteousness by good works, that would be salvation apart from grace. If works are the standard for entry into heaven or the kingdom, then they must be done according to God's standard, which is perfection (Matt. 5:48). But that is an impossible standard that even the fastidious scribes and Pharisees could not reach (Matt. 5:20). Then what is the will of the Father? It is to believe in the only One who could perfectly fulfill all the commandments in our place, Jesus Christ (John 6:28-29).

The context leads us to the conclusion that trusting in the perfect righteousness of Jesus Christ is the only way to salvation. In 7:13-15, Jesus spoke of a narrow gate that leads to life (cf. John 10:9). Luke 13:24-30 also mentions the narrow gate as the way to salvation in a parable with similar language. There, Jesus answers the question posed by an anonymous hearer, "Lord, are there few who are saved?" Jesus talks about entering the narrow gate and those who are shut out by a closed door. He explains that false professors are excluded from the way of salvation, and they will grieve deeply as they realize their exclusion from the kingdom of God (Luke 13:28).

The A Truth of Matthew 7:21-23 is that faith in Jesus Christ must be our only hope of eternal life. Doing good works are not a part of that saving message. Good theology, impressive deeds, and submission to Christ as Lord cannot save us. This group of professors had all these things, but they were not saved. All they had was self-righteousness instead of Christ-righteousness.

The sad result of trusting in theology, good works, or submission to Christ's Lordship without trusting in Christ for His righteousness is that many who think they are saved have never really been saved. This is as true today as it was then.

Passages on Discipleship

Are disciples born or made? In other words, is every Christian a disciple or only those who meet certain conditions? Whether we see conditions for discipleship as A Truth or B Truth is one of the most important distinctions we can make in how we understand the gospel and the Christian life.

Fishing and following. Matthew 4:18-22 (cf. Mark 1:16-20; Luke 5:1-11)

> [18] *And Jesus, walking by the Sea of Galilee, saw two brothers, Simon called Peter, and Andrew his brother, casting a net into the sea; for they were fishermen.* [19] *Then He said to them, "Follow Me, and I will make you fishers of men."* [20] *They immediately left their nets and followed Him.*
>
> [21] *Going on from there, He saw two other brothers, James the son of Zebedee, and John his brother, in the boat with Zebedee their father, mending their nets. He called them,* [22] *and immediately they left the boat and their father, and followed Him.*

A Truth Interpretation: Jesus' call to follow Him is a call to salvation.

B Truth Interpretation: Jesus' call to follow Him is a call to become a disciple.

Since in the Synoptics this encounter with the first disciples at the Sea of Galilee is the first recorded, it is sometimes assumed that Jesus is inviting Andrew, Peter, James, and John to salvation. In that view, the assumption is that salvation is obtained by following Jesus, since that is His invitation in

Matthew and Mark's accounts. Is Jesus' call to follow an A Truth or B Truth invitation?

On the face of it, we can easily deny that salvation is the invitation, because Jesus clarified it with "I will make you fishers of men." This obviously speaks of evangelism that leads others to Jesus Christ. If this is A Truth, here is where the logic takes us: We are saved by following Christ in such a way that we are leading others to Christ. This would be a unique condition for salvation—only soul-winners would be saved! It would also make many Christians who have not led anyone to Christ doubt their salvation.

But there is no reason to assume that this is Jesus' first encounter ever with the disciples. In fact, John 1:35-42 is good evidence that Andrew and Peter, at least, had encountered Jesus earlier since it is Peter's first introduction to the Lord. In John, they met Jesus "beyond the Jordan" where John the Baptist was baptizing, not at the Sea of Galilee (John 1:28, 43). When we compare the setting and circumstances, we see two different stories. By the same measure, Luke 5:1-11 is a different story from Matthew and Mark's account. Though the seaside setting is similar, we find no crowd pressing Jesus; He is alone. He is also walking, not standing as in Matthew and Mark's account, and the fishermen are in the boat, not on shore washing their nets, and Luke alone mentions the miraculous catch of fish. Since all these men were fishermen in Galilee, they surely would have encountered Jesus and His teaching more than once.

By observing these details, we see that this call to follow Jesus is B Truth. Jesus is inviting these men, who had already met Him and evidently already believed (see John 2:11) to become His disciples. That means they had to commit to leaving their work, their source of income, and even their families, which they did. Salvation is free, but discipleship is costly.

Accepting this invitation to discipleship gives every Christian a purpose in this world. We are to help others come to Jesus Christ as Savior. For those who fear sharing their faith with others, there is comfort in Jesus' promise that *He* will make us fishers of men. It is His promise; all we have to do is follow.

Hating your family. Matthew 10:37; Luke 14:26

"He who loves father or mother more than Me is not worthy of Me. And he who loves son or daughter more than Me is not worthy of Me." (Matthew 10:37)

"If anyone comes to Me and does not hate his father and mother, wife and children, brothers and sisters, yes, and his own life also, He cannot be My disciple." (Luke 14:26)

A Truth Interpretation: If a person loves anyone, even a family member, more than Jesus, that person is unworthy of salvation and therefore cannot be saved.

B Truth Interpretation: If a believer loves anyone, even a family member, more than Jesus, that person is not worthy of Jesus' favorable recognition as His disciple.

Jesus would never advocate hating our family members, as Luke's wording might indicate. Matthew helpfully clarifies what Luke's version means. To "hate" is used as a familiar figure of speech in the first century that meant "to love less than;" in other words, Jesus is saying that to be His disciple, one must love Him more than any other person. When we compare the two accounts, to be worthy of Christ in Matthew is the equivalent of being a disciple in Luke's words, or worthy to be called a disciple of Christ. The worthiness spoken of is not in relation to Christ's righteousness, but denotes His favorable recognition of one who is His disciple. The condition for becoming a worthy disciple is that one must be devoted to Jesus Christ above every other human relationship, even family members.

Again, context helps us in Matthew's account because Jesus is preparing His disciples for a mixed response to their message as He sends them out to preach (Matt. 10:5-7). As some respond favorably to the gospel, it will put them at odds with even family members. Choosing to side with Jesus invites family conflict (Matt. 10:34-36).

If we understand this to be a condition of discipleship, then it is B Truth. In order for it to be A Truth, an unbeliever would have to know enough about Jesus Christ to be willing to love Him above all others, then he could be saved. But this reverses the biblical order: "We love Him because He first loved us" (1 John 4:19). Without experiencing the love of Jesus Christ in the salvation experience, how can we expect an unbeliever to respond with total devotion and love?

Not as much in the United States, but in other countries, I have seen wonderful examples of those who have identified with Jesus Christ even though they knew their family members would ostracize or disown them. I once had a church member, a Christian friend, ignore me in public because she was with her mother who did not approve of her faith in Christ. She did not put her relationship with Christ above her relationship with her mother. Does this mean she was not saved? No—as much as I could know, I think she was—but she wasn't much of a disciple!

We who know Jesus as our Savior and Lord should be devoted to Him above anyone else in this world. How can we do less when He gave His own life for us? The wonderful truth is that the more we love Jesus Christ, the more we will love our family members and all other people. After all, Jesus loved and died for them too!

Taking His yoke and learning. Matt 11:28-30.

> *"Come to Me, all you who labor and are heavy laden, and I will give you rest. Take My yoke upon you and learn from Me, for I am gentle and lowly in heart, and you will find rest for your souls. For My yoke is easy and My burden is light."*

A Truth Interpretation: The invitation to come to Jesus, take His yoke, and learn from Him are all invitations to become a Christian.

B Truth Interpretation: The invitation to come to Jesus is an invitation to salvation, but the invitation to take His yoke and learn from Him are invitations to discipleship.

This passage definitely teaches discipleship truth in its invitation to take the yoke of Christ and learn from Him. After all, *disciple* essentially means *learner*. But we observe a progression in this invitation: Come . . . Take . . . Learn. Before one can "take" and "learn," one must "come." The invitation to "come to" Jesus is used elsewhere as an invitation to come to Him as Savior, in other words, it is an A Truth invitation (John 5:40; 6:35. 37, 44, 65; 7:37) and is different from "come after," which is a B Truth invitation (we'll discuss "come after" in the next passage).

Jesus speaks these words after He acknowledges that the cities of Israel had rejected Him (Matt. 11:20-24). In general, the nation was under the sway of the Pharisees and their rigid interpretation of the Law of Moses. It made salvation impossible, as any system of performance does. The apostle Peter affirmed this when he defended salvation by grace against those who said the Law must be kept:

"Now therefore, why do you test God by putting a yoke on the neck of the disciples which neither our fathers nor we were able to bear? But we believe that through the grace of the Lord Jesus Christ we shall be saved in the same manner as they." (Acts 15:10-11)

Jesus' invitation recognizes the nation's rejection, but invites individual Jews within the nation to come to Him for salvation. Only in salvation by His grace can they find rest for their souls that they could never find under the Pharisaical Law.

After coming to Christ for salvation, the individual is invited to take Jesus' yoke, which evokes the image of a yoke that binds an ox to a plow. This is evidently meant to contrast the impossible yoke of the Mosaic Law and its rabbinic interpretations, which the scribes and Pharisees imposed on their followers. After one comes to Christ for salvation, he or she can learn how to walk in the love and grace of Jesus Christ. Though the demands of discipleship are stringent, they are at the same time "easy" and "light" because life in Jesus Christ is simpler than life under the Pharisees' interpretation of the Law. And God's grace, which provides salvation, also provides power to live righteously through the indwelling Holy Spirit (cf. Rom. 8:3-4). Yoked to Jesus, the burden seems light.

As much as we need to distinguish between salvation and discipleship for the sake of gospel clarity, we should also recognize that Jesus wants both and sometimes invites people to the whole package, but always in proper sequence as in this passage. When we share the gospel with people, it is good to tell them that Jesus offers not only a new birth, but also a new life. There is much to learn from Him after we are saved!

Following Jesus. Matthew 10:38; 16:24 (cf. Mark 8:34; Luke 9:23; 14:27)

"And he who does not take his cross and follow after Me is not worthy of Me." (Matthew 10:38)

Then Jesus said to His disciples, "If anyone desires to come after Me, let him deny himself, and take up his cross, and follow Me." (Matthew 16:24)

A Truth Interpretation: To "come after" or "follow" Jesus refers to becoming a Christian.

B Truth Interpretation: To "come after" or "follow" Jesus refers to becoming a disciple.

Since these statements from Jesus about becoming a disciple are similar, we will look at them together. We notice that while Jesus was addressing the crowds, the disciples were always present (the disciples exclusively in Matt. 10:1-11:1). Since the disciples were believers at this point (John 2:11), and probably many others in the crowd as well, we should suspect that these conditions address the commitments of a disciple, not the condition for salvation.

Jesus' invitation is to "come after Me," not "come to Me" as in Matthew 11:28 (see the previous discussion). To *come after* or *follow* Jesus is the language of discipleship. It speaks of a life committed to Him. It is different from coming *to* Him for salvation. That these conditions are in the category of B Truth becomes more apparent when we understand the implications of each of them.

The condition mentioned first in Matthew 16:24 (as also in Mark 8:34 and Luke 9:23) is that a person must "deny himself." As always, the context gives us insight into what this means. In both Matthew and Luke, Jesus has just predicted that He is going to suffer and even die. No one wants to die, not even Jesus (Luke 22:42), but He obediently goes to His death because it is God's will for Him. To deny oneself is to say "no" to our desires (good and bad) in order to say "yes" to God's will for us. It is a decision we make as we come to understand what God's will is, something an unsaved person really doesn't know. Clearly it is B Truth related to the Christian life.

A second condition mentioned in these two passages, but also in Mark 10:38 and in Luke 14:27, is that one must "take up his cross." Again, the contexts in which Jesus gives this condition have, as a background, His own suffering and death. The meaning is certainly not lost on the disciples and the crowds. Jesus is speaking of a willingness to suffer and die and He is inviting others to do the same in order to be His disciples. The emotional impact of His statement is dulled to our modern sensibilities. When the crowds heard the word "cross" they surely shuddered at the thought of being crucified by their Roman occupiers on wooden crossbars exposed to the elements in public, or lining the streets with other offenders and dying a slow humiliating death. In that day, crucifixion was the cruelest kind of death and included social and religious stigmas (such as God's curse, Deut. 21:23).

Though carrying one's cross is stringent enough as a condition for discipleship, Luke 9:23 adds that this must be done "daily" suggesting Jesus is speaking not just of someone's physical death, but also a daily willingness to suffer for identifying with Jesus Christ. Now we clearly see why this cannot be A Truth. How can someone be saved if it requires a daily commitment to suffer and die for Jesus Christ? And how does an unsaved person comprehend what suffering for Christ entails? Besides, salvation is possible because Jesus died for us, not because we die for Him."

The third condition in these passages is simply "follow Me." Again, as with His call to Peter, Andrew, James, and John at the Sea of Galilee while they were fishing, Jesus is inviting people to follow Him as disciples or learners. Normally, a first-century Jewish disciple would literally follow his master, live with him, eat with him, study with him. It meant giving up one's own agenda and goals for that of the master's or teacher's. Since this is obviously a process, not a single event, it cannot be A Truth.

You can see how confused people can become if we tell them that they can only be saved if they deny all their own desires and adopt God's, are willing to suffer or die every day for being a Christian, and follow God's agenda for their lives. For that matter, we who are Christians, rarely keep these commitments fully. For us, they are goals that guide our hearts as we seek to fulfill them perfectly. But to make such criteria conditions for unsaved people to obtain salvation will only result in doubt and insecurity about measuring up on the one hand, or pride because they think they have on the other. Salvation is not about our commitments and suffering for Jesus Christ; it's about His suffering and commitment to us.

You might wonder why those who are called disciples are given conditions for discipleship. The answer to this is that discipleship is a process, not an accomplishment; it is a journey, not a destination. The end goal is Christlikeness (Matt. 10:25), something that cannot be fully achieved in this life. There is a sense in which every disciple is challenged to be more of a disciple. Peter was challenged to follow Christ several times after his initial decision at the Sea of Galilee, with each challenge demanding more of a commitment. For example, one of the last challenges, which Jesus gave after His resurrection, was for Peter to follow Christ *after* he was told the manner in which he would die (John 21:19). For Peter, that certainly contained a specific commitment he had not yet encountered. For each of us as Christians, Jesus Christ challenges us to move to the next level of commitment, something that is relative to where each of us is at the present. We can always become more of a disciple.

Finding your life. Matthew 10:39; 16:25-26 (cf. Mark 8:35-38; Luke 9:24-26; John 12:25)

"He who finds his life will lose it, and he who loses his life for My sake will find it." (Matthew 10:39)

"For whoever desires to save his life will lose it, but whoever loses his life for My sake will find it. For what profit is it to a man if he gains the whole world, and loses his own soul? Or what will a man give in exchange for his soul?" (Matthew 16:25-26)

A Truth Interpretation: If a person lives for himself, he will not gain salvation or he will lose salvation. But if a person forsakes his selfish desires, he will gain eternal life.

B Truth Interpretation: If a believer lives for himself, he will miss the abundant life that God has for him. But if he forsakes his selfish desires, he will find the abundant life.

These statements explain why the invitation to discipleship that we discussed above should be accepted. Whoever does so saves his *life*, or his *soul*. Immediately, when some hear the language about *saving* (or *losing*) *one's soul* they assume an A Truth interpretation taking it as a reference to salvation of one's spirit from hell. This is a problem created by the English translations of the Bible. The word *soul* (*psychē*) is the same word translated *life* in these passages (which is how some Bible versions translate it). It refers to life in its essence, the immaterial part of a person comprised of mind, will, and emotions that forms one's identity. Your life is who you really are. Luke's version of this statement is helpful because it uses the word "himself" for "life:" "For what profit is it to a man if he gains the whole world, and is himself destroyed or lost?" (Luke 9:25).

It is also important to understand how the word *save* (*sōzō*) is used. As discussed earlier, it does not always refer to eternal salvation. It simply means *to deliver, to preserve* from some danger or loss. Usually we determine its meaning from the context. Here, Jesus has just talked about *losing* our own desires and subsuming them to His desires for us. If someone wants to hang on to his own desires and agenda in this world ("save his life") he will lose what life is really all about—experiencing the will of God and the fullness of God's life. He may gain everything this world has to offer, but miss the greater experience of God's life now and as a reward in the future (v. 27).

Taken in this way, we see that the word *lose* (*apollumi*) is the opposite of *save*. It does not mean to be eternally lost in hell, but has the idea of *ruin* or *forfeit*. To lose your life is to ruin it or forfeit what God would have it be. Someone can have eternal life yet waste the opportunity to enjoy life's fullness by living for God now.

If we interpret this statement by Jesus as A Truth, we miss a profound principle for the Christian life. If we seek the things this world has to offer while avoiding the hardships that can be involved with knowing Jesus Christ, we lose the very quality of life we really desire. It is only by losing our life to God that we get it back fuller and richer than ever. *When life ceases to be the issue, life becomes the reality.*

We may think it is too painful to give up a consuming habit, a toxic relationship, or our own ambitions and plans. What we will discover is that in losing our life, we find true life—the fullness of God's abundant life now and forever.

Ashamed to confess. Matthew 10:32-33; Mark 8:38 (cf. Luke 9:26; 12:8-9)

> *"Therefore whoever confesses Me before men, him I will also confess before My Father who is in heaven. But whoever denies Me before men, him I will also deny before My Father who is in heaven."* *(Matthew 10:32-33)*

> *"For whoever is ashamed of Me and My words in this adulterous and sinful generation, of him the Son of Man also will be ashamed when He comes in the glory of His Father with the holy angels."* *(Mark 8:38)*

A Truth Interpretation: If a person does not confess Jesus publically, he will be denied salvation, will prove he was never saved, or if saved, lose that salvation.

B Truth Interpretation: If a Christian does not confess Jesus publically or is ashamed of Him, that person will be denied the reward of Jesus' commendation before God the Father.

These passages have a similar theme: If someone denies the Lord Jesus or is ashamed of Him, he will be denied before God the Father and Jesus will be ashamed of him. These are tough words, so tough that many interpret them as A Truth: Jesus will deny entrance into heaven and be ashamed in such a way that implies the person is unworthy of heaven.

Again, context is the key. In Matthew 10, Jesus is sending out His disciples with instructions and warnings about how they will be received and how they should not fear opposition. The warning of verses 32-33 about confessing (acknowledging) Jesus Christ could apply to those who hear the disciples' message, or it could apply to the disciples themselves, or it could be a principle that applies to both. Comparing Jesus' statement in Matthew with His similar statement in Luke 12:8-9, we find in both a common context about not fearing to speak to others about Christ. Though this could be a general principle, it certainly is addressed to the disciples first as both a warning and an encouragement.

In both Mark 8:38 and Luke 9:26, the statement is a warning without a corresponding encouragement. But this too is addressed to the disciples after Jesus tells them to deny themselves, take up their cross, and follow Him in order to "save" their lives. As we saw earlier, these are B Truths. Jesus explains that believers have choices and those choices have their respective consequences. One can identify with the world, lose his life, and earn Christ's shame, or one can identify with Christ. Though Mark and Luke's accounts do not mention a reward other than that one's life will be saved, Matthew's version goes on to speak of rewards in 10:41-42. The parallel account in Matthew 16:24-27 ends with a promise that when Jesus Christ returns, "He will reward each according to his works." Jesus' confessing or denying a confession and being ashamed are issues of rewards deserved by believers.

The negative "reward" (from *misthos*, which can also mean *recompense, payment*) for those who deny their identification with Christ or are ashamed of Him is that Jesus will not confess (acknowledge) them before the Father, or similarly, will be ashamed of them before the Father. Since this is in the context of B Truth, what does this mean? Since Jesus Christ's confession of someone before the Father is an acknowledgment of his or her faithfulness in identifying with Him, the negative of that is Jesus will withhold acknowledgment of that person. He will be ashamed in the sense of refusing to acknowledge him or her with a commendation before the Father.

That this is a consequence experienced only by Christians makes sense. It is no motivation to an unbeliever who rejects Christ not to be confessed before the Father or for Christ to be ashamed. In light of his decision to have nothing to do with Jesus Christ, what would he or she care?

But to those who have a relationship with Jesus Christ, to earn a word of approval or disapproval, or to make Christ ashamed would have a great motivating impact. The believer knows the love of God and the sacrifice Jesus has made for him by dying on the cross. Disapproval and shame assume a degree of relationship. For example, imagine a boy misbehaving in a shopping mall. While others walk by nonplussed, one man's face is flushed with embarrassment and his head is lowered in shame. That is the boy's father. The son disappointed his father's expectations.

Our Savior's approval or disapproval of our conduct and choices should be a motivation to us who are children of a Heavenly Father. In the end, it is the only approval that really matters. Publically identifying with Jesus Christ may or may not win approval from others in this world, but either way, the effect is temporary. God's approval is eternal.

The rich young ruler. Matthew 19:16-22 (cf. Mark 10:17-27; Luke 18:18-23)

[16] *Now behold, one came and said to Him, "Good Teacher, what good thing shall I do that I may have eternal life?"* [17] *So He said to him, "Why do you call Me good? No one is good but One, that is, God. But if you want to enter into life, keep the commandments."* [18] *He said to Him, "Which ones?" Jesus said, "'You shall not murder,' 'You shall not commit adultery,' 'You shall not steal,' 'You shall not bear false witness,'* [19] *'Honor your father and your mother,' and, 'You shall love your neighbor as yourself.'"* [20] *The young man said to Him, "All these things I have kept from my youth. What do I still lack?"* [21] *Jesus said to him, "If you want to be perfect, go, sell what you have and give to the poor, and you will have treasure in heaven; and come, follow Me."* [22] *But when the young man heard that saying, he went away sorrowful, for he had great possessions.*

A Truth Interpretation: If a person is unwilling to forsake everything and follow Jesus, he cannot be saved.

Second A Truth Interpretation: If a person is unwilling to forsake everything and follow Jesus, he should know that this disqualification for discipleship also proves he fails to meet the perfect righteousness needed for salvation, and therefore needs a Savior.

This story is frequently used to teach that salvation comes only to those who are willing to commit everything to God. At first glance, it may seem that way. However, if we accept that interpretation, some pertinent questions arise.

First and foremost, if Jesus is telling this rich man how to be saved, why is there no discussion of Jesus as the Messiah, His saving work, or believing in Him as Savior? Second, if Jesus is giving the man the way of salvation, then isn't He insisting that he not only keep the law perfectly, but fulfill all its implications, such as give all he owns to the poor? Third, in this interpretation, isn't Jesus' reference to eternal salvation as "treasure in heaven" unusual and even unique as a reference to salvation? Fourth, if Jesus is teaching that salvation is difficult, doesn't He immediately contradict Himself in the subsequent discussion with the disciples when He says salvation is "impossible" apart from God's intervention? Fifth, wouldn't this interpretation directly contradict the Bible's clear teaching that salvation is not by keeping the Law or by doing works (Rom. 3:20-4:5; Gal. 2:16; Eph. 2:8-9; Titus 3:5)?

In no other personal encounter does Jesus tell anyone that he or she must sell everything and give all to the poor to be saved. He does mention that a disciple must be willing to forsake everything, even his own life (Luke 14:26, 33), but as we have already seen, this is a condition for discipleship, not salvation.

Context comes to the rescue. In all three synoptic accounts, this story is preceded by the story of the little children brought to Jesus, and His teaching that "of such is the kingdom of heaven" (Matt. 19:14; cf. 18:1-5), or more helpfully in Mark and Luke's account, "whoever does not receive the kingdom of God as a little child will by no means enter it" (Mark 10:15; Luke 18:17). Jesus is teaching that one can only receive the kingdom of God (not earn it) like a child—through simple faith born of humility.

The rich ruler doesn't appear to be arrogant, but sincere—yet sincerely deceived. He naively thought he had kept *all* the Law. He had both a subtle pride and a false interpretation of the Law. Jesus' interpretation of the Law evaluated not only one's conduct, but also one's inner thoughts and motives (see Matt. 5:21-22; 27-28). Now He tests the ruler's motives by applying the command which is not mentioned, but probably behind so many of the other commands: "You shall not covet." Though the man thinks he has also kept this command, his refusal to sell all and give it to the poor shows that he still covets, "for he had great possessions." It is likely that this man had adopted the contemporary Jewish notion that the rich were especially favored or blessed by God.

His deception is three-fold: First, he is trusting in his self-righteousness ("All these things I have kept from my youth"); second, he is most likely trusting in his riches as proof of God's acceptance; and third, he has a highly deficient view of God's righteousness. When he addresses Jesus as "Good Teacher," Jesus responds with a question to expose the man's concept of God's goodness. By responding "Why do you call Me good? No one is good but One, that is, God," Jesus sets the divine standard of acceptance as perfect goodness. In this challenge, Jesus could also be saying, "If you call Me good, then are you calling Me God?" But He is also telling the ruler that *he* is not good. In any case, Jesus challenges the man with his Law-keeping performance, which He then shows him is less than perfect.

The way that Jesus finally gets the man to realize his deficiency is by challenging him with a condition of discipleship and the reward of treasure in heaven. Jesus does not argue that the man has not kept the law, but for the sake of His illustration, assumes it as if He was saying, "Okay, if you have kept the law perfectly, then become My disciple by giving everything you own to the poor" (Mark adds the explicit language of discipleship, "and come, take up the cross, and follow Me," Mark 10:21; see also Luke 18:22). This the man would not do, showing he was less than perfect. If he could not keep all the implications of the Law that led to following Jesus as a disciple, then perhaps he was not good enough for heaven after all, much less its rewards (In Mark and Luke's account, the man asked about how to "inherit eternal life" showing that he had in mind not only entrance into heaven, but possession of its rewards; Mark 10:17; Luke 18:18). When the man finally realizes this, he goes away sad, not only because he had great possessions (that's nothing to be sad about!), but because his self-righteousness was exposed as insufficient for entrance into heaven.

Jesus had confronted all three of the man's self-deceptions, and all were found deficient.

We might say that Jesus' dialog with the rich man is pre-evangelistic. In other words, since the man thought he was good enough for heaven, he was closed to his need for righteousness outside of himself. He was not open to the gospel truth that the righteousness of Jesus Christ alone provides entrance into heaven, and that this could not be merited by one's conduct, but only accepted through faith. Jesus jumped to a discussion of discipleship (selling possessions and giving to the poor) that would make the man reconsider his self-righteousness. It worked. Jesus teaches A Truth by first appealing to B Truth, because the young ruler asked a B Truth question.

The story, when properly understood, underscores the A Truth that there is *nothing* we can do to earn eternal life. It also shows us that our self-righteousness is deceptively inflated, especially when compared to God's perfect standard of righteousness. The Bible says, "There is none who is good, no not one" (Rom. 3:12). Jesus says, "No one is good but One, that is, God." To enter heaven, we have to be as good as God. Since we can never be as good as God, Jesus was good for us—He fulfilled God's righteous requirements. We can now enter heaven on His merits instead of ours, if we believe in Him as our Savior.

That is the answer to the disciples' question that follows the encounter with the ruler, "Who then can be saved?" It is simply this: *no one* can, apart from God's righteousness provided in Jesus Christ, or in Jesus' words, "With men this is impossible, but with God all things are possible" (Matt. 19:26; also Mark 10:27; Luke 18:27).

Peter's implied question that follows probes Jesus' challenge to forsake all and follow Him (Matt. 19:27; Mark 10:28; Luke 18:28). It is basically this: "If entering the kingdom is only possible through God's work (implying by God's grace) and not by our work of forsaking all to follow Jesus, then what is our 'treasure in heaven' which You indicated to the young ruler was the reward for following You as a disciple?" (Matt. 19:21; Mark 10:21; Luke 18:22). Jesus answers Peter's B Truth question with B Truth: Those who forsake this world to follow Him will enjoy God's eternal life now and in the future. They will have "eternal life" as an abundant life in the present and a future possession to enjoy (as in Mark 10:30 and Luke 18:30). Matthew's wording, "inherit eternal life," emphasizes the disciples' future rewards in the kingdom that include possession of eternal life and ruling with Jesus (Matt. 19:28-30).

The story of the rich young ruler shows us that we cannot be true disciples of Jesus Christ until we acknowledge we are sinners who fall far short of God's perfect goodness and come to Jesus for that righteousness. We must experience A Truth before we can experience B Truth. Then, and only then, can we make the sacrifices of a disciple that earn us rewards in this life and the next. It is a great encouragement to know that our sacrifices and the forsaking of our own desires will bring God's abundant rewards. As for Peter, so also for us—indeed, it will be worth it!

Other Passages and Parables with Serious Consequences

Apart from the conditions for discipleship, there are many other passages, including parables, that are sometimes hard to understand because they involve serious consequences. The interpreter of the Bible must determine if these consequences are for the unbeliever or for the believer—A Truth or B Truth.

Some have interpreted these parables exclusively in relation to Israel since the church had not yet begun. However, we know that Jesus had already predicted the church (Matt. 16:18) and given instruction for it (Matt. 18:17). These parables are prophetic, so we should not be surprised that they include truth for the (then future) church as well as Israel.

The unforgiveable sin. Matthew 12:31-32 (cf. Mark 3:28-30)

> [31] *"Therefore I say to you, every sin and blasphemy will be forgiven men, but the blasphemy against the Spirit will not be forgiven men.* [32] *Anyone who speaks a word against the Son of Man, it will be forgiven him; but whoever speaks against the Holy Spirit, it will not be forgiven him, either in this age or in the age to come."*

A Truth Interpretation: A person can commit this sin that makes salvation impossible, or if he is saved, will cause him to lose his salvation.

Second A Truth Interpretation: A person can commit this sin that shows his heart is hardened to the Holy Spirit's convicting work that brings a person to salvation.

It is unfortunate that both unbelievers and believers have lived under the fear of committing this sin and thinking they have been disqualified from salvation. That this is A Truth is clear from whom Jesus is addressing. The audience are the unbelieving Pharisees and scribes who accuse Jesus of an allegiance with Satan (Matt. 12:24-30; Mark 3:22-27). Their verbal accusation prompts Jesus' reply about the sin that cannot be forgiven. Eternal salvation is at issue because this sin can never be forgiven and brings eternal condemnation (Matt. 12:32; Mark 3:29).

Jesus is not speaking of Israel's national rejection of Him, because He says "anyone," which denotes individuals. Also, the warning is about a sin more specific than unbelief in Jesus as Savior. Neither does it seem to be the specific sin of accusing Christ of satanic allegiance, as terrible as that is. Jesus says that blasphemies can be forgiven (Matt. 12:31; Mark 3:28). There is only one blasphemy that cannot be forgiven, and it is not specifically blasphemy against Christ, but against the Holy Spirit. Some interpret this as a sin that can only be committed by unbelievers when Christ is present performing miracles either in His lifetime or in the future kingdom. The issue, however, seems to be the heart attitude more than the time period.

What makes the most sense of this difficult saying is that Jesus speaks of a willful and slanderous rejection of the Holy Spirit's testimony about Christ. This sin is revealed in the perverse verbal accusation that Jesus Christ is in league with the devil. The Father witnesses to the Son both through prophecy and His verbal approval at Christ's baptism. The Son witnesses through His own words and works. These witnesses are external. But the Holy Spirit witnesses through His internal convicting ministry (John 16:7-11). When the Spirit convinces an unbeliever about who Jesus Christ is, and that person nevertheless accuses Him of being satanic, he has committed blasphemy against the Holy Spirit. Matthew's discussion that follows this warning emphasizes how one's words reveal one's heart condition so that "*by your words you will be condemned*" (Matt. 12:33-37). The accusation that Jesus is of the devil reveals the moral blindness of a person who would call light darkness. It displays a heart hardened beyond hope of forgiveness, because there is nothing left to appeal to the conscience when the Holy Spirit's testimony is rejected and slandered. Any unbeliever who blasphemes the Holy Spirit demonstrates a spiritual condition that precludes a receptive attitude toward the gospel.

According to this interpretation, someone who knowingly and maliciously rejects and slanders the Holy Spirit's convicting ministry about the person of Christ could commit this sin today. It would be hard to know when someone knowingly rejects the Holy Spirit's testimony and is not doing it out of ignorance, but God knows.

If there is a B Truth present in this warning, it is by implication. If you are a believer, then you have responded positively to the Holy Spirit's testimony about Christ. This should bring assurance that you cannot commit this sin and your salvation is not in jeopardy. If a believer worries about committing this sin, it is a testimony that he is still responding positively to the Holy Spirit's witness. Also, as believers, we have the assurance that

God's grace covers every sin (Rom. 5:20; Col. 2:13). As for an unbeliever, if he worries about committing this sin, it is also a testimony that he is prone to respond positively to the Holy Spirit's testimony about Christ. We can say this emphatically: Those who believe in Jesus Christ as Savior are saved and have *all* their sins forgiven.

He who endures to the end. Matthew 24:13 (cf. Matt. 10:22; Mark 13:13; Luke 21:19)

"But he who endures to the end shall be saved."

A Truth Interpretation: Only someone who continues in good works and faith to the end of his life will receive salvation or prove he was saved.

B Truth Interpretation: Only those of Israel in the Tribulation who are able to endure persecution until the time of Christ's return will be delivered from the hostile nations.

This saying in Matthew and Mark is used by some to teach that professing Christians must persevere in faith and good works in order to prove their salvation is genuine, which is an A Truth interpretation.

While those who say professing Christians must persevere in order to prove that they are genuinely saved, they would not admit that perseverance is a work that earns salvation. Of course, this is flawed reasoning, because if perseverance is necessary to prove salvation, then perseverance is necessary for salvation. This is in addition to one's initial faith in Jesus Christ as Savior. Salvation would be by faith plus one's performance, which contradicts the free nature of God's grace. Some might try to avoid this charge by modifying their view to say that true saving faith is a faith *that performs*, but this does not avoid the error of making works necessary for salvation.

The A Truth interpretation understands "the end" to mean the end of one's physical life. But this ignores the unique order and events of the end times about which Jesus is speaking. The context indicates what "the end" refers to. It is clear that Matthew (and Mark) is speaking about conditions in the time of Israel's great Tribulation (which also seems to be the context of a similar saying in Matt. 10:22). In answering the disciples' question about His return (24:3) Jesus answers the last question about the end of the age first. When Jesus refers to "the end" in verses 6, 13, and 14, it has the same meaning—the end of the age which concludes with the Tribulation period. In that time of great sorrow, the Jews will be hated and killed by all the nations (24:9), betrayed by their own countrymen (24:10), deceived by false prophets (24:11), and experience lawlessness and lack of natural affection (24:12). After verse 13, Jesus' prophecy reveals the details that actually describe His coming (24:14ff.). Though many of Israel will be killed, those who endure these perils to the *end of the Tribulation* (not to the end of their physical lives, which is the A Truth interpretation) will be delivered ("saved") from their enemies, the nations who hate them. This "last minute rescue" of Israel by Jesus Christ is a clear biblical prophecy (Zech. 12:2-9; Rom. 11:26). This is an example of the word *saved* referring to deliverance from a danger, not deliverance from hell. Indeed, hell is not mentioned in the passage. This is obviously B Truth because enduring to the end does not relate to eternal salvation but temporal deliverance of God's people. In verse 22, Jesus says, "And unless those days were shortened, no flesh would be saved…" It appears that "no flesh" includes Gentiles among those delivered. The parable of the sheep and goats in Matthew 25:31-46 shows that Gentiles ("nations") will be present at the end of the Tribulation.

Israel's story is a story of God's grace. They were chosen by Him to be a special people. In spite of constant sin, God preserved them throughout their history. He will preserve them in the future as well, not because they deserve it, but because He is faithful to His promise to do so. We who are saved by God's grace are kept saved by grace, and will be glorified ultimately and finally by His grace, not because we deserve it, but because that is God's promise to all who believe (John 3:16; 5:24; Rom, 8:29).

Parable of the soils. Luke 8:4-8, 11-15 (cf. Matt. 13:1-9; Mark 4:2-20)

> [4] *And when a great multitude had gathered, and they had come to Him from every city, He spoke by a parable:* [5] *"A sower went out to sow his seed. And as he sowed, some fell by the wayside; and it was trampled down, and the birds of the air devoured it.* [6] *Some fell on rock; and as soon as it sprang up, it withered away because it lacked moisture.* [7] *And some fell among thorns, and the thorns sprang up with it and choked it.* [8] *But others fell on good ground, sprang up, and yielded a crop a hundredfold." When He had said these things He cried, "He who has ears to hear, let him hear!"*

[11] *"Now the parable is this: The seed is the word of God.* [12] *Those by the wayside are the ones who hear; then the devil comes and takes away the word out of their hearts, lest they should believe and be saved.* [13] *But the ones on the rock are those who, when they hear, receive the word with joy; and these have no root, who believe for a while and in time of temptation fall away.* [14] *Now the ones that fell among thorns are those who, when they have heard, go out and are choked with cares, riches, and pleasures of life, and bring no fruit to maturity.* [15] *But the ones that fell on the good ground are those who, having heard the word with a noble and good heart, keep it and bear fruit with patience."*

A Truth Interpretation: The parable teaches that there are some who profess Christ but are not truly saved, or they are saved but lose their salvation because they do not go on to bear fruit.

B Truth Interpretation: The parable teaches that there are some who believe and do not go on to produce fruit and some who do.

This is the first of Christ's parables, and it is intended to explain the purpose of all parables and show how people respond to God's truth. Jesus uses parables to enlighten those who are receptive to the truth and to obscure it from those who are not receptive to it. Christ explains this purpose before He interprets the parable for his disciples (Matt. 13:10-17; Mark 4:10-12; Luke 8:9-10). In the larger context of the preceding chapters 11-12, the leaders of Israel have rejected Christ's teaching, and He has condemned them. He now speaks truth they will not comprehend, but His followers will. If Jesus is compared to the sower, the seed sown is truth about His claims as Israel's Messiah, which is the issue in the context.

There is no disagreement that the first soil, which has its seed snatched away by the birds representing the devil, represents those who were never saved. Luke helps us in this interpretation by adding that these are people from whom the devil keeps the truth "lest they should believe and be saved" (Luke 8:12). Neither is there much disagreement about the fourth soil that represents those who accept the truth and continue in it to bear fruit (though some would say we cannot know if they are saved unless they produce fruit until the end of their lives).

Speaking of the first soil, Jesus demonstrates that salvation is based on believing. It is only in this first soil that no germination occurs because there is no belief. It is the second and third soils where interpretations diverge, because these two soils bear life implying there was belief. The second soil produces life, but it quickly withers because the soil is mostly rock with no moisture. The third soil also produces life, but thorns that represent the cares and pleasures of this life choke it. It is "unfruitful" according to Matthew and Mark (Matt. 13:22; Mark 4:19), but Luke is more ambiguous saying those represented "bring no fruit to maturity" (Luke 8:14). It is possible they have fruit, but it never matures. Do the second and third soils represent people who simply profess Christ as Savior, or were they truly saved?

We observe several things that help our interpretation. First, both soils demonstrate the presence of life, as opposed to the first soil that never demonstrates life because the devil does not allow the truth to reach their hearts. This would argue that the truth reaches the hearts of the second and third groups and divine life is brought forth. Luke clearly says that the second group "receive the word with joy . . . who believe for a while" (Luke 4:13). The issue is not the sincerity of their faith, but its duration. The third group also shows life, but it is choked out—not out of existence, but out of fruitfulness.

The B Truth interpretation makes more sense because the issue the parable illustrates is not perseverance unto salvation, but perseverance unto fruitfulness. Some people who believe in Christ do not go on to be very fruitful. The reason is the nature of their hearts. Those who go on to fruitfulness have hearts that remain responsive to God's truth, so responsive that challenges and distractions to their faith do not prevent growth to fruitful maturity.

The parable reveals important truth to believers: Everyone has the opportunity to respond to God's truth, and He desires everyone who responds to His truth to persevere in faith for a fruitful life. The reality is, many are distracted by trials that challenge their faith, or distractions of worldly pleasures that choke out strong growth. It is a lesson for us to stay in the truth of God's Word and to monitor our own hearts so that we are always responsive to what God says.

Parables of the hidden treasure and pearl of great price. Matthew 13:44-46

[44] *"Again, the kingdom of heaven is like treasure hidden in a field, which a man found and hid; and for joy over it he goes and sells all*

that he has and buys that field. [45] *Again, the kingdom of heaven is like a merchant seeking beautiful pearls,* [46] *who, when he had found one pearl of great price, went and sold all that he had and bought it."*

A Truth Interpretation: These two parables teach that to enter the kingdom of God a person must give up everything and pay a great price.

B Truth Interpretation: These two parables teach that a mystery of the kingdom is that it will include both of God's treasured people, Israel and the Gentiles, whom He bought at a great price.

The first interpretation sees the parables as teaching about the great worth of the kingdom and the high cost of entering it—an evangelistic purpose. However, the context does not support this view. The purpose of these parables is to hide truth from unbelievers and reveal truth to believers (Matt. 13:10-17; Mark 4:10-12; Luke 8:9-10). It is to teach "the mysteries of the kingdom of heaven," that is, a new truth about the kingdom of God. Jesus is teaching about the nature of the kingdom that reveals something new about it. If He is only teaching about how to enter the kingdom by paying the price of discipleship, this teaching is nothing new to the disciples because Jesus previously spoke of the conditions of discipleship (Matt 10:32-33; 37-39; 11:28-30). Besides, God does not hide the truth of the gospel from unbelievers.

The new "mystery" teaching is that those who are Jews and those who are Gentiles will be together in the kingdom. In the first parable, the treasure in a field represents Israel in the world. They are hidden for a time because they are dispersed among the nations, but will be re-gathered and restored by the One who paid a great price for them—Jesus Christ. In the second parable, the precious pearl speaks of the church that is never hidden, but is also purchased by the highest price—the death of Jesus Christ.

Jesus came to "seek and to save that which was lost" (Luke 19:10). He purchased Israel and the church through His death on the cross. An unbeliever has nothing of value to God by which he can purchase the kingdom of God (By the way, in the first parable, not just the treasure is purchased, but also the field, which would have to be explained if this is A Truth).

B Truth teaches something precious that has not been previously revealed, but which believers need to know. God's people, Israel, and God's people, the church, will be together in the kingdom. God so values both groups that He paid the highest price for them—His own Son. As Christians, we can marvel at God's sovereignty, wisdom, and grace that redeems Israel and also raises up the church from among the Gentiles to be together in one kingdom.

Parable of the unforgiving servant. Matthew 18:21-35

[21] *Then Peter came to Him and said, "Lord, how often shall my brother sin against me, and I forgive him? Up to seven times?"* [22] *Jesus said to him, "I do not say to you, up to seven times, but up to seventy times seven.* [23] *Therefore the kingdom of heaven is like a certain king who wanted to settle accounts with his servants.* [24] *And when he had begun to settle accounts, one was brought to him who owed him ten thousand talents.* [25] *But as he was not able to pay, his master commanded that he be sold, with his wife and children and all that he had, and that payment be made.* [26] *The servant therefore fell down before him, saying, 'Master, have patience with me, and I will pay you all.'* [27] *Then the master of that servant was moved with compassion, released him, and forgave him the debt.* [28] *But that servant went out and found one of his fellow servants who owed him a hundred denarii; and he laid hands on him and took him by the throat, saying, 'Pay me what you owe!'* [29] *So his fellow servant fell down at his feet and begged him, saying, 'Have patience with me, and I will pay you all.'* [30] *And he would not, but went and threw him into prison till he should pay the debt.* [31] *So when his fellow servants saw what had been done, they were very grieved, and came and told their master all that had been done.* [32] *Then his master, after he had called him, said to him, 'You wicked servant! I forgave you all that debt because you begged me.* [33] *Should you not also have had compassion on your fellow servant, just as I had pity on you?'* [34] *And his master was angry, and delivered him to the torturers until he should pay all that was due to him.* [35] *So My heavenly Father also will do to you if each of you, from his heart, does not forgive his brother his trespasses."*

A Truth Interpretation: The servant who is forgiven a great debt but refuses to forgive his debtors represents someone who was never really saved, or someone who was saved and loses salvation, and will be tortured in hell.

B Truth Interpretation: The servant who is forgiven a great debt but refuses to forgive his debtors represents someone who is saved but will receive little mercy from the Heavenly Father in the kingdom.

What probably causes people to see hell in this passage is verse 34 that speaks of the unforgiving servant delivered to "the torturers." A severe consequence is undeniable. However, we carefully observe that it does not say the unforgiving servant is actually tortured. Torture may be implied, but even so, we also observe that his penalty is only until all his own debt is paid to his own master, making it an unlikely reference to hell. The principle here is summed up in verse 35 by noting that those who do not forgive others will not be forgiven by God. This is the same principle discussed earlier from Matthew 6:14-15 (also Mark 11:25-26), so there is no need to elaborate it further except to remind that this speaks of fellowship forgiveness between God and the believer (B Truth), not positional forgiveness at justification (A Truth). After all, what prompted Jesus' parable was Peter's question about how often we should forgive a "brother" (Matt. 18:21).

As always, when interpreting a parable, it is important to understand the main point and consider the figures of speech or analogies used to make it. We should be careful about investing the details with literal understanding. In this parable, the torturers certainly represent a severe consequence, but the point seems to be that the unforgiving servant will face severe consequences, not that he will be literally tortured.

Not only is the B Truth interpretation preferred here, but corroboration for this conclusion comes from James 2:13 written to "brethren" (Jas. 2:1). We who are believers, who will be judged by the law of liberty, will receive judgment without mercy if we have shown no mercy to others (Jas. 2:12-13). The only judgment believers face is the Judgment Seat of Christ (cf. Jas. 3:1 used of teachers of God's Word).

As Christians who are forgiven all our sins in Christ, it is incongruous and displays ungratefulness if we do not forgive those who sin against us. God will take this into account in the kingdom and deal severely with those who were unforgiving.

Parable of the wedding feast. Matthew 22:1-14

¹ *And Jesus answered and spoke to them again by parables and said:*
² *"The kingdom of heaven is like a certain king who arranged a marriage for his son,* ³ *and sent out his servants to call those who were*

invited to the wedding; and they were not willing to come. [4] *Again, he sent out other servants, saying, 'Tell those who are invited, "See, I have prepared my dinner; my oxen and fatted cattle are killed, and all things are ready. Come to the wedding."'* [5] *But they made light of it and went their ways, one to his own farm, another to his business.* [6] *And the rest seized his servants, treated them spitefully, and killed them.* [7] *But when the king heard about it, he was furious. And he sent out his armies, destroyed those murderers, and burned up their city.* [8] *Then he said to his servants, 'The wedding is ready, but those who were invited were not worthy.* [9] *Therefore go into the highways, and as many as you find, invite to the wedding.'* [10] *So those servants went out into the highways and gathered together all whom they found, both bad and good. And the wedding hall was filled with guests.* [11] *But when the king came in to see the guests, he saw a man there who did not have on a wedding garment.* [12] *So he said to him, 'Friend, how did you come in here without a wedding garment?' And he was speechless.* [13] *Then the king said to the servants, 'Bind him hand and foot, take him away, and cast him into outer darkness; there will be weeping and gnashing of teeth.'* [14] *For many are called, but few are chosen."*

A Truth Interpretation: The man at the wedding feast who had no proper garment is unsaved so he is thrown into hell, which is referred to as outer darkness.

B Truth Interpretation: The man at the wedding feast who had no proper garment is saved but does not deserve special privileges in the kingdom.

This parable challenges our powers of observation and our theological traditions. It also challenges us to properly interpret parables.

When we interpret a parable, we should resist the temptation to make a point of every detail. Usually a parable has one or two main points which the details of the story support. In the case of this parable, what we need to know is simple and clear. There is a king who invites people to his son's wedding, but they refuse to attend. The king then invites others outside of that group and there is a great response. Many attend the wedding, but one man attends without proper dress. He is excluded from the banquet celebration.

For the sake of brevity and to get quickly to the controversial statement at the end of the parable, let's state what is obvious. The parable shows that Pharisees and Jewish leaders are invited to the kingdom first, but they reject the invitation and even murder the king's servants (22:1-6). Jesus had just said the kingdom would be taken from the Jewish leaders and given to others (Matt. 21:43), so that thought sets up this parable. The king responds by killing the murderers and burning their city (22:7), a probable prophetic reference to Jerusalem's destruction by the Romans in A.D. 70 (see Matt. 24:2). The invitation then goes to those beyond Israel's corrupt leadership to anyone and everyone ("both bad and good"), and the response is great; the wedding hall is filled with these guests (22:8-10). This pictures all who believe in Jesus Christ as Savior during the church age, a time predicted by Christ in Matthew 16:18. These enter the kingdom.

Now the focus turns to one guest among the many. Certainly in the story he represents a certain kind of believer in the kingdom. The king notices this man and calls him into account for not having dressed properly for the wedding. This reminds us of the Judgment Seat of Christ where believers' works will be scrutinized and their preparation or lack of it is called into account. The man is then bound and cast into "outer darkness."

There are some who interpret the central point of this parable as who does and doesn't get into heaven. From this A Truth perspective, they claim the improperly dressed man does not have the imputed righteousness of Christ and is therefore cast into hell. Some would argue that salvation is not simply responding to the gospel invitation; good works must accompany true salvation. But this poses an enormous problem in the parable—How did an unsaved man get into the wedding, that is, the kingdom? And if he is saved, casting him out must mean that he loses his salvation. Both options are unacceptable.

Some other details make that interpretation untenable. First, the man *did* respond to the invitation, unlike the others who had rejected it. Second, there was also to be a wedding feast (22:4) within the wedding, but he was excluded from only that. Third, the king calls him "friend," a term of endearment. From these details we conclude that this man represents believers who, though saved and in the kingdom, do not participate in the full celebration with the King and His Son, Jesus Christ. Contrary to interpreting the wedding garment as Christ's imputed righteousness, it is better to view it as the garments described in Revelation 19:7-8--the righteous acts of the saints. Notice that the host does not give out the wedding garments. They are the responsibility of each guest. However, this careless man neglected preparation for this important event. Notice also that this man is speechless with no defense (22:12). He knew better; he did not prepare; he was guilty.

This accords perfectly with the expectation at the Judgment Seat of Christ. Though all believers will be in the kingdom, some will have prepared themselves with a life of good works while others will be found unprepared. Using the Judgment Seat imagery of 1 Corinthians 3:11-15, some will appear with apparel of gold, silver, and precious stones, while others will wear shabby garments of wood, hay, and straw. Believers have been warned (Rom. 14:10-12; 2 Cor. 5:10) and will be without excuse if they are not prepared.

What forces many to an A Truth interpretation is the imagery of this unprepared guest being bound and "cast" into "outer darkness" where there is "weeping and gnashing of teeth." This is usually interpreted as a reference to hell. But we must admit the story is full of symbolism not to be taken literally. Certainly the food, the king's armies, the servants, the highways, the wedding garment, the imagery of a wedding itself, as well as the binding, are figurative expressions of spiritual, not physical, truths.

An A Truth conclusion comes from imposing one's theology on the story and reaching beyond the limits of the terms themselves. For example, the verb for "cast" (*ekballō*) in 22:13 does not necessarily represent a violent rejection, but can mean simply *to send or lead* (see Mark 1:12, 43; 9:38). Also, if the interpreter's theology has no category for the judgment of a believer's works at the Judgment Seat of Christ, then hell is the only option. Then the outer darkness becomes hell and the weeping and gnashing of teeth the torment of those in hell. But the torment, fire, and worms of hell are not mentioned in this friend's fate, though he has severe regret.

If we allow for the biblical teaching about the Judgment Seat of Christ, then we know that all believers will be in the kingdom, but not all will enjoy the same privileges. We also know that there will be experiences and expressions of regret (1 John 2:28), because the believer's bad deeds will be judged along with the good (2 Cor. 5:10), and there will be loss of rewards (1 Cor. 3:15). We are not told how long the regret endures, but it is likely very brief.

The imagery of this wedding parable agrees with the B Truth of the believer's accountability at the future Judgment Seat of Christ. The binding probably speaks of an inability to participate in the activity of the King, Jesus Christ. The outer darkness speaks of exclusion from the festive banquet at the wedding. Hebrew weddings usually extended into the night, so the central banquet celebration would be well lit. To be in the darkness outside of that light does not exclude the believer from the wedding (the kingdom), but from participation in the central festivities. *Outer* darkness does not mean *outermost* darkness. Besides, this experience is probably best understood not in spatial terms, but in terms of spiritual experience as the loss of participation in some benefits of Christ's rule. Matthew uses the phrase "outer darkness" two other times. It can be argued that both instances apply to believers, or at least those who were the legal heirs of the kingdom (called "sons of the kingdom" in Matt. 8:12; cf. 13:38; and a "servant" of the master in 25:30). All believers will be in the kingdom, but faithful ones will have central roles such as ruling with Jesus Christ.

Likewise, weeping and gnashing of teeth is traditionally over-interpreted as the torment of hell when it is simply a figure of speech meaning deep regret. Unlike the western world, it is common for people of the Middle East (both then and now) to show great emotion and weeping when grieved. We see this throughout the book of Lamentations. It is true that those in hell experience suffering, but it is usually associated with fire and destruction (e.g., Luke 16:22-24; 2 Thess. 1:9; Rev. 20:14). The association of regret and intense emotion with weeping and gnashing of teeth does not in itself make this phrase a technical term for eternal torment. The cause of this response is determined by the context where it occurs.

The central lesson of the parable is stated at the end: "For many are called, but few are chosen" (22:14). Of the many people "invited" to the kingdom of God, some will accept the invitation and believe in Christ as Savior, but fewer of those will prove faithful enough to be awarded ruling privileges with Christ in His kingdom. This teaching is similar to Jesus' teaching about rewards in Matthew 20:16 (according to the Majority Text of the NKJV). It is also reflected in 2 Peter 1:1-11 where the readers are told to add various virtues (1:5-10) to their faith that saved them (1:1-4) so that they do not just enter the kingdom, but have an *abundant* entrance (1:11). Peter refers to "call" before "election" just as Jesus does, tying the idea of choosing ("election") to rewards not salvation (1:10-11). We should not equate Jesus and Peter's teachings about rewards with Paul's teaching about the order of predestination before calling for salvation (Rom. 8:30).

You have believed in Christ—welcome to the wedding in the future kingdom! But are you clothed in the garments of a righteous life so that you can also sit with Christ in His kingdom banquet? Entering the kingdom is a free gift, but ruling with Christ in His kingdom as a close companion is a privilege earned by faithfulness and righteous deeds. This B Truth is a wonderful prospect for believers.

Parable of the evil servant. Matthew 24:45-51 (cf. Luke 12:42-48)

[45] *"Who then is a faithful and wise servant, whom his master made ruler over his household, to give them food in due season? [46] Blessed is that servant whom his master, when he comes, will find so doing. [47] Assuredly, I say to you that he will make him ruler over all his goods. [48] But if that evil servant says in his heart, 'My master is delaying his coming,' [49] and begins to beat his fellow servants, and to eat and drink with the drunkards, [50] the master of that servant will come on a day when he is not looking for him and at an hour that he is not aware of, [51] and will cut him in two and appoint him his portion with the hypocrites. There shall be weeping and gnashing of teeth."*

A Truth Interpretation: Those people who are not prepared for the coming of Jesus Christ will not enter the kingdom of heaven.

B Truth Interpretation: Those believers who are not prepared for the coming of Jesus Christ will be judged severely at the Judgment Seat of Christ.

The background of this parable is the imminent coming of the Lord Jesus Christ. Jesus has just told His disciples that no one knows the time of His coming, so they must always be ready and prepared for that event (Matt. 24:42-44). This event could only speak of the Rapture of the church immediately preceding the seven-year Tribulation, because the time of the Second Coming can be calculated from the beginning of the Tribulation and the mid-point abomination of desolation, and therefore is known (Dan. 9:27; Matt. 24:15; Rev. 12:4-6). Jesus predicted a coming era for His church, but the end of the era and the time of its Rapture is unknown (Matt. 16:18; 1 Thess. 4:13-5:6).

The issue in the parable is "Who then is faithful and wise?" Both these virtues, as well as the designation of "servant," apply most naturally to believers in Christ making this parable B Truth. The servant does, after all, believe in the return of his master, who in the story represents Christ. He is also given responsibility in the master's house. There is only one servant in view with two hypothetical choices ("that servant" in vv. 46 and 48 signifies the same servant as v. 45). If the servant does good in anticipation of his master's arrival, he is blessed with more responsibility, but if he does evil because he thinks his master is delaying, he is punished. Describing the servant as "evil" seems an unbecoming description for a Christian, but the Bible and life experience is full of believers who choose to do evil.

Another difficulty in seeing this evil servant as a believer in Christ is his fate. He is cut in two and assigned a portion with hypocrites where he weeps and gnashes his teeth (Matt. 24:51). Again, we encounter symbolic language, because not even unbelievers are literally cut in two. The metaphor speaks of a severe and intense judgment. The basis of this servant's hypocrisy is not that he claims to be a believer when he is not, rather, he claims to be a servant of the Master when in reality he is not--he is serving his own purposes and desires. Instead of "hypocrites," Luke's version uses the word "unbelievers" (*apistos*), but that word can also be translated "unfaithful," which better fits the context raised by the Lord's opening question (Matt. 24:45; Luke 12:42). We have already seen in our discussion of Matthew 22:1-14 that "weeping and gnashing of teeth" is a metaphorical expression for intense regret, which could be short-lived. Luke adds the interesting information that the evil servant is "beaten with many stripes" while the servant who does not completely understand the master's will is "beaten with a few" (Luke 12:47-48). This would be an odd way to describe the punishment of unbelievers in hell, but fits comfortably with the relative experiences of the Judgment Seat of Christ.

An important application from this B Truth parable is that we cannot discount the negative consequences for unfaithful and unprepared believers at the Judgment Seat of Christ. There, the Word of God will be like a sword that cuts painfully into their deepest thoughts and motivations (Heb. 4:12; 1 Cor. 4:5). There also, they will experience shame (1 John 2:28) and have a fiery experience as their unworthy works are burned (1 Cor. 3:11-15). There is a definite loss to the unfaithful servant's future experience in the kingdom as he shares the fate of other hypocrites who were not prepared for the Lord's return.

The Lord may return at any time. We must be ready, prepared for His coming by continuing in good works. We cannot grow lax as He delays His return lest we encounter a severe judgment at the Judgment Seat of Christ.

Parable of the ten virgins. Matthew 25:1-13

> [1] *"Then the kingdom of heaven shall be likened to ten virgins who took their lamps and went out to meet the bridegroom.* [2] *Now five of them were wise, and five were foolish.* [3] *Those who were foolish took*

their lamps and took no oil with them, [4] *but the wise took oil in their vessels with their lamps.* [5] *But while the bridegroom was delayed, they all slumbered and slept.* [6] *And at midnight a cry was heard: 'Behold, the bridegroom is coming; go out to meet him!'* [7] *Then all those virgins arose and trimmed their lamps.* [8] *And the foolish said to the wise, 'Give us some of your oil, for our lamps are going out.'* [9] *But the wise answered, saying, 'No, lest there should not be enough for us and you; but go rather to those who sell, and buy for yourselves.'* [10] *And while they went to buy, the bridegroom came, and those who were ready went in with him to the wedding; and the door was shut.* [11] *Afterward the other virgins came also, saying, 'Lord, Lord, open to us!'* [12] *But he answered and said, 'Assuredly, I say to you, I do not know you.'* [13] *Watch therefore, for you know neither the day nor the hour in which the Son of Man is coming."*

A Truth Interpretation: Those who are not prepared (through faith in Christ) for the Lord's return will be shut out from eternal life.

B Truth Interpretation: Those believers who are not prepared (through faithfulness to Christ) for the Lord's return will be shut out from honor at the Lord's return.

This parable presents a challenge to interpreters. It is here that we remind ourselves that the interpretation of parables must look for the main point and then interpret details in light of that. The meaning of many of this parable's details are less than clear, but we can understand them well enough in light of how they contribute to the central point, which is essentially the same as the previous parable on the evil servant—preparedness for the Lord's return (made clear in Matt. 25:13).

However, the crucial divide in interpretation is whether this depicts A Truth or B Truth. Of the ten virgins, are the five unprepared ones unsaved or saved? Is this a warning to unbelievers or to disciples?

We remember that Jesus is speaking here privately to His disciples (Matt. 24:3) who are saved, with the exception of Judas. But certainly, Jesus is not tailoring this lesson to Judas alone as a warning to be saved. That approach would have to apply to all of Christ's teaching (except part of the Upper Room Discourse after John 13:30 when Judas left). This leads us to understand this parable as B Truth for disciples.

Eschatology, or one's understanding of the end times, also influences the interpretation. Some interpret the virgins as Jewish believers in the Tribulation who meet the Lord at His second coming. The foolish virgins are excluded from ruling with Christ in the Kingdom. However, the unknown time of His arrival and the lesson about preparedness seem to indicate the same event as the previous parable of the evil servant--the Rapture event that begins the Tribulation. Some who believe that this is the Rapture interpret the foolish virgins as professing Christians who do not really know Christ as Savior. At the Rapture, they are shut out from heaven and the kingdom altogether. The first word of the parable, "Then" (*tote*), may be significant in that it is only found here in the sequence of four parables and may indicate events following the Rapture, which is the focus of the previous parable.

Who are the virgins? In the weddings of those times, a bride would have a wedding party of young women. She and the women would meet the bridegroom who comes for his bride to take her to his house. This usually occurred at night, thus the lamps. The approach of the bridegroom was announced with a shout, and after a festive welcome, the formal wedding celebration would begin. The church is compared to the bride of Christ in the New Testament (2 Cor. 11:2; Eph. 5:25-27). It is interesting that the bride herself is not mentioned, but it makes sense that as the church, she is pictured as ten virgins so that distinctions can be made among those who comprise the church. So it seems best that the virgins picture the church. That these are genuine believers is supported by several observations. First, they are part of the bride and the wedding party (cf. 1 Cor. 11:2). Second, they are called "virgins" which at least suggests they are pure in the sense of having been cleansed and set apart to Christ. Third, they anticipate the coming of the bridegroom. Fourth, they are told to "buy" oil, which implies they must pay a cost, something characteristic of discipleship, but not the free gift of salvation.

What differentiates the five virgins with oil and the five without is the central point of the parable--preparedness. While it is commonly understood that the five unprepared virgins ran out of oil, Jesus actually said they took lamps but "took no oil with them" (Matt. 25:3). If so, the lamps were not used in the daytime journey, but when night fell and the bridegroom arrived, they lit the wicks to their lamps only to realize that they had no oil to sustain the flame. It is possible that they had some oil in their lamps if their journey was at night, but not enough and they carried no extra. Nevertheless, the main point is that they were not adequately prepared. The other five virgins, however, were well prepared (cf. Rev. 19:7-8 where the Bride's preparedness is related to righteous acts of the saints). While we can speculate on the symbolism and meaning of the oil, all we can say for certain is that it pictures readiness. Readiness in the previous parable and the one to follow equates to faithfulness and good stewardship.

The bridegroom's arrival has several aspects that point to the Rapture of the church. First, it is unexpected (unlike the timing of Christ's second coming, which could be known from prophecy once the Tribulation begins). Second, it is announced by a shout, which also accompanies the Rapture (1 Thess. 4:17). Third, it brings the bridegroom and the bride together at the end of the church age. Fourth, at the Rapture it will be too late to show faithfulness (buy oil). An interesting observation is that the Rapture happens too quickly to afford anyone time to believe and be saved (1 Cor. 15:52), while at the second coming of Christ there are Jews who see Him and believe (Zech. 12:10).

A crucial interpretive question concerns the meaning of the shut door in verse 10 and the bridegroom's pronouncement "I do not know you" in verse 12. Both of these actions happen after the bridegroom's appearance, so they do not seem to be an exclusion of the five unprepared virgins from the Rapture. More difficult is the meaning of "I don't know you," so it may help to understand that first. This reminds us of the Lord's words to the unbelieving professors in Matthew 7:23, but there is a significant difference. There, Jesus said, "Depart from Me, I never knew you." Here, He does not send the virgins away, and does not use the word "never." Also, in Matthew 7:23, Jesus uses the word *ginōskō* for *know*, but here He uses the word *oida*. The first can denote a more intimate knowledge of someone, while the latter a more cognitive knowledge. In fact, *oida* can have the meaning *acknowledge, respect,* or *honor* (cf. 1 Thess. 5:12-13). This meaning fits well since Jesus consistently taught that those who honored Him will be honored by Him before the Father (Matt. 10:32-33).

Putting these observations together, it seems that Jesus is excluding the unprepared virgins from the wedding celebration. "Afterward" (v. 11) could mean after the wedding or after the door is shut. It was the practice of Jewish weddings at the time to celebrate after the formal wedding service with a feast and festivities. These special privileges would not be extended to the unprepared virgins (just as they were also withheld from the unprepared wedding guest in Matt. 22:11-13).

In summary, this parable is B Truth that concerns the faithfulness of believers of the church age. All will be present at the Rapture and make it into the kingdom, but not all will be able to participate in special privileges there.

They were not faithful in preparing for the Lord's return. This emphasis is consistent with the two parables that surround it.

As believers, we have the exhortation to be alert for the Lord's return and always ready (1 Thess. 5:1-11). This posture helps us to be faithful, active in good works, and live a godly life (1 John 3:3). The Lord has special privileges awaiting those who prove to be faithful followers, privileges not enjoyed by those caught unprepared.

Parable of the talents. Matthew 25:14-30 (cf. Luke 19:11-27)

[14] *"For the kingdom of heaven is like a man traveling to a far country, who called his own servants and delivered his goods to them.* [15] *And to one he gave five talents, to another two, and to another one, to each according to his own ability; and immediately he went on a journey.* [16] *Then he who had received the five talents went and traded with them, and made another five talents.* [17] *And likewise he who had received two gained two more also.* [18] *But he who had received one went and dug in the ground, and hid his lord's money.* [19] *After a long time the lord of those servants came and settled accounts with them.* [20] *"So he who had received five talents came and brought five other talents, saying, 'Lord, you delivered to me five talents; look, I have gained five more talents besides them.'* [21] *His lord said to him, 'Well done, good and faithful servant; you were faithful over a few things, I will make you ruler over many things. Enter into the joy of your lord.'* [22] *He also who had received two talents came and said, 'Lord, you delivered to me two talents; look, I have gained two more talents besides them.'* [23] *His lord said to him, 'Well done, good and faithful servant; you have been faithful over a few things, I will make you ruler over many things. Enter into the joy of your lord.'* [24] *Then he who had received the one talent came and said, 'Lord, I knew you to be a hard man, reaping where you have not sown, and gathering where you have not scattered seed.* [25] *And I was afraid, and went and hid your talent in the ground. Look, there you have what is yours.'* [26] *But his lord answered and said to him, 'You wicked and lazy servant, you knew that I reap where I have not sown, and gather where I have not scattered seed.* [27] *So you ought to have deposited my money with the bankers, and at my coming I would have received back my own with*

interest. [28] *So take the talent from him, and give it to him who has ten talents.* [29] *For to everyone who has, more will be given, and he will have abundance; but from him who does not have, even what he has will be taken away.* [30] *And cast the unprofitable servant into the outer darkness. There will be weeping and gnashing of teeth."*

A Truth Interpretation: When Christ returns, those people who are not faithful stewards prove they are not saved and will not enter the kingdom, while faithful stewards prove they are saved and will be rewarded in the kingdom.

B Truth Interpretation: When Christ returns, those believers who are not faithful stewards will be excluded from kingdom rewards, while faithful stewards will be rewarded in the kingdom.

This parable continues the theme of anticipating the Lord's return as an answer to the disciples' question in Matthew 24:3. It emphasizes the virtue of faithful stewardship in light of Christ's return.

The master who leaves and returns obviously pictures Jesus Christ. As in the previous parables involving servants, there is good reason to view these servants as believers. They belong to the master, they are entrusted with money, "each according to his own ability," and they are held accountable for faithfulness. The issue *is not* their faith in who the master is. Jesus is speaking this B Truth privately to His disciples about an issue of Christian living—faithfulness and stewardship.

The servants who receive five talents and two talents invest them wisely and are not only commended as "good and faithful servants," but are promised a share in kingdom rule (vv. 21, 23). The reward is not entrance into the kingdom. That would condition entrance upon performance, which is contrary to salvation by unconditional grace. The reward is co-ruling with Christ and accompanying joy. This reward for faithful believers is not unfamiliar to Bible students (see Rom. 8:17; 2 Tim. 2:12; Rev. 2:26-27). It is noteworthy that the reward is the same for the two servants though they each had different amounts to invest. Each was held accountable for what he had received.

What influences the interpretation for many is the master's words to the unfaithful servant, calling him "wicked and lazy" (v. 26) and consigning him to "the outer darkness" where there is "weeping and gnashing of teeth"

(v. 30). Admittedly, this is severe language addressed to a Christian, but not without precedent. We saw this in relation to the unforgiving servant (Matt. 18:21-35), the improperly clothed guest at the wedding (Matt. 22:1-14), the evil servant (Matt. 24:45-51), and the five unprepared virgins (Matt. 25:1-13). In those discussions, we argued that Christians can be unforgiving, be unfaithful, do evil, and be unprepared for the Lord's return. Likewise, we have seen that "the outer darkness" speaks of exclusion from kingdom blessings, and "weeping and gnashing of teeth" is a metaphor for profound regret at the Judgment Seat of Christ.

The additional statements that might give some pause are in verses 28-29. What is taken away from the unfaithful servant? Salvation does not fit the context in any way—would Jesus take salvation away from a believer or entrust anything to an unbeliever? What is taken is the talent that was entrusted to the lazy servant who did not produce a profit for the master. The master takes it and gives it to the servant who made a profit from his ten talents. The master is, after all, a good steward himself! As a picture of a believer's relationship to Jesus Christ, the Master in His absence, has entrusted to each believer many things: a new life, spiritual gifts, abilities, ministry, opportunities, resources, etc. When Jesus returns, each believer will be held accountable for how he used these things "each according to his own ability" (v. 15) while he waited for the Lord. There will be rewards in the kingdom for those who use them faithfully and an exclusion from rewards for those who do not use them.

We should note the similarities and differences that this parable of the talents has with the parable of the minas in Luke 19:11-27. Both parables address a question or thought about the timing of the coming kingdom. Other similarities include a master who leaves, trusts his wealth to his three servants, and later returns to hold them accountable for how they used it. Also, both parables show rewards in the kingdom for the two faithful servants and a loss in the kingdom for the unfaithful third servant. Both unfaithful servants make the same excuse to the master, both are called "wicked," and both have the money taken from them and given to a faithful servant. We can make the same inferences here, that the master represents the Lord Jesus Christ, and the servants represent believers.

Differences between the parables include the amount the master gives to each servant—a mina was substantially more money than a talent. While in the parable of the talents, the servants are given different amounts, in the parable of the minas, the servants are given the same amount. However, the two who were faithful with the differing amounts of talents receive the same reward whereas the two who were faithful with the same amount (one mina) receive different rewards proportionate to their profitability (ten cities and five cities; Luke 19:16-19). There is a little difference in how the fate of the unfaithful servants is stated, because the servant in Luke's parable of the minas is not threatened with "the outer darkness." One significant addition in the parable of the minas is the contrast between the three servants and those called the "enemies" of the master who did not want him to reign over them. The master commands that they be slain (Luke 19:27). This contrast shows the difference between believers (the three servants) and unbelievers.

The B Truth message of these two parables is similar: Believers should be faithful in how they use their lives while the Lord is away, because when He returns, there will be consequences, good and bad, in the kingdom. However, there seems to be a different emphasis in each. The parable of the talents teaches us that believers must be faithful to use whatever different resources are given to each, while the parable of the minas teaches us that believers must be faithful to use the same opportunity given to each.

The apostle Paul wrote this relevant B Truth to the Corinthian church:

Let a man so consider us, as servants of Christ and stewards of the mysteries of God. Moreover, it is required in stewards that one be found faithful. (1 Cor. 4:1-2).

As believers waiting for Christ's return, we must be faithful as servants and stewards to invest our lives to profit Him. This gives every Christian a purpose in life. The Lord will not accept any excuse for not investing our lives for His glory. Each Christian will be held accountable for what God has entrusted to him.

Judgment of the sheep and the goats. Matthew 25:31-46

[31] *"When the Son of Man comes in His glory, and all the holy angels with Him, then He will sit on the throne of His glory. [32] All the nations will be gathered before Him, and He will separate them one from another, as a shepherd divides his sheep from the goats. [33] And He will set the sheep on His right hand, but the goats on the left. [34] Then the King will say to those on His right hand, 'Come, you blessed of My Father, inherit the kingdom prepared for you from the foundation of the world: [35] for I was hungry and you gave Me food; I was thirsty and you gave Me drink; I was a stranger and you took Me in; [36] I was*

*naked and you clothed Me; I was sick and you visited Me; I was in
prison and you came to Me.'"*

A Truth Interpretation: Those people who help the needy will enter
the kingdom, but those who do not help the needy will go to hell.

Second A Truth Interpretation: Those Gentiles who help the Jews
in the Tribulation are faithful believers who will enter the kingdom,
while those Gentiles who do not help the Jews in the Tribulation are
unbelievers who will go to hell.

B Truth Interpretation: The Gentiles are judged to be saved or
unsaved, then each group is respectively rewarded or punished
according to their conduct toward the Jews in the Tribulation.

It is very common to hear this parable cited as evidence that works
are the necessary evidence that determines one's eternal salvation or
condemnation. More specifically, many well-meaning advocates for the poor
use Jesus' statements about helping the disadvantaged as the distinguishing
mark of genuine Christians and true Christianity.

It is very important to observe the context and timing of this event.
Since Jesus most likely taught the four parables of Matthew 24-25 with
chronological sequence in mind, this judgment follows the Judgment
Seat of Christ and the bestowment of kingdom rewards at the beginning
of or during the Tribulation period, as seen in the previous parables. The
judgment of Matthew 25:31-46 is evidently at the end of the Tribulation
because it reflects the events and sequence of Jesus' teaching in Matthew
24:5-31. There we learn that there will be a great persecution of the Jewish
people by the Antichrist. Revelation 12-13 adds more information about the
terrible plight of the Jews and believers. During this period, the beast will
prohibit those who do not follow him from buying or selling anything (Rev.
13:16-17). Jesus says that Jews who endure the persecution to the end of the
Tribulation will be delivered from their enemies (though we acknowledge
some Jews and Gentiles will die from persecution; see Rev. 20:4-5 and the
previous discussion of Matt. 24:13). The time is so terrible, if it were not
shortened, "no flesh" would survive (this includes Gentiles in those who
survive; Matt. 24:22). This judgment is evidently not the same as the Great
White Throne Judgment in Revelation 20:11-15 because that is only for the
unbelievers of past ages and the millennium. This is a special judgment

specifically for the Gentiles at the end of the Tribulation when Jesus returns to earth in His second coming.

In this parable, we observe three groups. Since the term "nations" (*ethnē*) refers to all Gentiles, it is they who are separated into sheep and goats. Jesus names the third group as "My brethren," an obvious reference to the Jewish people, perhaps the 144,000 Jews who are actively spreading the gospel (Matt. 24:14; Rev. 7:3-8; 12:17; 14:1-7). The judgment of the Gentiles is determined by their treatment of the Jews during the Tribulation. Does this mean that their works determines their salvation?

An important key to interpreting this judgment is found in the revelation Jesus gave shortly before: Some Jews and Gentiles will live until the end of the Tribulation and be delivered from their enemies (Matt. 24:13, 22). The mention of good deeds by the saved Gentiles (sheep) refers to them helping the Jews endure the persecution of the Tribulation. These Gentiles' faith is demonstrated by their help given to the Jewish refugees who had been displaced and were in great need of food, clothes, medical attention, and visitation in prison (vv. 35-36). Perhaps Jesus emphasizes the believing Gentiles' deeds because He describes their future as entering "into eternal life" (v. 46) as well as inheriting a kingdom specially prepared for them (v. 34). The idea of entering and inheriting may emphasize their transformation from mortal to immortal, so they can enter and possess their joy in the kingdom of God (Matt. 24:21, 23; 1 Cor. 15:50).

When we observe the context, we should see that this passage does not simply describe a judgment on peoples' salvation determined by how they treat needy people as the first A Truth interpretation views it. Salvation is never by works, nor can works definitely prove one's salvation (see the discussions on Matt. 7:15-23). The second A Truth interpretation would say that works do not determine or prove that Gentiles are either saved or unsaved, but works are evidence of their state. While this view claims to remove works from the salvation equation, it may not do so convincingly. If there are only two judgments in view, one for sheep and one for goats, and the only criterion that seems to make the difference is how each group treated the Jews, then it appears that works determine salvation,

The B Truth interpretation would explain this judgment differently. This view would propose that three judgments are in view. The first judgment is the separation of all the Gentiles into sheep (believers) and goats (unbelievers) before any deeds are mentioned. We have argued previously that the only basis for distinguishing believers from unbelievers is faith in Jesus Christ as Savior. It is this separation that determines where each group will spend eternity.

When deeds are mentioned, however, the emphasis is on the consequences of each group's conduct toward the Jews. The second judgment is for the sheep (believers), those Jesus calls "blessed of My Father." They are invited to "inherit the kingdom" (v. 34). The word "kingdom" has no modifiers such as "of God" or "of heaven" so it may refer to the more general aspect of Christ's rule or kingship. Then the invitation is to enjoy the reward of participation in Christ's kingdom rule, a theme of the previous parable (cf. Matt. 24:21, 23) and a teaching found in other passages (e.g. Luke 22:27-30; Rom. 8:17; and 2 Tim. 2:10-13 which is discussed later). As we have also seen, the term "eternal life" (used in v. 46 for the fate of the "righteous") should be thought of in terms of quality of experience, not just quantity of time (see the discussions of Gal. 6:7-8 and 1 Tim. 6:17-19). The third judgment concerns the consequence for those unbelieving Gentiles (the goats) who neglected the Jews. They will experience "everlasting fire" (v. 41) and "everlasting punishment" (v. 46). Though the lake of fire is the final habitation of all unbelievers, the additional mention of "punishment" implies more than a final habitation. It implies divine retribution or degrees of punishment determined by former conduct, as is true of the Great White Throne Judgment that comes later (Rev. 20:12-13; see also Matt. 23:14/Mark 12:38-40/Luke 20:46-47).

This B Truth interpretation has much to commend it and keeps works out of the determination of who is saved (sheep) and who is unsaved (goats). One objection to this view would be that the passage does not explicitly distinguish degrees of faithfulness in the sheep or degrees of wickedness in the goats--this could only be implied. In answer, it can be argued that Jesus was speaking in generalities about what characterized each group as a whole. We know that there will be varying degrees of faithfulness when believers are judged at the Judgment Seat of Christ (Matt. 25:20-23), especially with those who endure persecution (Matt. 5:19). This judgment would be similar. As pointed out in the previous paragraph, there are also varying degrees of punishment for unbelievers.

The second A Truth interpretation sees the deeds mentioned not as the condition for the Gentiles' salvation, but a demonstration of their faith that assumes their salvation. The B Truth interpretation does away with any role of works for determining salvation, but suggests they determine degrees of reward for believers or punishment for unbelievers. With either view, there is an important application for us who are believers today: God cares about how we treat His people, the Jews. They are crucial to His plan for the world, therefore His promise to Abraham and his descendants remains: "I will bless those who bless you, and I will curse him who curses you" (Gen. 12:3).

Parable of the Prodigal Son. Luke 15:11-32.

[11] *Then He said: "A certain man had two sons.* [12] *And the younger of them said to his father, 'Father, give me the portion of goods that falls to me.' So he divided to them his livelihood.* [13] *And not many days after, the younger son gathered all together, journeyed to a far country, and there wasted his possessions with prodigal living.* [14] *But when he had spent all, there arose a severe famine in that land, and he began to be in want.* [15] *Then he went and joined himself to a citizen of that country, and he sent him into his fields to feed swine.* [16] *And he would gladly have filled his stomach with the pods that the swine ate, and no one gave him anything.* [17] *But when he came to himself, he said, 'How many of my father's hired servants have bread enough and to spare, and I perish with hunger!* [18] *I will arise and go to my father, and will say to him, "Father, I have sinned against heaven and before you,* [19] *and I am no longer worthy to be called your son. Make me like one of your hired servants."'* [20] *And he arose and came to his father. But when he was still a great way off, his father saw him and had compassion, and ran and fell on his neck and kissed him.* [21] *And the son said to him, 'Father, I have sinned against heaven and in your sight, and am no longer worthy to be called your son.'* [22] *But the father said to his servants, 'Bring out the best robe and put it on him, and put a ring on his hand and sandals on his feet.* [23] *And bring the fatted calf here and kill it, and let us eat and be merry;* [24] *for this my son was dead and is alive again; he was lost and is found.' And they began to be merry.* [25] *Now his older son was in the field. And as he came and drew near to the house, he heard music and dancing.* [26] *So he called one of the servants and asked what these things meant.* [27] *And he said to him, 'Your brother has come, and because he has received him safe and sound, your father has killed the fatted calf.'* [28] *But he was angry and would not go in. Therefore, his father came out and pleaded with him.* [29] *So he answered and said to his father, 'Lo, these many years I have been serving you; I never transgressed your commandment at any time; and yet you never gave me a young goat, that I might make merry with my friends.* [30] *But as soon as this son of yours came, who has devoured your livelihood with harlots, you killed the fatted calf for him.'* [31] *And he said to him, 'Son, you are always with me, and all*

that I have is yours. ³² It was right that we should make merry and be glad, for your brother was dead and is alive again, and was lost and is found.'"

A Truth Interpretation: The son is saved when he repents of his sin by returning home to his father.

B Truth Interpretation: The son may represent someone who is either saved or unsaved, but the emphasis is that a father's grace forgives and receives sinners who repent.

One aspect of this story may be debated—does the prodigal son represent a believer or an unbeliever? One could argue he represents a believer because he is, after all, a son. Another might argue that he could not at first be a saved person since he lives in sin and has to repent of his sins in order to be saved.

The A Truth interpretation would claim that the son is unsaved but gets saved. He repents of his sin and returns to his father. This teaches that any sinner must repent of his sin when he comes to God for salvation. Often the emphasis is that one can only be saved when he turns from his sin, because in that view, repentance is not only a change of mind, but also a change in the direction of one's conduct.

The B Truth interpretation would argue that the son is already in the family, but he has sinned and broken fellowship with his father. His repentance happened when he "came to himself" (Luke 15:17) and changed his mind about his worthiness to be called a son. His return to his father is a result of his repentance. As previously discussed, this separates the inner aspect of repentance from outer conduct, making works a consequence not a condition of the gospel. Though it seems to be primarily B Truth, there is application for unbelievers.

It seems the main emphasis of the story is that this father, who represents God, joyfully receives his son who comes to him. Whether the son is saved or unsaved is not crucial to this point. He once was lost, but now is found—just like the lost sheep and the lost coin are found in the preceding stories (Luke 15:4-10). The parable is spoken to the Pharisees and scribes in the context of Israel's rejection of the Messiah. To them the message would be that God welcomes back a rebellious nation as well as rebellious individuals. We also note that the story is recorded only in Luke who is thought to have written to a predominantly Gentile audience. Any Gentile could see what God's attitude toward him is as well. Every sinning person, whether he already belongs to God or not, needs to know that God loves and welcomes him.

The main lesson is that God the Father loves sinners, forgives them, rejoices greatly when they repent and come to Him, and restores them. In Luke 5:32, Jesus says, "I have not come to call the righteous, but sinners to repentance." This parable is part of Jesus' response to the Pharisees and scribes who criticized him for eating with sinners (Luke 15:1-3). The three stories Jesus tells in Luke 15 show the value of every sinner to God. We should not forget the prominent role of the elder brother in this story. He criticizes the father's grace shown toward his prodigal brother, just as the scribes and Pharisees criticized Jesus' attitude toward sinners.

It is hard to sequester the interpretation of this parable to either only an unsaved person or only a saved person. There seem to be elements of both A Truth and B Truth. The point is, God rejoices when a sinner is saved or when a son is restored.

While we may not have been cognizant of God's joy when we were initially saved, we can now understand how much He rejoices when we behave as errant children who repent of our sinfulness and return to Him.

Passages on Baptism

The significance of baptism in the Bible persists as a controversy, especially in the interpretation of some specific passages in the Synoptic Gospels. There are many who either claim that baptism is a necessary condition of salvation, or that it is a necessary fruit of salvation. In either case, they believe that baptism has A Truth significance. Here, we examine a couple key passages on baptism in the first three Gospels.

John's baptism of repentance. Matthew 3:1-12 (cf. Luke 3:3-17)

[1] *In those days John the Baptist came preaching in the wilderness of Judea,* [2] *and saying, "Repent, for the kingdom of heaven is at hand!"* [3] *For this is he who was spoken of by the prophet Isaiah, saying: "The voice of one crying in the wilderness: 'Prepare the way of the Lord; Make His paths straight.'"* [4] *Now John himself was clothed in camel's hair, with a leather belt around his waist; and his food was locusts and wild honey.* [5] *Then Jerusalem, all Judea, and all the region around the Jordan went out to him* [6] *and were baptized by him in the Jordan,*

confessing their sins. ⁷ *But when he saw many of the Pharisees and Sadducees coming to his baptism, he said to them, "Brood of vipers! Who warned you to flee from the wrath to come?* ⁸ *Therefore bear fruits worthy of repentance,* ⁹ *and do not think to say to yourselves, 'We have Abraham as our father.' For I say to you that God is able to raise up children to Abraham from these stones.* ¹⁰ *And even now the ax is laid to the root of the trees. Therefore every tree which does not bear good fruit is cut down and thrown into the fire.* ¹¹ *I indeed baptize you with water unto repentance, but He who is coming after me is mightier than I, whose sandals I am not worthy to carry. He will baptize you with the Holy Spirit and fire.* ¹² *His winnowing fan is in His hand, and He will thoroughly clean out His threshing floor, and gather His wheat into the barn; but He will burn up the chaff with unquenchable fire."*

A Truth Interpretation: John the Baptist baptized unbelievers who repented of sins and changed their conduct so that they would be saved.

B Truth Interpretation: John the Baptist baptized Jews who wanted to show their repentance under the Mosaic Covenant, separate from sinful Israel, and prepare for the coming Messiah.

This is a passage where it is important to understand the setting and context. John the Baptist has a message for the nation of Israel about repentance and baptism. But is he telling them as well as people today how to be saved?

At the time that John preached, the nation of Israel was still under the Mosaic Covenant. For God's covenant people, the way to be restored from departing from God was to repent—to change their minds or attitudes about their sin (Deut. 30:2, 10; 2 Chr. 7:14). At that point, they are prepared to receive the Messiah that John would introduce. His baptism was a witness to their repentance and anticipation of the Messiah. The works he tells the Pharisees, Sadducees, and others to do (Matt. 3:7-9; Luke 3:7-14) are works that are consistent with true repentance, not works that will save them. This passage clearly differentiates between repentance as an inner attitude and "fruits worthy of repentance" which is the outer conduct (v. 8).

It helps to see what the apostle Paul says about John's baptism in Acts

19:4. Speaking to Ephesians who had received John's baptism but had not believed in Jesus Christ, he said, "John indeed baptized with a baptism of repentance, saying to the people that they should believe on Him who would come after him, that is, on Jesus Christ." Those who had received John's baptism were Jewish believers who needed to become Christians through faith in Jesus Christ. They were in the transition period between the era of Law and the era of grace.

As recorded in Acts 13:24, Paul said in Psidian Antioch before Christ officially presented Himself to Israel as the Messiah, that John preached "the baptism of repentance to all the people of Israel." If we understand the Jewish audience and the covenantal background for John's preaching of baptism and repentance, we should not make this a template for preaching the gospel in the church age. First, this does not at all speak of Christian baptism. Second, repentance does not save anyone in and of itself, but the change of heart that it reflects is well prepared to believe in the Savior. Though it addresses God's people under His covenant, we can learn from this as a general B Truth that teaches the way back to God begins with a change of mind and heart.

He who is baptized will be saved. Mark 16:16

"He who believes and is baptized will be saved; but he who does not believe will be condemned."

A Truth Interpretation: Salvation requires belief in Jesus Christ plus water baptism.

B Truth Interpretation: Salvation requires belief in Jesus Christ with water baptism serving as a witness to that faith.

(Though Mark 16:9-20 is not included in a couple early manuscripts of the New Testament, it is in nearly all manuscripts of Mark, so we will treat it here.)

The statement seems straightforward in its saying, "He who believes and is baptized will be saved." However, it is just as straightforward in the next statement: "but he who does not believe will be condemned." One would expect that if baptism is a condition for salvation in the first statement, the lack of baptism would be a reason for condemnation. Yet no mention of baptism is connected to condemnation.

That is a pretty solid indication that baptism is not a condition for salvation. The close connection of belief and baptism was due to the close connection these two things had in the early converts. When one believed, he was baptized. That is the pattern seen so clearly in Acts (Acts 2:41; 8:35-37; 10:44-48; 16:14-15).

But this is also a situation where we must compare clear Scriptures with those less clear. This statement that seems to make baptism a saving act contradicts the overwhelming teaching of the New Testament that salvation is through faith alone in Jesus Christ. The Gospel of John, written to tell unbelievers how to be saved (John 20:31), makes belief the only condition of salvation and never adds baptism. Also, the Apostle Paul could not be clearer than he is in Romans 3:24-4:5, that we are justified through faith, not works. Furthermore, he said baptism was not part of his gospel preaching (1 Cor. 1:14-17).

The correct A Truth in Mark 16:16 is that those who believe will be saved and those who do not believe will be condemned. The B Truth is that those who believe and are saved should automatically testify to that faith through water baptism. While we do not believe that baptism saves, we do not diminish the importance of baptism that testifies to our salvation.

The Gospel of John

6

J OHN'S GOSPEL DIFFERS from the Synoptic Gospels in the uniqueness of its content and purpose. Its content is rarely shared with the other Gospels—only ten percent is repeated in them. Also, it's purpose is clearly stated for us in John 20:30-31:

> [30] *And truly Jesus did many other signs in the presence of His disciples, which are not written in this book;* [31] *but these are written that you may believe that Jesus is the Christ, the Son of God, and that believing you may have life in His name.*

John wrote to bring people to faith in Jesus Christ. That was probably an implicit and partial purpose for the Synoptic Gospels as well, but John uniquely and emphatically states it. The choice of stories, metaphors for Jesus Christ, emphasis on His deity, the fact that John uses the word "believe" almost one hundred times (always in verbal form, never as a noun) usually as the condition for eternal life shows this purpose. John also uses analogies for believing to emphasize how the free gift of eternal life is appropriated. He compares believing to looking (John 3:15), asking (John 4:10), eating and drinking (John 6:47-58), and entering (John 10:9), all of which are simple activities that avoid any appearance of merit or work.

Because of the emphasis on eternal life, we might be tempted to say that the Gospel of John is an A Truth book, but it also contains some very clear B Truth, truth for Christian living and discipleship. Chapters 13-17, known as the Upper Room Discourse, are an intimate conversation between Jesus and His disciples mostly about the Christian life. This is also consistent with the purpose statement in John 20:31, which ends in "that believing you might have life in His name." The present tense of "believing" shows that sanctifying faith must continue after initial justifying faith in order to *experience* the new life that was received. This thematic purpose is also seen at the beginning of the book in John 1:4: "In Him was life, and the life was the light of men." Life that is gained becomes life that gives the believer light to live by. Eternal life is not just something to possess, it is something to experience, because it is God's life.

Jesus does not trust some people. John 2:23-25

> [23] Now when He was in Jerusalem at the Passover, during the feast, many believed in His name when they saw the signs which He did. [24] But Jesus did not commit Himself to them, because He knew all men, [25] and had no need that anyone should testify of man, for He knew what was in man.

A Truth Interpretation: Jesus did not entrust Himself to some Jews and give them eternal life because He knew those who did not really believe in Him.

B Truth Interpretation: Jesus did not entrust Himself to some Jews who had received eternal life and give them deeper fellowship because He knew their hearts were not ready.

Almost all commentators favor an A Truth interpretation. They do not believe these Jews were saved, even though it says they had believed in Christ. They claim it is a false faith because 1) They only believed in Jesus' name not His person, 2) They only believed because of the signs Jesus did, and 3) Jesus refuses to entrust Himself to them.

Their argument sounds convincing—until we start to compare other Scriptures. For example, in relation to the first argument that the Jews had believed only in Jesus' name, that very language is used for salvation in the prologue as a condition for becoming a child of God (John 1:12). Likewise, the purpose statement says we have "life through His name" (John 20:31). Not believing in His name is grounds for condemnation (John 3:18). Amazingly, the same commentators who say that believing in Jesus' name is not enough to save, usually assert that a person must "believe in Him" to be saved, yet they deny that meaning in John 2:23. What they fail to understand is that believing in Jesus' *name* means believing in all that Jesus is and represents— the significance attached quite often to *name* in the Bible.

The second argument—that faith induced by signs is not inadequate for salvation—falls to the evidence as well. Signs are not the object of faith anyway—Jesus Christ is. Signs only point people to Jesus. Besides, faith prompted by signs is seen elsewhere in John (John 1:47-49; 2:11; 4:52-53; 10:41-42; 11:42, 45; 20:26-29) and Jesus Himself encourages faith based on signs (John 1:50-51; 10:37-38; 14:11). The apostle John expects signs to prompt faith (12:37), and even says so in his purpose statement for the Gospel (20:30-31).

It appears that the only reason people interpret the Jews' faith as a false faith is because Jesus does not entrust Himself to them. So why doesn't Jesus trust these new believers?

First, we should recognize that there is a play on words here, because the word translated *commit* is the same word translated *believe (pisteuō)* used of the Jews, but in this reference to Jesus it is not used in a soteriological sense. We could say that even though the Jews believed in Him, Jesus did not yet believe in them because he knew what was in them. They were new believers who were unproven and for some reason known only to Jesus, not ready for Him to share more of Himself with them. It is a principle we see taught later in John that those who respond well to truth are granted more truth (John 14:21; 15:14-15). Jesus' refusal to commit Himself says absolutely nothing explicit about the genuineness of these Jews' faith and their salvation. The clear statement is that they believed, which in John can be shown to result always in eternal life.

By interpreting this passage as A Truth, many have missed the marvelous B Truth related to the Christian life and discipleship, that obedience brings us into a deeper more intimate relationship with Jesus Christ in which He makes Himself known to us more and more. But Christ will only give us this knowledge when we prove that we are ready for it.

Born of water and the Spirit. John 3:5

Jesus answered, "Most assuredly, I say to you, unless one is born of water and the Spirit, he cannot enter the kingdom of God."

A Truth Interpretation: A person must be baptized to receive the Holy Spirit and be born again.

Second A Truth Interpretation: A person who receives the promise of the Holy Spirit is born again.

If context means anything (and of course, it means everything!), then the new birth seen in John 3:1-16 comes through faith in Jesus Christ as Savior, not by baptism. Most are very familiar with belief as the condition for salvation in John 3:16. But the necessity of belief is mentioned as early as 1:12. It is also amplified in 3:15 by reference to the incident in Numbers 21 with the serpents in the wilderness under Moses. It is the simple look at God's provision that saved the Israelites from death, just as it is simple faith that looks to Jesus Christ as God's provision for eternal salvation today. Nothing else is involved and there is certainly no mention of baptism.

So what does the reference to "born of the water and of the Spirit" mean in verse 5? There are a number of interpretations offered by commentators. Some say water refers to the baptism of John the Baptist that prepares people for faith in Christ by which they get the Holy Spirit, but there is no mention of John or baptism. Others think this is a reference to Christian baptism, but that certainly is premature since we don't see baptism in Jesus' name until Acts. Some believe water refers to the Word of God because of the "washing of water by the word" mentioned in Ephesians 5:26, but this is also reaching far from the context. A more contextual interpretation is that water refers to physical birth, because Jesus does refer to "that which is born of the flesh" and Nicodemus also offers a misguided question about the plausibility of a person retreating into his mother's womb to be born a second time. So at least this interpretation comes from the context.

However, another interpretation supported by the context is that water is a reference to the Holy Spirit. The emphasis is, after all, on spiritual birth. Jesus essentially chided Nicodemus that as *the* teacher of Israel, he should know this truth about the new birth. How would Nicodemus know about the new birth? It would have to be from the Old Testament, and the most likely passage would be the very familiar New Covenant promises in Ezekiel 36:25-27:

> [25] *Then I will sprinkle clean water on you, and you shall be clean; I will cleanse you from all your filthiness and from all your idols.* [26] *I will give you a new heart and put a new spirit within you; I will take the heart of stone out of your flesh and give you a heart of flesh.* [27] *I will put My Spirit within you and cause you to walk in My statutes, and you will keep My judgments and do them.*

So Nicodemus should have known that the kingdom required the forgiveness of sins and a new ministry of the Holy Spirit in each person who believes in the Messiah. John 3:5 can be translated "water, even the Spirit" or "water, that is, the Spirit," as sometimes the connector "and" (*kai*) is translated into English. The spiritual aspects of the New Covenant promises to Israel, like the ministry of the Holy Spirit, were shared with Gentiles who believed in Jesus Christ.

Much more could be said, but we have established that water baptism does not suit this context. The story and commentary that follows it (John 3:1-18) make it very clear that the new birth, entrance into the kingdom, and eternal life are all on the basis of believing in Jesus Christ as Savior and nothing else.

Believe and obey. John 3:36

"He who believes in the Son has everlasting life; and he who does not believe the Son shall not see life, but the wrath of God abides on him."

A Truth Interpretation: A person is saved if he or she believes in Christ and obeys Him.

Second A Truth Interpretation: A person is saved if he or she obeys the command to believe in Christ.

The NKJV version cited above does not seem to present a problem, because its translators understand the Greek word *peithō* in "does not believe the Son" to have a meaning equivalent to *believe*. However, the NASB and ESV translate *peithō* as *obey* ("whoever does not obey the Son shall not see life" ESV), which prompts the first A Truth interpretation. Because of the language of verse 36 which associates *believe* and *obey*, some insist that the only faith that saves is a faith that obeys God, that is, a faith that guarantees obedience.

It helps to view a similar passage seen in the context, verse 18, where unbelief is the reason for present condemnation: "whoever does not believe is condemned already." This compares with the statement in verse 36: "the wrath of God abides on Him". When we consider this and the fact that the Gospel of John's presentation is overwhelmingly presented in terms of belief for eternal life and unbelief for condemnation, the NKJV translation makes perfect sense. All John is doing in the context is presenting Jesus Christ as one who has been given the authority of God the Father and therefore should be obeyed as such. The first and foremost obedience God requires is to believe in Jesus Christ whom He has sent.

Those who equate faith with obedience or say faith guarantees obedience make works of obedience an essential condition for salvation by making works essential to faith. This is against the entire teaching of the New Testament that salvation is by grace through faith not by works, much less the clear emphasis in John's Gospel on the sufficiency of faith alone as the condition for eternal life.

Two resurrections. John 5:28-29

[28] *"Do not marvel at this; for the hour is coming in which all who are in the graves will hear His voice* [29] *and come forth—those who have done good, to the resurrection of life, and those who have done evil, to the resurrection of condemnation."*

First A Truth Interpretation: Those who have done good works will experience the resurrection of life while those who have done evil deeds will be condemned.

Second A Truth Interpretation: Those who have done good works as evidence of their faith will experience the resurrection of life while those who have done evil deeds as evidence of their unbelief will be condemned.

Third A Truth Interpretation: At their resurrection, those who have done good—believed in Jesus Christ—will experience their eternal life while those who have done evil—rejected Jesus Christ—will experience their condemnation.

At first glance this passage seems to indicate a judgment will take place at the resurrection of all people where everyone's works will be examined to determine if they receive the resurrection of life or the resurrection of condemnation. The first A Truth interpretation assumes that one's salvation is based on one's conduct in this life. However, we quickly realize this is contrary to the emphasis in John's Gospel on salvation through believing only. In John, believing results in eternal life while *not* believing condemns (John 3:18, 36). This is a case where an unclear passage must be interpreted in light of clearer passages.

Those who hold the second A Truth interpretation would say that works are not the basis of salvation, but they are the basis of judgment. An examination of one's works will affirm or deny whether that person has truly believed in Jesus Christ as Savior. As in a court of law, the evidence will acquit or convict. We have argued earlier that this does not adequately separate works from salvation. In the end, with this interpretation it is works that determine one's fate. But is that what the context leading up to this passage teaches?

In the context that precedes verses 28-29, Jesus explains to the Jews trying to kill Him (5:16-18) that He has the Father's authority to judge and to give life (5:19-22). He contrasts two different groups of people—those who honor the Son and the Father, and those who do not (5:23). Then Jesus describes in emphatic fashion ("most assuredly" from *amēn amēn*) the group that honors Him and the Father: it is those "who hear My word and believe in Him who sent Me." This group "has everlasting life, and shall not come into judgment, but has passed from death to life" (5:24). This a clear statement that those who believe in Jesus Christ have eternal life in the present and will not come into judgment in the future.

Jesus then addresses two future resurrections awaiting mankind. While Jesus does not distinguish them in time, we see in Revelation 20:4-15 that these resurrections are separated by one thousand years. This alone tips us off that these resurrections are not the time of determining one's salvation, but only the time of delivering each one's fate. Jesus' preface to the mention of the resurrections is that He has "life in Himself" implying that those who have everlasting life are safe in Him as the Life (5:25-26). The resurrections parallel the consequences of believing and not believing in 5:24. The resurrection of life parallels eternal life that is given to anyone who believes. The resurrection of condemnation parallels the judgment mentioned in 5:24 as that which the believer escapes ("shall not come into judgment").

When Jesus refers to "those who have done good" (literally, "the good things;" *ta agatha*), the context leads us to understand this in the light of verses 23-34. This group honors the Son, hears (listens to) His word, and believes in Him. Conversely, "those who have done evil (literally, "the evil things;" *ta phaula*) is the group that does not honor the Son, does not hear (listen to) His word, and does not believe in Him. The fate of each group is settled by their previous responses. Their fate is not *decided* at their resurrection; their fate is only *delivered* at their resurrection. In the contrast of these two groups, we see John's fondness for stating things in contrasting absolutes. We see the same contrast with similar expressions in John 3:18-21. There, a person's fate is also sealed according to his response:

"He who believes in Him is not condemned; but he who does not believe is condemned already" (v. 18a).

Contextually, the third A Truth interpretation has more support than the second interpretation that considers doing good or evil as evidence of belief or unbelief. In John 3:21, the one who escapes condemnation is described as "he who does the truth" and in 6:29 believing in Jesus Christ is spoken of as doing good or doing the "work of God" (see the discussion of Matt. 7:21-23 and the next discussion). In other words, believing in Jesus Christ is the right thing to do, and it results in the experience of eternal life now as well as the resurrection of life in the future. On the other hand, doing evil would be rejection of Jesus Christ as Savior (cf. John 3:20). No one can *do* better than believing in Jesus Christ as Savior!

The work of God. John 6:28-29

[28] *Then they said to Him, "What shall we do, that we may work the works of God?"* [29] *Jesus answered and said to them, "This is the work of God, that you believe in Him whom He sent."*

A Truth Interpretation: Believing in Jesus Christ for salvation requires a working faith.

Second A Truth Interpretation: Believing in Jesus Christ for salvation requires simple faith.

This passage has been used to argue that faith is obedience or work, because when the Jews ask Jesus what they must "do that we may work the works of God?" Jesus answers, "This is the work of God, that you believe on Him whom He sent."

The question reflects a typical Jewish mindset of that time which assumed something had to be done in order to earn salvation. They had the Mosaic Law as their reference point, but because there were many commandments (613) the discussion often centered on which ones were the most important to keep in order to be righteous before God (cf. Matt. 22:34-36). Different rabbis had different answers about what God required. Jesus, seen in the role of another rabbi, was put to the test: "Okay, Rabbi Jesus, we know the other rabbis' lists, so what is your list of things to do in order to be righteous before God?"

Jesus answers simply, "This is the work of God…" Jesus does not concede to their request for a list of works, but in a play on their request for "works" He uses only the singular word "work" as something that must be done. In other words, He answers, "If you want to know what you have to *do* to become acceptable to God, simply believe in the Me whom He sent." Jesus gives nothing else to "do" but believe; that is all that God commands and all that God requires (cf. 1 john 3:23).

In a world full of religions that all have a different list of things to do in order to know God, get to heaven, or find salvation, how refreshing it is that Jesus teaches we must only and simply believe that He was sent by God to be our Savior from sin. If biblical Christianity loses this clear teaching, we become like all the other religions of the world that teach we must work to earn our eternal salvation.

Eat Jesus' body, drink His blood. John 6:48-58

[48] *"I am the bread of life.* [49] *Your fathers ate the manna in the wilderness, and are dead.* [50] *This is the bread which comes down from heaven, that one may eat of it and not die.* [51] *I am the living bread which came down from heaven. If anyone eats of this bread, he will live forever; and the bread that I shall give is My flesh, which I shall give for the life of the world."* [52] *The Jews therefore quarreled among themselves, saying, "How can this Man give us His flesh to eat?"* [53] *Then Jesus said to them, "Most assuredly, I say to you, unless you eat the flesh of the Son of Man and drink His blood, you have no life in you.* [54] *Whoever eats My flesh and drinks My blood has eternal life, and I will raise him up at the last day.* [55] *For My flesh is food indeed, and My blood is drink indeed.* [56] *He who eats My flesh and drinks My blood abides in Me, and I in him.* [57] *As the living Father sent Me, and I live because of the Father, so he who feeds on Me will live because of Me.* [58] *This is the bread which came down from heaven—not as your fathers ate the manna, and are dead. He who eats this bread will live forever."*

A Truth Interpretation: A person is saved when he receives the holy Eucharist of Christ's body and blood.

Second A Truth Interpretation: A person is saved when he believes in Christ, which is pictured as eating His flesh and drinking His blood.

This passage from Jesus' Bread of Life discourse is a premise of the Roman Catholic teaching that the holy Eucharist, the ritual of ingesting bread and wine blessed by a priest, actually become the body and blood of Jesus Christ. Those who eat the elements, or receive Christ, obtain eternal life. There are a number of other problems with this view that are not addressed by the passage itself. One problem is that this is only one of the seven Roman Catholic sacraments that supposedly convey God's saving grace, and in their system salvation depends on keeping not just this sacrament, but others as well. Catholics are faced with the dilemma that this passage teaches (in their view) that a person receives eternal life through the Eucharist, but there are other sacraments necessary also. A second issue that plagues this view is that the bread and wine actually become the body and blood of Jesus Christ when the priest blesses them (called *transubstantiation*). Of course, there is no biblical support for this whatsoever.

In the context before this passage, Jesus makes it very clear that eternal life is through faith in Him (John 6:29, 35, 40, 47). These claims are made within His use of the Old Testament story of the manna in the wilderness and the analogy of Himself as the bread of life. The comparison to bread invites the analogy between eating and believing, just as He earlier used the story of the serpents in Numbers 21 to make an analogy between looking and believing (John 3:15). The analogy of eating and drinking emphasizes the reception or internalization of the truth Christ teaches about Himself. The result of never hungering and thirsting emphasizes the eternal life one enjoys.

As always with John, his analogies of believing are simple acts that convey no hint of works or merit before God. It strains the analogy to say that eating and drinking (or elsewhere in John receiving, looking, hearing, entering) are anything more than simple illustrations of what it means to accept the Truth. No one considers eating and drinking work; that is simply how sustenance is appropriated. I was once explaining through a translator in Ghana, Africa, that *believe* means to be convinced or persuaded of a truth such that the person receives it or depends on it. He interrupted me saying, "Oh, we have a good word for *believe* in our language—we say it means *take God's words and eat them.*" When a person believes in Jesus Christ as Savior, he is appropriating or depending upon Jesus' promise to give eternal life.

Disciples abide in Christ's word. John 8:30-32

[30] *As He spoke these words, many believed in Him.* [31] *Then Jesus said to those Jews who believed Him, "If you abide in My word, you are*

My disciples indeed. [32] *And you shall know the truth, and the truth shall make you free."*

A Truth Interpretation: Only those who continue to obey Christ's word are truly saved.

B Truth Interpretation: Only believers who continue to obey Christ's word are truly His disciples.

The A Truth interpretation sees nothing beyond salvation in this passage. Those who profess to believe must actually obey God's Word in order to prove they are genuinely saved. In other words, the many Jews who believed had only a superficial faith that must be proved by obedience to God's Word. Only true believers are disciples and only true believers are "free" from eternal condemnation for their sins.

There are several reasons that many commentators take the A Truth interpretation. Their argument goes like this: Jesus later tells these Jews "You are of your father the devil" (v. 44), so they could not have been saved. Also, verse 31 only says that they "believed Him," not that they "believed *in* Him." Besides, the commentators say, becoming a true believer and a disciple are only two ways of saying the same thing.

When we look at the context that surrounds this passage, we run into difficulties with this interpretation. Yes, the dialogue immediately turns hostile again in verse 33 and continues hostile until the end of the chapter when the Jews try to kill Jesus. Clearly the majority of the audience was hostile even though some of the Jews had believed in Him. Verses 31-32 is Jesus' brief address to the faction of the crowd who had believed, an important acknowledgement that furthers the dialogue with His enemies, because Jesus introduces the possibility of freedom.

We should view verse 30 as an interjection of John's editorial comment designed to help the reader understand the context of Jesus' remarks that follow in verses 31-32 (We see the same pattern used by John in vv. 27-29). The dialogue resumes with the hostile Jews without introducing them again, because their opposition has driven the dialogue from verse 13 and continues to the end of the chapter.

The second reason many say this passage is A Truth is because they claim these Jews only "believed Him" which indicates an inadequate faith because they did not "believe *in* Him." But earlier, Jesus did not use the preposition "in" when He said those who "do not believe that I am He" will die in their sins, implying they perish. Nor is the preposition used in a very clear salvation verse, John 5:24: "Most assuredly, I say to you, he who hears My word and believes [in] Him who sent Me has everlasting life, and shall not come into judgment, but has passed from death to life" (in the NKJV, the "in" is supplied though not in the Greek). The preposition is also not used in John 8:24: ". . . if you do not believe that I am He, you will die in your sins." More importantly, there is no preposition used in the clear offer of salvation in John's purpose statement in 20:31. We must conclude that there is no difference between *believe in* and *believe that* in John, which is consistent with similar language used of salvation in other New Testament passages (There is no preposition in the original language of Acts 16:34; 18:8; Rom. 4:3; Gal. 3:6; 2 Tim. 1:12; Titus 3:8; and Jas. 2:23, and "believe that" is used in Matt. 9:28; Rom. 10:9; and 1 Thess. 4:14).

In answer to the third and last argument, it should be obvious by now that there is a clear distinction in the Bible between the *condition* for salvation and the *conditions* for discipleship. It is clear that verses 31-32 is addressed to believers (v. 30), and that it is conditional for them ("If you"). It is also clear that this is not an invitation to *enter* His Word, but to *abide* in it. These believers entered the truth of the Word when they believed in Jesus. But they must abide in it to become true disciples. If Jesus' statement here is a condition for salvation, consider the consequences: Salvation is by works because the word "abide" (*menō*) means *to adhere to, continue in, remain in,* implying obedience. Also, no one would be sure he is saved until he dies, because he would not know if he has continued obeying God's Word faithfully until the end of his life.

The B Truth aspect of this passage is amplified by the result of abiding and becoming true disciples: knowing and being set free by the truth. True disciples are in a position to know more truth and find freedom in it. Intimate knowledge of Jesus Christ and God the Father is a privilege of those who obey the truth (John 14:15, 21, 23; 15:4, 7, 10, 14). Abiding in truth not only frees the disciple *from* the shame and guilt of sin, the bondage of legalism and the error of false doctrine, but also frees him *to* experience love, joy, peace and the other blessings of the spiritual life.

Those of us who have believed in Jesus Christ for salvation have a fuller and richer life awaiting us when we abide in (live in obedience to) God's Word. We will have a more intimate relationship with God in which He will manifest Himself more and more to us. We will also enjoy the freedom of living under grace and in the power of the Holy Spirit. To remain in God's Word certainly implies that we hear it, read it, study it, even memorize it, but most importantly, *obey it.*

Jesus' sheep follow Him. John 10:27-28

> [27] *"My sheep hear My voice, and I know them, and they follow Me.* [28]
> *And I give them eternal life, and they shall never perish; neither shall*
> *anyone snatch them out of My hand."*

A Truth Interpretation: Those who follow Jesus Christ will be given
eternal life.

B Truth Interpretation: Those who hear Jesus Christ are those who
believe in Him and they follow Him and are given eternal life.

Some who see obedience as a condition for salvation use this passage as
support. If sheep represent believers, then it is only those who follow Christ
in obedience who have eternal life.

Several observations are necessary. First, this passage is within a larger
context using the metaphor of sheep and a shepherd. Second, two activities
are described—hearing and following. Third, these two activities are
descriptive of the sheep, not commands or conditions imposed on the sheep.

The metaphor of sheep and the Shepherd, who is Jesus Christ, pictures
trust in the right voice, the issue that is established early in the metaphor
(10:3-5). When sheep know the right voice, they follow. Of the two activities
described, hearing and following, it is clear that hearing pictures believing
(10:3, 5) and that following is a subsequent response to believing: "the sheep
follow him, for they know his voice" (10:4). How else would sheep show
their trust in the right shepherd? That hearing pictures believing is clear
when we compare verse 16 and verse 26:

> [16] *And other sheep I have which are not of this fold; them also I must*
> *bring, and they will hear My voice; and there will be one flock and*
> *one shepherd.*

> [26] *But you do not believe, because you are not of My sheep, as I said to*
> *you.* [27] *My sheep hear My voice, and I know them, and they follow Me.*

The condition for being in the true Shepherd's flock is hearing His voice,
an A Truth. The natural result of hearing is following, a B Truth. It is important
to make this distinction in the passage and keep conduct out of the gospel
of salvation through faith alone. Following, or obedience, is a natural result

of trusting someone, but it is not what determines the initial relationship. Hearing (believing) the gospel positions one in the flock, while following (obeying) is the expected practical result (cf. Luke 6:47; 8:21). Hearing is used elsewhere in the Bible to picture faith in Jesus Christ for eternal life because hearing is often used in the sense of perceiving and agreeing, which is essential to believing (Matt. 10:14; 11:15; 13:23; Luke 10:16; John 5:24; Acts 28:27-28; Rom. 10:14-17; Gal. 3:2, 5; 1 John 4:6). In verse 26, the result of hearing Christ (believing in Him) is that He knows these people. This implies their salvation and explains their subsequent choice to follow Him. Again, it is important to note that hearing and following simply describe what the sheep are doing; they are never stated as imperatives for conditions for eternal life.

We know our Good Shepherd, Jesus Christ, and He knows us when we hear His voice, or believe in Him. Why would we not follow the One we trust with our eternal destiny, who is truly the Good Shepherd who cares about us? Unfortunately, not all of us are always *good sheep*. Thank God that our eternal destiny does not depend on our obedient following!

Some believe but do not confess. John 12:42

> *Nevertheless even among the rulers many believed in Him, but because of the Pharisees they did not confess Him, lest they should be put out of the synagogue.*

A Truth Interpretation: Those who do not confess Jesus Christ are not true believers.

B Truth Interpretation: True believers may not confess Jesus because of fear.

Can people not confess Jesus Christ publically, fear for their lives and futures, and love the praise of men more than the praise of God, and yet be saved? This was the conduct of the Jewish rulers in this passage, and yet we are told that they had believed in Jesus Christ. We need to sort out the A Truth issue from the B Truth issues.

A Truth relates to initial salvation that comes only through faith in Jesus Christ as our Savior. John tells us that these rulers had believed in Christ. So far we have seen that in John, there is good reason to understand every reference to believing in Christ as a genuine offer or reception of salvation. This passage would be no different.

B Truth relates to conditions for discipleship that come through following Christ. The conduct of these rulers does not fulfill the conditions for discipleship stated elsewhere in the Gospels. They do not confess Christ publically (Matt. 10:32-33), they are not willing to take up their cross or suffer for their identity with Christ (Luke 9:23b), and they are not willing to deny themselves the praise of men (Luke 9:23a).

We conclude that these rulers were saved, but in their new and immature state they were not ready to advance into the commitments necessary to become disciples of Jesus Christ. The immature faith of untrustworthy believers is a subtle motif in John seen already in 2:23-25. The story of Nicodemus is another example. He goes from secret inquirer (John 3:1-4), to feeble defender of Christ (John 7:47-52), to full public identification with Christ (John 19:39-42). The parents of the blind man and Joseph of Arimathea also acted discreetly about their faith (John 9:22; 19:38).

This B Truth should be understood by many Christians around the world who experience the fear that comes from confessing Christ to their families and their communities. In many situations, their lives are at stake. We need to be careful not to impose a western Judeo-Christian society interpretation on this passage or on the actions of other believers who live in places hostile to Christians. God saves weak and fearful Christians. Courage is not a condition for salvation, but it is a condition for discipleship. Those who want to be true disciples will follow Jesus in spite of persecution and even their own death.

Branches that do not bear fruit. John 15:1-8

[1] *"I am the true vine, and My Father is the vinedresser.* [2] *Every branch in Me that does not bear fruit He takes away; and every branch that bears fruit He prunes, that it may bear more fruit.* [3] *You are already clean because of the word which I have spoken to you.* [4] *Abide in Me, and I in you. As the branch cannot bear fruit of itself, unless it abides in the vine, neither can you, unless you abide in Me.* [5] *"I am the vine, you are the branches. He who abides in Me, and I in him, bears much fruit; for without Me you can do nothing.* [6] *If anyone does not abide in Me, he is cast out as a branch and is withered; and they gather them and throw them into the fire, and they are burned.* [7] *If you abide in*

*Me, and My words abide in you, you will ask what you desire, and it
shall be done for you. ⁸ By this My Father is glorified, that you bear
much fruit; so you will be My disciples."*

A Truth Interpretation: Those described as branches without fruit
are not believers and are cast into hell.

B Truth Interpretation: Believers who do not bear fruit are not
useful to the Savior.

The decisive interpretive question here is whether John's reference to the
fruitless branches cast into the fire relates to believers or unbelievers. If the
fruitless branches refer to unbelievers, then they are cast into hell because
their faith was superficial, and they did not bear fruit, or have the good
works true faith would have produced.

The A Truth argument is based on several assumptions. First, "abide"
means *believe*. Second, the *taking away* in verse 2 refers to unbelievers taken
away to the judgment of hell fire, which is supposedly described in verse 6.
Third, "fruit" refers to visible and measurable good works. Inevitably, in this
view, works determine whether one is saved or not.

As we would expect, knowing whether Jesus is addressing believers or
unbelievers is crucial to a correct interpretation. Some might argue that
Jesus is addressing both in such a way that "If the shoe fits, wear it." It is
universally recognized that chapters 13-17 of John form a distinct unit
usually called The Upper Room Discourse because Jesus is isolated with
his disciples in an upstairs room to observe the Passover supper. But the
only unbeliever, Judas Iscariot, departs immediately after the supper (John
13:30), leaving only the believing disciples. In light of His own imminent
absence, Jesus is encouraging His disciples to keep His commandment to
love and to bear the fruit of love.

Jesus speaks to them as saved—He calls them branches in the true vine
(v. 2), and He pronounces them "already clean" (v. 3). These terms speak of
their union with Christ and their justification or forgiveness and cleansing
from sin. These strong assurances preclude the idea that they were spurious
believers.

As we saw in John 8:31, *abide* is not a synonym for *believe*. Jesus shows
no reluctance to use the word *believe* in relation to His offer of eternal life,
so why doesn't He use it here if He is speaking of salvation? And besides,
why would He tell His saved disciples that they need to believe in Him

if that's what *abide* means? We should note that Jesus and His word also abide in them (vv. 4, 5, 7), and Jesus abides in His Father's love (v. 10). It is clear that *abide* cannot mean *believe*, but means *to adhere to, dwell with, continue in a close relation with*. It is a condition for answered prayer (v. 7), and as a condition ("if" vv. 6, 7) shows the possibility that a believer may not comply.

How, then, do we understand the fate of the fruitless branches that the Divine Vinedresser "takes away" in verse 2? This cannot refer to losing salvation and being thrown into hell fire because Jesus says these branches are "in Me." The latter part of the verse hints at a different meaning for "takes away." It pictures the tender care of the Vinedresser who prunes fruitful branches to make them more fruitful. How does He make the fruitless branches more fruitful? The Vinedresser does not take away, but "lifts up" these branches. This is a better translation of the Greek word (*airō*) and is used that way in other places in John (5:8-12; 8:59; 10:18; 11:41). It pictures the common viticultural practice of lifting vines off the ground to keep them from damage and to expose them to more sunlight. As verse 2 states, once fruit is seen, the branch can be pruned to encourage more fruit. This presents a seamless picture of God encouraging fruitfulness in His people (vv. 1-3) if they cooperate by abiding (vv. 4-8).

But what about the fire in verse 6? There is no need to assume this is hell fire, as so many quickly conclude. Jesus is not threatening His disciples with hell. Fire is used often in the Bible to represent God's discipline, anger, or jealousy toward His own people. It is also used in references to the judgment that faces all Christians, the Judgment Seat of Christ, where unworthy works are burned up (1 Cor. 3:12-15; 2 Cor. 5:10). In this passage, the fire is figurative as are the vine and the branches. The burning of useless branches was a common agricultural practice. Fruitless branches that do not bear fruit even after being lifted off the ground have no practical purpose, so they are burned or disposed of. This compares to the burning of useless works at the Judgment Seat of Christ in 1 Corinthians 3:15.

Of course, if bearing fruit is a measure of salvation, then we have problems, such as what exactly fits the description of fruit, are fruit always visible or measureable, and how much is needed? The biggest problem is the intrusion of works into the gospel of grace, especially in John, which purposes to show that believing is the only condition for salvation. The only interpretation that fits this passage and the clear teachings of Scripture is a B Truth interpretation. In B Truth, bearing fruit is an important way to be useful and to glorify God.

Believers who are slack in their walk with God and not producing fruit do not need to fear hell, but they should fear being useless in God's service and should fear facing Jesus Christ on that Day of Judgment when they will have to account for how they lived their lives. On the other hand, believers who abide with Christ in an intimate relationship will bear fruit, have prayers answered, show themselves to be disciples, and glorify God (vv. 7-10).

Keep on believing for eternal life. John 20:30-31

> [30] *And truly Jesus did many other signs in the presence of His disciples, which are not written in this book;* [31] *but these are written that you may believe that Jesus is the Christ, the Son of God, and that believing you may have life in His name.*

A Truth Interpretation: A person must keep on believing in Jesus Christ to have eternal life or that person was never really saved, or loses his salvation.

B Truth Interpretation: A person must keep on believing in order to experience the eternal life they received when they believed in Jesus as Savior.

As already noted, it is usually recognized that John 20:30-31 forms the purpose statement for the Gospel. Some might prefer to see John's purpose in 1:4 of the prologue: "In Him was life, and the life was the light of men." If we consider them together, we have neat bookends (an inclusio) for John's material. Both allow us to see that the preponderance of John's material is designed to bring people to faith in Jesus Christ as Savior (resulting in "life") and that the distinct unit of chapters 13-17 is an intimate discussion with the disciples about B Truth issues (resulting in "light" for living). It makes sense that any purpose statement for John should declare the primary A Truth purpose, yet allow for the secondary B Truth purpose.

The A Truth purpose is clear in 20:31, that if one believes in Jesus Christ, the Son of God, he has eternal life. But the B Truth comes in the next phrase, "and that believing you may have life in His name." Some argue that the present participle "believing" indicates continuing belief. In other words, one must *keep on believing* in order to have eternal life, and if one does not, then that person loses salvation or proves he was never really saved. But is that what the present tense indicates? No, not if we understand the nature of eternal life and the B Truth purpose within John's Gospel.

Eternal life is God's life given as a permanent possession, but it is also God's life given as something to enjoy. It is both a quantity of life as well as a quality of life. Jesus says, "I have come that they may have life, and that they may have it more abundantly" (John 10:10b). He also prays about those who believe in Him: "And this is eternal life, that they may know You, the only true God, and Jesus Christ whom You have sent" (John 17:3). Besides an initial possession that brings a relationship to God, eternal life is also an abundant life and a life of knowing God, which indicates fellowship or enjoyment of that life. The condition for continual enjoyment of God's eternal life is also faith. The exercise of faith is the key principle not only in initial salvation, but also in the Christian life (Rom. 1:17; 5:2; Gal. 2:20). John 20:31 therefore represents both A Truth and B Truth.

John's statement in 20:31 declares that belief is how one receives God's eternal life, but also how one experiences God's life in the present. Those who believe in Jesus Christ must never treat eternal life as merely a ticket to heaven to be used at a future time. They must also realize they are in a new relationship with God as their Father, a relationship that is enhanced and enjoyed as they live by faith.

Acts

AN IMPORTANT FACT to remember about the book of Acts is that it is the narrative of a transitional time in history as God introduced the church. We must therefore be careful about using the descriptive accounts as prescriptive for conduct today. We must also observe carefully to whom specific messages were addressed, because we meet various groups: unsaved Jews, unsaved Gentiles, Disciples of John the Baptist, and Christians. Also, when we deduce theology from narrative accounts, we are mindful that not everything that happened or was said is necessarily reported to us. Theological deductions from Acts must be scrutinized in light of the didactic epistles of the New Testament.

Repent and be baptized. Acts 2:37-39

37 Now when they heard this, they were cut to the heart, and said to Peter and the rest of the apostles, "Men and brethren, what shall we do?" 38 Then Peter said to them, "Repent, and let every one of you be baptized in the name of Jesus Christ for the remission of sins; and you shall receive the gift of the Holy Spirit. 39 For the promise is to you and to your children, and to all who are afar off, as many as the Lord our God will call."

A Truth Interpretation: People must turn from sins and be baptized to be saved.

First B Truth Interpretation: People must change their minds about (believe in) Jesus Christ as their Savior and then be baptized to show that they are forgiven their sins.

Second B Truth Interpretation: The Jews who realized they crucified their Messiah have believed in Him and must now repent of that sin to be forgiven for the purpose of fellowship with God, and be baptized to identify with those who are forgiven and saved.

Third B Truth Interpretation: The Jews who realized they crucified their Messiah must now believe in Him as their Savior and declare their faith through baptism to escape judgment on their sinful generation and identify with the new Christian community.

This has been the "go to" passage for those who argue that baptism is necessary for salvation. But that interpretation meets immediate resistance from those who say baptism is a work that contradicts salvation by grace through faith alone. The latter view is supported by Acts 10:43-44 and 15:7-9 where people believed and received the Holy Spirit before they were baptized, and many occasions where people were saved with no mention of baptism as a condition in the narrative or in the preaching of the gospel (Acts 4:4; 13:38-49; 15:1-11; 17:2-4, 10-12; 18:27-28; 20:18-21).

Overall, it is important to view the book of Acts as a transitional book. The gospel message now included the cross and resurrection as well as the promise of the Holy Spirit. Jews who believed in Jesus Christ in the Gospels didn't necessarily know about His work on the cross and His resurrection since those events had not yet happened. In the Gospels, Jesus also promised the giving of the Holy Spirit as something still future. In Acts, the Samaritans (half Jews) and Jews who believed received the Spirit in a subsequent event (Acts 8:14-18; 9:17; 19:5) while Gentiles received the Spirit immediately (Acts 10:44-48).

Though a notoriously difficult passage, there are several interpretations that preserve the gospel of salvation by grace through faith alone. In the first B Truth interpretation, baptism "for the forgiveness of sins" is not seen as a condition for salvation, because "for" (*eis*) is given the meaning "on the basis of" or *because* one has been forgiven. However, the causal use of *eis* in the New Testament is debatable.

A second B Truth interpretation considers the historical and transitional nature of the narrative. Peter is addressing the Jewish nation that has just crucified the Messiah. When they are convinced of what they had done, they believed in Jesus Christ, indicated by the fact that "they were cut to the heart," and asked what they should do next. Peter's command to repent and be baptized is what they need to do to identify with the new Christian community in order to escape judgment for their terrible sin of crucifying Christ. They would then receive forgiveness for that sin and receive the promised Holy Spirit. Some may think it a stretch to assume "cut to the heart" is the same as believing in Jesus Christ for eternal life because knowing you have sinned is not the same as believing in Christ for forgiveness and eternal life.

The third interpretation that keeps salvation through faith alone also considers the transitional aspect of Peter addressing the Jewish nation. When they are "cut to the heart," the Jews realized their sin of killing the Messiah, but had not yet embraced His promise of eternal life. Peter says they still need to repent or change their minds about (which is essentially saying "believe in") Jesus Christ as their Savior who will forgive all their sins and give them the Holy Spirit. Baptism is how they show both their repentance that separates them from the sinful nation and their faith that identifies them with the new community of believers. Baptism is a visible display of their faith, not a condition for salvation. In support, it is noted that the command to "repent" is in the plural, which corresponds to the plural in "you shall receive the gift of the Holy Spirit," but the command to be baptized is singular and thus parenthetical.

Each of these B Truth interpretations has their strengths and weaknesses. However, in light of clear biblical teaching, any one of them is stronger than the interpretation that makes baptism a condition for eternal life.

As Acts shows later, Gentiles who believed received the Holy Spirit immediately apart from baptism (Acts 10:40-44). That is the way God works today. Anyone who believes in Jesus Christ is saved immediately (A Truth), but should be baptized as soon as possible to declare that faith and to publically identify with the Christian community (B Truth). Though baptism is not a condition for salvation, we should not minimize its importance; it is the first step of obedience in following Jesus Christ.

Simon the sorcerer. Acts 8:17-24

[17] *Then they laid hands on them, and they received the Holy Spirit.* [18] *And when Simon saw that through the laying on of the apostles' hands the Holy Spirit was given, he offered them money,* [19] *saying, "Give me this power also, that anyone on whom I lay hands may receive the Holy Spirit."* [20] *But Peter said to him, "Your money perish with you, because you thought that the gift of God could be purchased*

with money! [21] *You have neither part nor portion in this matter, for
your heart is not right in the sight of God.* [22] *Repent therefore of this
your wickedness, and pray God if perhaps the thought of your heart
may be forgiven you.* [23] *For I see that you are poisoned by bitterness
and bound by iniquity."* [24] *Then Simon answered and said, "Pray to
the Lord for me, that none of the things which you have spoken may
come upon me."*

A Truth Interpretation: Simon's faith was false because he sinned
greatly and was eternally cursed by Peter; therefore, he needed to
be saved.

B Truth Interpretation: Simon's faith saved him, but his great sin
almost brought a temporal curse; therefore, he needed to repent.

Once again, the A Truth interpretation demands that we deny the clear
statement of Scripture that says, "Then Simon himself also believed" and was
baptized (Acts 8:13). However, those who deny Simon's salvation probably
do not question the preceding statement that the Samaritans "believed
Philip as he preached the things concerning the kingdom of God and the
name of Jesus Christ, both men and women were baptized" (Acts 8:12). That
statement is taken at face value while the statement about Simon is not. In
the next story, the same Phillip preaches the gospel to the Ethiopian eunuch
(8:26-36) and he also believes (8:37-39). No one questions that conversion.
So we have a problem: why assume salvation is genuine for the Samaritan
group and the Ethiopian eunuch, but false for Simon? His salvation is
mentioned in the same way as the Samaritans in the very next verse. If
anything, singling out Simon emphasizes his salvation rather than denies it.
There is a contrast in this section of Acts designed to show us that the gospel
saves both evil-hearted people (Simon who was steeped in sorcery) as well
as good-hearted ones (the Ethiopian who was steeped in Scripture).

Were it not for Peter's words, "Your money perish with you," there would
probably be no question about the genuineness of Simon's salvation. What
caused Peter's statement was not Simon's rejection of Jesus Christ, which
is never indicated, but Simon's specific sin of avarice born of jealousy for
the unique apostolic power of bestowing the Holy Spirit on new believers.
Simon had certainly experienced his own reception of the Holy Spirit with
the other Samaritans (8:14-17), which is probably why he sought the ability
to bestow this wonderful gift of the Spirit on others. However, he sought to

purchase this unique apostolic power with money (v. 20). Thus when Peter says, "You have neither part nor portion in this matter" (v. 21), Peter was speaking of the apostolic privilege of giving the Holy Spirit, not salvation. Peter also says that his heart was not right with God (Acts 8:21), which would be an odd way of describing a non-believer. He is told to repent of a specific sin, "of this your wickedness," and find God's forgiveness (Acts 8:22)—again, an odd way to address a non-believer who is condemned by all sin, not any one sin. Simon's problem is not described as him being dead in sin or separated from God, but as him being "poisoned by bitterness and bound by iniquity," both obvious references to his jealousy and avarice (Acts 8:23). Believers can succumb to bitterness and sin (Eph. 4:32; Heb. 12:15).

How then do we understand Peter's threat, "Your money perish with you" in verse 20? While the word "perish" (from *apoleia*) sometimes refers specifically to eternal destruction in hell, it has the general meaning of *ruin* or *waste* (see Mark 14:4/Matt. 26:8; Acts 25:16; 2 Pet. 3:16) and is used in reference to a saved person in 1 Corinthians 8:11. Certainly, Simon's misguided request shows such a perverted view of the apostolic position and the gift of the Holy Spirit that it would lead to his ruin or waste in this life. Two observations support the interpretation of a temporal curse. First, it would be odd to consign money to eternal damnation in hell with Simon. Second, Simon's request for the apostles' prayer shows repentance of some kind, an attitude consistent with being regenerate. The B Truth interpretation fits this narrative best.

Simon's misunderstanding about the uniqueness of the apostolic gift and God's prerogative in how and when He bestows the Holy Spirit should be a warning today to those who claim apostolic gifts and the power to bestow the Holy Spirit upon people. Acts is a book that describes unique events in the transitional period between the Law and the Church age. We cannot interpret these events as the norm for today. As is clear in Paul's epistles, every believer in Jesus Christ receives the Holy Spirit immediately without apostolic agency (Rom. 8:9; 1 Cor. 12:13; Gal. 3:2; Eph. 1:13).

Believe in the Lord Jesus Christ. Acts 16:30-31

[30] *And he brought them out and said, "Sirs, what must I do to be saved?"* [31] *So they said, "Believe on the Lord Jesus Christ, and you will be saved, you and your household."*

A Truth Interpretation: The jailer was told that submitting to Jesus Christ as the Lord of his life would save him.

Second A Truth Interpretation: The jailer was told that believing in Jesus Christ who is the Lord would save him.

The emphasis of the first interpretation is a subjective one: to believe in the *Lord* Jesus Christ for salvation means to submit to Him as the Master of all of your life. This view is called Lordship Salvation because those who hold it define *believe* in terms of submission, commitment, and surrender (to Jesus as Master). The emphasis of the second interpretation is objective: to believe in the one who can save you *because* He is the Lord Jesus Christ.

The first interpretation focuses on one aspect of the word "Lord." It is interpreted in terms of Christ ruling over one's life. However, the primary meaning of *Lord* (*kyrios*) is deity (see v. 34). Of course, deity includes a lot of other aspects of divinity such as King, High Priest, Messiah, etc., so it is somewhat arbitrary—or theologically biased—to assume *Lord* has the subjective meaning of ruling over one's life in this passage. It is better to see it as an objective reference to Jesus Christ, His title. We see the same word used as a title of respect for Paul and Silas in verse 30 when the jailor says, "Sirs (*lords*, from *kyrios*), what must I do to be saved?"

We must ask, what would a pagan Roman jailer understand about submitting his life to Jesus as Master anyway? Unbelievers only need to understand what it means that the Son of God has died for their sins, risen from the dead, and offers eternal life. They do not need to know the multitude of commands and conditions for following Jesus as Master. That is the substance of discipleship.

Those who hold the second interpretation are sometimes accused of teaching that a person can reject the Lordship of Jesus Christ and only believe in Him for salvation. This is a straw man argument. The position of Jesus Christ as Lord is essential to our salvation in every way. As divine Lord, only Jesus could live a perfect life, die for all people, and offer eternal salvation. However, the issue of subjectively submitting to His lordship is just not presented as a condition in Paul's answer, which is simply and only "Believe." Every believer should submit to Jesus Christ as Lord, but first they must come to know Him as Savior.

Another misinterpreted aspect of verse 31 is by those who take it as a promise that if a person believes in Jesus Christ for salvation, then his or her whole family will be saved, because Paul said, "you and your whole household." Since there is no such thing as salvation by proxy (someone else's faith) taught or seen in the Bible, this view can be rejected. Besides, the idea of a household in those days included servants, making that view even more problematic (I can hear someone jokingly ask if in-laws would be included!). Every person in every family must believe individually in Jesus Christ as Savior. Salvation is not automatically perpetual through the generations. We have an obligation to share the gospel message with all, especially our families.

Be baptized to wash away sins. Acts 22:16

"And now why are you waiting? Arise and be baptized, and wash away your sins, calling on the name of the Lord."

A Truth Interpretation: Paul was told he had to be baptized to have his sins washed away so that he could be saved.

B Truth Interpretation: Paul was told that he had to be baptized to show his new identity in Christ and be forgiven of His former sins.

In this passage, the apostle Paul recounts his conversion on the Damascus Road to a crowd of people in Jerusalem. The result of his story is the same as the original narrative in chapter 9: Paul is saved. The difference is that this passage mentions baptism and calling on the name of the Lord for the washing away of sins.

It is clear from Luke's account in Acts 9 and in Paul's account in Acts 22 and 26 that Paul was saved at the time of his experience on the Damascus Road and not later. His own testimony in Galatians 1:11-12 is that he received the gospel directly from Jesus Christ, not Ananias. It is also critical to look at the timing in the account and its retelling. Paul called Jesus "Lord" *after* the revelation on the road. He says, "What shall I do, Lord?" which also indicates his submission to Christ's will. After the experience, the only instruction the Lord has for Paul concerns what he is now "to do" (Acts 22:10). In his retelling in chapter 22, Paul mentions several things Ananias did that indicate Paul is saved before his baptism: He calls Paul "bother," restores his sight, and relays God's commission for him to go to the Gentiles (Acts 22:13-15). So Ananias' command to "Arise and be baptized" is told to a saved Paul just as Jesus foretold to him that he would be told what to do (Acts 9:6).

The command to be baptized here is not then a condition for salvation, but as the text indicates, a condition for having sins washed away. The best explanation for this is to recall our discussion of Acts 2:38, where baptism is a way for Jews to show they are identifying with the Christian community and forsaking the generation of Jews who crucified the Messiah. Paul needs to be baptized to show his repentance for supporting the crucifixion of the Messiah and to have that sin forgiven (and perhaps also his sins of persecuting Christians and Christ, Acts 9:1, 5). "Calling on the name of the Lord" is not for salvation, but expresses an appeal for God's help, which Paul will need to fulfill his new ministry.

Again, we find a situation in Acts that is transitional in nature. The Jews of Jesus' generation shared in the sin of His crucifixion and received forgiveness for that sin only as it was confessed and forsaken in baptism. For the Jew, the Holy Spirit was given after salvation, as in Paul's case, while Gentiles received the Holy Spirit immediately upon believing in Christ and before baptism (Acts 10:43-44; 15:7-9).

It is important to see the transitional nature of the book of Acts and not view its events as normative for the church today. If we took Acts as the norm today, we would all speak in tongues (Acts 2:1-4; 19:1-6), sell all that we own and distribute it to the poor (Acts 2:45), meet in temples and homes (daily! Acts 2:46), have a morgue in the church basement for those who drop dead from lying in church (Acts 5:1-10), and receive the Holy Spirit subsequent to salvation. Our knowledge of the context rescues us from such conclusions.

The Epistles of Paul

8

T HE APOSTLE PAUL was the chief expositor of the gospel and its implications for salvation and Christian living. His logical and theological approach to issues helps us greatly in interpreting the various controversial passages below as A Truth or B Truth.

Obedience of faith. Romans 1:5; 16:26

Through Him we have received grace and apostleship for obedience to the faith among all nations for His name. (Romans 1:5)

But now made manifest, and by the prophetic Scriptures made known to all nations, according to the commandment of the everlasting God, for obedience to the faith. (Romans 16:26)

A Truth Interpretation: Faith in Christ is obedience to Christ.

Second A Truth Interpretation: Faith in Christ is obedience to the command to believe.

The phrase "obedience of faith" is common to both passages. Also common to both passages is Paul's concern for all the nations who are without Christ.

If Paul is saying that the unbelievers in the nations must be saved by a faith that obeys, consider the problems that confront us. First, this view wrongly conflates the meanings of faith and obedience. These words are distinct lexically, though they are related experientially in that faith is what generates obedience to God's commands. Second, Paul would be telling unsaved Gentiles (the usual meaning of "the nations") that they must obey

God's commands when they would not be expected to know any of them except the command to believe. Third, in his section on justification (Rom. 3:21-4:25) Paul does not use the words obey or obedience at all, much less as a condition of salvation (justification) or to qualify the meaning of faith. His emphasis is the freeness of the gospel (Rom. 3:24). In fact, he is adamant about the contrast between faith and works (Rom. 4:4-5). As we have seen, salvation by obedience and works is not consistent with salvation by grace through faith. Paul makes it clear that it is not by our obedience, but by Jesus Christ's obedience that we are given God's righteousness (Rom. 5:19).

The phrase "obedience to the faith" (sometimes "obedience of the faith" in other translations) puts the two words "obedience" and "faith" in close relationship (there are no intervening words as in the English translations). But it does not mean obedience to the faith in the sense of obeying Christian truth or doctrine, because in the original language, we would expect to see the article *tē*, translated "the," before the word "faith" as in Acts 6:7, which speaks of priests who had become disciples and were continuing to obey the new Christian teachings. It is possible that the phrase could refer to obedience that comes from faith as two separate responses the nations could have. (We see the two responses in Romans 6:17, but that verse does not use this phrase and in its context is referring to the sanctification of the readers who had believed. See that discussion later.) Probably the best interpretation of the phrase is "obedience which is faith (that is, *believing*)," which is one response not two. This is called an appositional relationship, like saying "the act of kindness" to refer to one deed.

Only one response to the gospel is required for salvation and that is to believe it. To believe the gospel obeys God's command that is implicit in the nature of man's predicament and the offer of salvation, and is also explicitly stated as God's will (Mark 1:15; Acts 16:31; 1 John 3:23). For the people of the nations to be saved, they must obey God by believing the gospel. Preaching the gospel is not just declaring good news; it is also calling unbelievers to obey God by believing in His Son.

Doing good for eternal life. Romans 2:6-7, 10, 13

> [6] who "will render to each one according to his deeds": [7] eternal life to those who by patient continuance in doing good seek for glory, honor, and immortality.

[10] *but glory, honor, and peace to everyone who works what is good, to the Jew first and also to the Greek.*

[13] *(for not the hearers of the law are just in the sight of God, but the doers of the law will be justified).*

A Truth Interpretation: Those who continue to obey the law will be saved or prove they are saved.

Second A Truth Interpretation: God's ideal standard for salvation is perfect obedience.

These verses seem to say that eternal life can be obtained or proved by good deeds or keeping the Law. But that view flatly contradicts Paul's assertion in Rom. 3:12 that "There is none who does good" and the subsequent argument that justification is through faith alone, not by keeping the law because no one can keep the law (Rom. 3:20-4:25). Surely Paul would not be so careless.

These verses appear in a discussion about the principles of God's justice and judgment (Rom. 2:2-3, 5). Paul is telling the self-righteous that their judgment of others and themselves is imperfect, but God's judgment is perfect, according to "truth" (Rom. 2:2). According to His principle of absolute and perfect justice, God would give eternal life to anyone who earns it by doing good deeds and keeping the law perfectly. The problem is, as Paul goes on to show, *no one can.* (His argument builds from Rom. 2:17 to the inclusive statement that "all have sinned" in Rom. 3:23).

These verses do not teach salvation is obtained by good works, but are part of Paul's argument to show that since "There is none righteous, no, not one" and "There is none who does good, no, not one" (Rom. 3:10, 12), justification is only possible through faith in Jesus Christ (Rom. 3:22-24).

How futile it is for people to try to obtain eternal life by their own efforts. They do not understand that God's standard is not 51% obedience or 99% obedience, but 100%. If someone never sinned and always did right, then God would have to be fair and give them eternal life. But we all know that no one on earth fits that description. Thus, we have a problem that God can only solve with a free gift, which is why we are "justified freely by His grace through the redemption that is in Christ Jesus" (Rom. 3:24). When we could not be perfect, Jesus Christ lived perfectly and fulfilled all the law while paying for our sins through His death on the cross. All we can do is believe in His person, provision, and promise for eternal life.

Saved by His life. Romans 5:9-10

> [9] *Much more then, having now been justified by His blood, we shall be saved from wrath through Him.* [10] *For if when we were enemies we were reconciled to God through the death of His Son, much more, having been reconciled, we shall be saved by His life.*

A Truth Interpretation: A person is eternally saved by the death and the life of Christ.

B Truth Interpretation: A person is justified eternally by the death of Christ and saved from the power and consequences of sin in this life by living in the power of His resurrected life.

This passage is a good example of how the word "saved" should be interpreted in its context. Many would interpret this as salvation from hell in the sense of justification salvation. If Paul had said "we *were* saved," then it would be a clear example of A Truth relating to justification salvation. However, he says, "we *shall be* saved," which emphasizes the future aspect of our salvation experience. But, is Paul referring to the eternal future after the Christian's death, or the future of the Christian's experience after justification?

There are good reasons to not interpret this as future salvation from hell or A Truth. In the immediate context, Paul expresses the finality of our eternal salvation in the past tense as an accomplished event: believers have been justified (Rom. 5:1) and reconciled to God (Rom. 5:10). We should also observe the larger context. The first use of the word "wrath" in Romans is after the prologue in the beginning of the body of the book where it describes a present reality: "For the wrath of God is revealed from heaven against all ungodliness and unrighteousness of men, who suppress the truth in unrighteousness" (Rom. 1:18). The word "wrath" simply means anger and does not necessarily or only refer to God's eternal punitive anger toward unbelievers (see its use in Rom. 9:22; 12:19; 13:4, 5). While wrath may be spoken of as a future eternal consequence for those who are impenitent (Rom. 2:5, 8), the implication of 1:18 is that all who practice ungodliness can experience an aspect of God's wrath in this life. In his discussion of the believer's sanctification (Romans chapters 6-8), Paul does not use the word "wrath," but explains that there are negative consequences for believers who sin, which are expressions of God's anger toward sin (Rom. 6:21, 23; 7:13; 8:6).

So if God's wrath is a possible future experience of the Christian life after justification, how can we be saved from God's wrath, and what does it mean to be "saved by His (Jesus Christ's) life"? First, we recall that the word *saved* simply means *delivered,* and the context must decide what that deliverance is from. Second, when we examine the context and the flow of Paul's argument, we see he is speaking to those who have been justified (Rom. 5:1, 9), but moves on to a discussion of sanctification. Romans 5:9-10 is a "hinge" or transition from his discussion of justification to the believer's ongoing sanctification, which depends on the life of Jesus Christ as it is lived through us by the indwelling Holy Spirit (Rom. 5:18-21; 6:5-11; 7:4, 6, 24-25; 8:1-11). As we allow Christ's life to dominate ours, we are "saved" from God's anger and its consequences in this life.

This is an important B Truth for Christians to know and apply. We must avoid sin and confess it, and live righteously with the enablement of God's Spirit who manifests Christ's life in us. As Christians, we are used to saying "I have been saved," but we can also say "I am being saved" or "I will be saved" as we allow Christ to live His live through us and deliver us from God's angry expressions toward sin.

Slaves of sin or righteousness. Romans 6:17

> But God be thanked that though you were slaves of sin, yet you obeyed
> from the heart that form of doctrine to which you were delivered.

A Truth Interpretation: People must obey and submit to God as slaves in order to be saved.

B Truth Interpretation: Believers should submit to God as slaves in order to experience His holiness and His life.

If this verse is A Truth referring to salvation, then Paul is reminding the readers that they were saved by obeying Christian truths and submitting themselves to God as slaves. However, in the context that we have established for this section, Paul addresses the believing readers about their sanctification. They are "under grace" (Rom. 6:15) which gives them two possibilities: they can submit to obedience or submit to sin (Rom. 6:16).

Paul then reflects on the past experience of the readers and is thankful that they had chosen to obey the new Christian teaching (v. 17). But was that a condition for their salvation or a result of their salvation?

The text indicates that the readers' obedience was subsequent to their deliverance to the Christian truth; therefore, this must be B Truth. The passive voice of "were delivered" points to God who saved them and delivered them into Christian teaching. It was at that time they also broke free from slavery to sin. As a result of their new standing, the readers chose to obey the truth to which they had been delivered. Verse 18 confirms that the choice to become "slaves of righteousness" was because they had "been set free from sin." Verse 19 then exhorts the readers to continue to present themselves as slaves of righteousness. Surely this is not exhorting them to be saved. Paul's desire is that they continue to submit to God in order to gain holiness and a greater experience of God's life (Rom. 6:22).

Grace sets believers free, and therefore it is always risky. Every believer should submit to God to experience holiness and the abundant life of God, but not all do. Submission to God is not a condition for salvation. Neither is it a one-time commitment. It is something that must be done continually.

The wages of sin is death. Romans 6:23

For the wages of sin is death, but the gift of God is eternal life in Christ Jesus our Lord.

A Truth Interpretation: Sin brings eternal death to unbelievers and causes believers to lose their salvation, but eternal life comes through the salvation that is in the Lord Jesus Christ.

B Truth Interpretation: Sin brings spiritual deadness to believers, but they can experience the fullness of God's life through the Lord Jesus Christ.

This verse is traditionally interpreted as A Truth, and so it finds its way into most evangelistic presentations. While it may have an A Truth application, it may surprise many that there are good reasons for interpreting this primarily as B Truth.

We have already established that the argument of Romans has progressed from justification salvation in chapters 3-4 to sanctification salvation in chapters 5-8. Chapter 6 is clearly written to believers who were baptized into or united with Christ (6:3-5), and who have died with Christ and now live with Him (6:6-11). The admonition to these believers is not to serve sin but God, because they are no longer under sin's authority, but under grace (6:12-14). In verse 15, an imaginary objection is raised about whether being under grace might encourage believers to sin. While 6:16-23 grants the possibility that believers can choose to sin, it also gives reasons why believers should not serve sin. Simply put, sin leads to death (6:16, 21) while serving God leads to "righteousness" (6:16), which leads to "holiness" (6:19), which leads to "everlasting life" (6:22). This latter is the choice that the Roman believers had made, as we saw in our discussion of verse 17. Obedient believers are set apart in a closer experience with Christ and a fuller experience of His life which they already possess as a gift. It is hard to escape verse 23 as a summary word to believers.

If this is written to believers, why are they told that sin leads to death, or better, that sin pays off ("wages") in death. In light of other affirmations about their eternal security in Romans, this cannot mean that believers who sin will lose their salvation and be separated from God in hell (cf. Rom. 4:16; 8:18-39). As we discussed earlier, it is biblical and crucial to understand death here in the sense of separation rather than cessation. On the spiritual level, death for unbelievers means they are separated from God's life now and potentially forever. Death for believers means they are separated from the benefits of God's life in their present experience. Believers have eternal life as a present possession and a future promise. While they cannot be separated from the *possession* of eternal life either in the present or future, they can be separated from its *experiential benefits* (e.g. peace, joy, power over sin, etc.). When believers sin, they experience the same effects that sin produced when they were unsaved (6:19-21), such as shame and spiritual deadness.

While the initial possession of eternal life comes at the moment of justification through faith in Christ (Rom. 3:24; 5:18), the enjoyment or ongoing experience of that life is the reward for godly living. As said before, eternal life is sometimes described as a relationship with God (John 17:3) that can be experienced in abundance (John 10:10a). Jesus Christ, with whom we are risen, has given the free gift of His life to us who believe and manifests that life in us as we live for Him.

If written to believers as B Truth, can this verse be applied to unbelievers as A Truth in an evangelistic presentation? It seems that it can, because it is stated as a general principle that is true for all people whether saved or unsaved. The verse applies to unbelievers in the sense that they, in their sin, are dead to God. The solution to their separation from God is the free gift of eternal life that comes through faith in Jesus Christ (cf. Rom. 3:22-26). Both believers and unbelievers can experience death, though in different ways, and the only solution for both is the free gift of God's life through Jesus Christ.

While we recognize an application to unbelievers, believers should not overlook the primary purpose of verse 23, which is to move them to serve God and not sin. Believers have been given a wonderful gift of God's life which they can only enjoy as they live for Him.

Die by the flesh or live by the Spirit. Romans 8:13

For if you live according to the flesh you will die; but if by the Spirit you put to death the deeds of the body, you will live.

A Truth Interpretation: Those who live in the flesh will go to hell because they lose their salvation or were never saved, but if the Spirit is in them, they will be saved.

B Truth Interpretation: Believers who live by the flesh experience deadness in their fellowship with God, but if they live by the power of the Spirit, they will experience the fullness of God's life.

Romans 8 continues Paul's discussion of sanctification and how the believer can have victory over sin. Verse 1 states, "There is therefore now no condemnation to those who are in Christ Jesus, who do not walk according to the flesh, but according to the Spirit." Though commonly understood as a reference to eternal hell, "condemnation" in this context of sanctification (as it is also used in Rom. 5:16 and 18) speaks of the tragic effects of sin on the believer's life in Christ. The second clause of verse 1 is not in many modern translations, but it has strong manuscript evidence and says the same thing as verse 4. The emphasis of this section is living according to the Spirit as opposed to living according to the flesh and the consequences of each.

In Romans 8 Paul is speaking to Christians (he calls them "brothers" in v. 12 and says they had received the Holy Spirit in v. 15) about their sanctification experience that delivers them from sin and its consequences, so we can easily see which interpretation fits best here. Living in the flesh is the choice (expressed by "if") a Christian makes when he sides with his old sinful flesh. "You will die" expresses a consequence of God's anger at sin. The significance of death here is the same as in Romans 6:23 (see the previous discussion). There will be a deadness in that Christian's experience and a separation from the vitality of divine life. On the other hand, if the believer submits to the indwelling Holy Spirit, he will "live" or experience God's invigorating and enriching life.

According to Romans 8:9, the test of salvation is not whether one lives in the Spirit but whether the Spirit lives in him: "Anyone who does not have the Spirit of Christ does not belong to him." Verses 9-11 are stated as assurances that the readers do indeed have the Holy Spirit, therefore they have the power to have victory over sin. Verses 12-13 give the readers two possibilities. To live according to the flesh is to have a fleshly mindset and to live according to the Spirit is to have a spiritual mindset. A fleshly mind-set leads to spiritual deadness, but a spiritual mindset leads to a victorious life of righteousness.

The strong assumption and designation of these readers as believers is contrary to the interpretation that they could lose their salvation or prove to have never been saved. We have shown earlier that death does not automatically refer to eternal death, but in its essence speaks of separation. In this case, the context shows that death refers to the believer's separation from God's life-giving power, thus it is B Truth, not A Truth.

As believers, we can choose to live fleshly or sinful lives, but that only brings a deadening of the experience God wants for us. Better to choose to let Jesus Christ live out His life through us and experience the power of His resurrected life.

Led by the Spirit. Romans 8:14

For as many as are led by the Spirit of God, these are sons of God.

A Truth Interpretation: Only those who are led by the Spirit are saved.

B Truth Interpretation: Those who are led into a righteous life by the Spirit exemplify their position as sons of God.

Those who take the A Truth interpretation for this verse say that one of the proofs of salvation is that a person is led by the Holy Spirit. In this view, to be a son of God is to be a saved person, and to be led by the Spirit may be interpreted as led away from sins and into godly practices, or even to be led in other non-moral decisions of life.

There are some obvious arguments against the A Truth interpretation. That view of verse 14 would make salvation and assurance of salvation depend on something other than faith in Jesus Christ. But faith is sufficient grounds for salvation and assurance (e.g., John 5:24; Eph. 2:8; 1 John 5:11-13). Also, that interpretation makes the test of salvation subjective. How could anyone know definitively if he is led by the Spirit in all the decisions of life? Is the Spirit leading when there are failures and sins?

Most obvious is the argument from the context. Those who take a B Truth interpretation note that Romans 6-8 is addressing Christians about their sanctification. Romans 8 answers the frustration expressed in Romans 7 about the inability to live a godly life in the flesh, or one's own strength. Those who have the victory over the flesh and the law are those whose minds and lives are controlled by the Spirit of God (8:1-6), and they have the Spirit because they are believers (8:9-11). In verse 12, Paul addresses the readers as "brothers" who are not indebted to live according to the flesh. Rather, they have the Spirit who can give victory over the flesh and the fullness of life (v. 13). Therefore, when Paul refers to "all who are led by the Spirit of God," he is referring to believers who live by the Spirit who leads them into victory, holiness, and life.

But what about the last part of verse 14 that says those "who are led by the Spirit of God are sons of God?" The term *son of God* does not refer simply to a saved person. In verse 16, we see those who are saved referred to as "children of God," a different term evidently used for all Christians. To be a *son of* something is to exhibit the same characteristics or to be like something or someone. Paul is simply saying that in as much as those who have the Spirit allow Him to lead them into a life of holiness, they are exhibiting the characteristics of their Heavenly Father. In fact, verse 15 assures the readers that they belong to the Father as children by adoption implying that they should live like it, that is, like His sons. Another important observation is that the designation of "sons" has implications of those who enjoy the full rights of adoption, which include being an heir of God (not just a child of God) and a co-heir of Jesus Christ when we suffer with Him (v. 17).

Romans 8:17 deserves a special note since it is often misunderstood. It begins with a simple particle (*ei*) denoting conditionality based on fact: *if* we are children, then we are heirs of God. Every child of God enjoys adoption privileges in God's family. The second statement uses a contrastive particle (*men...de*) to emphasize the different condition for becoming joint heirs of Christ (denoted by the strong particle *eiper*, "if indeed"). That condition is the believer's co-suffering: we are joint heirs with Christ *if indeed* we suffer with Him. The best understanding comes when the comma is placed after "God" and not after "Christ"—"heirs of God, and joint heirs of Christ if indeed we suffer with Him." To be a joint heir with Christ is to co-rule with Him in His kingdom. This verse teaches that all children of God are heirs of God, but only those who endure suffering for Christ will rule with Him in His kingdom (see the discussion of 2 Tim. 2:10-13).

The idea of sonship in relation to God implies adult status that is not in need of a tutor (or the law—see Gal. 3:22-4:1-7 which develops the difference between children of God and sons of God). So "sons of God" implies maturity and godliness, not simply salvation. Believers can only become mature if they allow the Spirit to lead them there. Romans 8:14 is not a verse to determine one's salvation.

To interpret the difficult passages in Romans 6-8, we should never forget the context. Paul discussed justification in Romans 3-4. Chapter 5 is a transition into a new section on sanctification (see the discussion on Rom. 5:9-10). Therefore, we expect Romans 6-8 to focus on B Truth for believers.

To be like God our Father, we must allow His Spirit to lead us into righteousness and a greater experience of the life of Christ who is in us. As believers, we are God's children; we should behave as mature sons (and daughters) of our Father.

Confess with your mouth. Romans 10:9-10

[9] *that if you confess with your mouth the Lord Jesus and believe in your heart that God has raised Him from the dead, you will be saved.* [10] *For with the heart one believes unto righteousness, and with the mouth confession is made unto salvation.*

A Truth Interpretation: To be saved eternally, a person must submit to the lordship of Jesus Christ and confess Him by words and/or deeds.

Second A Truth Interpretation: To be saved eternally, a person must believe in Jesus Christ, agreeing that he is the divine Savior.

B Truth Interpretation: To be saved from God's temporal wrath, those who have believed in Jesus Christ must also call on Him for help.

This very well-known passage is also very misunderstood. Misunderstanding centers on two key words in the passage, "confess" and "Lord." For example, based on a faulty view of what it means to confess, many preachers will call for people to get saved by coming to the front of the church to verbally proclaim their faith in Christ publically. Others say this teaches that a person is not saved until he confesses his faith publically through baptism. Still others say that confession refers not so much to one's words as much as one's conduct. A person is not saved unless he conducts himself according to Christian teaching.

The view called Lordship Salvation usually understands *confess* in one of these ways, but also takes the confession of "the Lord Jesus" as submission to Jesus as Master of one's life. In other words, it is not merely confessing that Jesus is *the* Lord, but that Jesus is *my* Lord.

The problem with these interpretations of *confess* is that they make something besides faith a necessary condition for salvation. Public confession of any kind and submitting oneself to the mastery of Jesus Christ all fit into the category of works or something done to merit salvation. This of course puts the apostle Paul in the awkward position of contradicting his argument in chapters 3-4 that a person is justified through faith alone, not works.

A better interpretation, one consistent with salvation by grace through faith (the second A Truth interpretation), comes from a proper understanding of what it means to confess the Lord Jesus. This simply means that one acknowledges (believes) Jesus is the Lord God. For the Jew in the context of Paul's argument in chapter 10, this meant acknowledging Jesus as the divine Messiah.

The word "confess" (*homologeō*) means to "agree, acknowledge." The word itself does not demand a public confession or an oral confession. More reasonably, it is a confession to God, not man (see Rom. 14:11 and 15:9, and compare its use in 1 John 1:9). As such, it expresses faith, which is prominent in the context (cf. Rom. 10:4, 6, 11, 14, 17). The fact that Paul uses *confess and believe* in verse 9, then inverts the order to *believe and confess* in verse 10 suggests that they refer to the same thing. As we read on, verses 11, 12, and 13 also merge the idea of believing and confessing.

Why, then, does Paul choose to identify faith with confession? First, we must admit that being persuaded that something is true (believing) is essentially the same as agreeing that something is true (confessing). But confession also fits Paul's argument and his use of Deuteronomy 30:12-14 in verses 6-8 which connect the mouth and heart with faith:

> [6] But the righteousness of **faith speaks** in this way, "*Do not say in your heart, 'Who will ascend into heaven?'*" (that is, to bring Christ down *from above*) [7] or, "'*Who will descend into the abyss?*'" (that is, to bring Christ up from the dead). [8] But what does it say? "*The word is near you, in your mouth and in your heart*" (that is, the **word of faith which we preach**)... (bolded emphasis mine)

The Deuteronomy passage is a message to Israel that says God's righteousness is readily available and near, as near as their mouths and hearts. In other words, the Deuteronomy passage is similar to saying that the Jews do not need to strenuously "search heaven and hell" for salvation, but simply agree with what has already been taught them and which they can even recite. Verse 9 explains the intention of Deuteronomy 30:12-14—salvation is simple and readily available. All one needs to do is agree with God about what He has told them about the coming Messiah. We might use the expression "It's on the tip of your tongue."

To confess "the Lord Jesus" is to admit that Jesus is who God said He is—the Messiah and Savior. The chief significance of the term "Lord" is deity. It speaks of Jesus' position as God over all. "Jesus is Lord" was a creedal confession of the early church (Acts 2:36; 1 Cor. 12:3) that recognized Jesus as the divine messianic Savior. In verse 13, the quote from Joel 2:32 translates the divine name YHWH as "Lord" which shows deity is the primary significance. Paul's designation of Jesus as Lord (or God) was intended primarily for his Jewish readers (Rom. 10:1-3), but has application for all people (Rom. 10:4, 11-13). To the Jews, a chief hindrance keeping them from obtaining God's righteousness was their unwillingness to accept Jesus as the Messiah (who would also be their divine King).

"Lord" refers primarily to Jesus' deity, not His mastery. Ruling is certainly one function of deity, but so are other functions such as eternal priesthood, intercessor, and advocate. It is somewhat arbitrary to choose His ruling as the aspect one must acknowledge and submit to. Contrary to Lordship Salvation, it is not submission to Jesus as Master that saves, but agreement that He is the divine Savior.

Consider the problem with the Lordship Salvation interpretation. If *confess* means to live out our belief in Jesus as Master, then we are left with a subjective and open-ended condition for salvation. How does one ever know when he has submitted enough to be saved? We are left to doubt or examine our commitment. But any time we take our eyes off of the Savior and put them on our faith or performance, we get mired in a swamp of subjectivity. We can know when we have believed in Christ as Savior, but we can never know when we have done enough to earn our salvation.

Sadly, the Lordship Salvation interpretation of this passage totally contradicts its original intention. The Lordship view that salvation is obtained by confessing the lordship of Christ and submitting to His mastery over all of one's life makes salvation difficult (or impossible!) to obtain. But Paul's intention was to show that salvation for the Jews was as simple as agreeing with God about what they have already been taught.

Though I prefer the second A Truth interpretation, there is another view of this passage that is consistent with the unconditional grace of the gospel. This B Truth interpretation says that the terms *confess* and *call on the name of the Lord* are not synonymous with belief, but refer to how the Jews (and Gentiles) can appeal to God for deliverance from sin. Those who hold this view would argue that calling on the name of the Lord in verse 13, which quotes Joel 2:32 in a passage about God's deliverance of the remnant of Israel from their enemies in the Tribulation, has temporal deliverance in view, not eternal salvation. It seems, however, that Joel 2:32 is cited as a general principle that God will deliver (save) those who call on Him for help, which Paul could certainly apply to calling on Him for eternal salvation.

To further support their view, those who prefer the B Truth interpretation argue from the sequence in verse 14 that faith and calling on the name of the Lord are separate events. The reverse order used in verse 14 mentions *call, belief, hearing,* and *preaching* as if one event depends sequentially on its chronological antecedent. There are certainly logical and chronological aspects to the order in this list, but it may be freighting the passage with too much chronological significance if we see these events strictly separated in time. After all, when someone is preaching, another person is simultaneously hearing him, and while hearing, he can simultaneously believe, and when believing, he can simultaneously appeal to God for eternal salvation. There is an overlap of activities. For example, in John 4:10 Jesus tells the Samaritan woman, "If you knew the gift of God, and who it is who says to you, 'Give Me a drink,' you would have asked Him, and He would have given you living water." Asking is certainly intended as an analogy for believing which would only happen when the woman recognizes God's gift and Christ's identity. It is more of a logical than strictly chronological sequence (for some examples of overlapping activity, see Acts 20:21; 26:18; Rom. 1:24-25; 4:5; 5:1-2)

It is also argued that in Romans chapter 5, Paul moves on from his discussion of justification to sanctification, therefore the word *saved* cannot be used synonymously for *justified*. While it is true that Paul's discussion progresses from justification to sanctification, this does not prevent him from re-visiting justification when he needs to make a point (cf. 8:30, 33). A major issue from 9:30 through chapter 11 is how the Gentiles and Jews might attain to God's righteousness. The verb *justify* (from *dikaioō*) means *to be declared righteous*, (from *dikaiosunē*), so though *justify* or *justification* are not mentioned explicitly, the idea of attaining God's righteousness is. Clearly, the word "salvation" in 1:16 of the prologue to Romans encompasses justification as well as sanctification when it expresses the theme of the epistle.

The more immediate context is clearly controlled by the discussion of the Jews' attempt to establish their own righteousness before God (Rom. 10:1-3), and this concern governs verses 9-13 which follow. Believing in the gospel is also the point of verses 14-17. Because of the immediate and larger contexts surrounding 10:9-10, I prefer the second A Truth interpretation while appreciating the arguments and intent of the B Truth interpretation.

God does not want to make eternal salvation difficult, or obscure it, or create obstacles to it. He wants to make it as simple and available as He possibly can. Such is the greatness of His love and the wonder of His grace. Many people know the Bible facts about Jesus Christ, and even the facts of the gospel, but they have never believed in Jesus Christ as *their own* Savior. The gospel is "on the tip of their tongues." They don't have to make any strenuous effort to find it—they've known it all along; they only need to personally appropriate its promise. Could this passage be speaking to *you*?

Works that are burned. 1 Corinthians 3:11-15

> [11] *For no other foundation can anyone lay than that which is laid, which is Jesus Christ.* [12] *Now if anyone builds on this foundation with gold, silver, precious stones, wood, hay, straw,* [13] *each one's work will become clear; for the Day will declare it, because it will be revealed by fire; and the fire will test each one's work, of what sort it is.* [14] *If anyone's work which he has built on it endures, he will receive a reward.* [15] *If anyone's work is burned, he will suffer loss; but he himself will be saved, yet so as through fire.*

A Truth Interpretation: Professing Christians will have their works tested by God's future judgment and some will prove not to be saved, or will have to suffer and be purified by fire in order to be saved.

B Truth Interpretation: Believers' works will be tested by God's future judgment so that unworthy works are burned but good works are rewarded.

The words "fire," "burn," and "suffer loss" push this passage into the A Truth category for many. They see it as a description of the judgment that sends people to hell because their unworthy works prove they were never really saved. The Roman Catholic church has a unique take on it; they understand the fire as a purging punishment, which they call Purgatory. After enough time in Purgatory, paying for some of their sins, believers will then go on to heaven.

The problem with both of these views is that they make the sacrifice of Jesus Christ and His payment for our sins inadequate. If these people whose works are burned are deemed unsaved because of their unworthy works, then works become necessary for their salvation. These works are not frontloaded at the initial reception of the gospel, but they are backloaded at the end of one's life. When the fire of God's discerning judgment tests them, they are found lacking and are burned up.

The problems with this A Truth interpretation are not only theological but biblical. As mentioned, this view contradicts the biblical teaching that we are saved by grace through faith apart from works. Requiring good works at the end of one's life is no different from requiring them at the initial reception of the gospel. In either position, the sufficiency of Christ's substitutionary atonement and His propitiation for our sins is denied.

From a biblical perspective, when we look at the details of the text, we see other problems. First, Paul is talking to believers whose salvation he never questions but affirms (1 Cor. 1:2, 4, 9; 3:16; 4:14; 6:11, 15, 19-20; 11:1; 12:13; 15:1-2). In fact, he admits that their foundation is Jesus Christ. Second, it is unworthy works that are burned, not the person. Third, the person whose works are burned nevertheless is ultimately saved (v. 15).

At least the Roman Catholic view sees the person with unworthy works as ultimately saved. But their route there is just as problematic. If a person must suffer for his sins in Purgatory, then that is a denial of the sufficiency of Christ's sacrifice to cover all our sins. Like the previous view, it makes works an essential part of salvation. It also ignores the fact that it is the works that burn, not the person. There is nothing in the text that says the person suffers a purging punishment or pain of any kind.

This is not to deny negative consequences for a life misspent. The judgment in view here is not the Great White Throne Judgment after Christ's return—that judgment is for unbelievers only (Rev. 20:11-15). This judgment is the Judgment Seat of Christ where all Christians and only Christians will be judged according to the worthiness of their deeds. Some believe this happens either at the believer's death, Christ's return for the church, during the Tribulation period, or at the beginning of the millennial kingdom. In any case, fire is associated with this judgment because it is sometimes used as a symbol of God's testing and purifying discernment (cf. Isa. 66:16; Zech. 13:9; Mal. 3:2; 1 Pet. 1:7; Rev. 3:18). There are negative consequences for those Christians who have lived irresponsibly. In this passage, the works they have done, perhaps because of wrong motives, are burned up. There is no reward for them in heaven as with those whose works are worthy and withstand the fire like gold, silver, and precious stones. This would certainly imply that some regret will be experienced by those whose works are lost. But it goes beyond the Bible's revelation to say they themselves will be painfully burned.

The B Truth interpretation of this passage teaches a principle important for all Christians. God holds us accountable for what we do, how we do it, and why. If our deeds are worthy, we will store up treasures in heaven (Matt. 6:19-21). If not, we will suffer the loss of our reward. All of this will be determined at the great assessment called the Judgment Seat of Christ where we must all appear and give account for our lives. Are you ready to give an account for your life?

Deliver to Satan. 1 Corinthians 5:1-5

> [3] *For I indeed, as absent in body but present in spirit, have already judged (as though I were present) him who has so done this deed.* [4] *In the name of our Lord Jesus Christ, when you are gathered together, along with my spirit, with the power of our Lord Jesus Christ,* [5] *deliver such a one to Satan for the destruction of the flesh, that his spirit may be saved in the day of the Lord Jesus.*

A Truth Interpretation: A sinner in the church should be exposed as an unbeliever so that he may repent and be saved.

B Truth Interpretation: A saved sinner in the church should be placed under God's discipline so that he may repent and be delivered from a negative judgment at the Judgment Seat of Christ.

It is hard to imagine that a believer would do as this man has done—have sexual relations with his stepmother (1 Cor. 5:1). That is one reason many think this man is unsaved. Another reason is because Paul tells the Corinthian church to deliver this man to Satan for the destruction of his flesh, which many take as a reference to consignment to hell.

As hard as it is to imagine such a sin, reality and biblical history tell us that Christians are capable of this and far worse. The B Truth interpretation considers this man saved, and here's why. First, Paul is writing to the church in Corinth about one of them, so there is some identity as a Christian on this man's part. However, that alone does not mean he is saved. But it is clear from the passage that those in the church were also sinful in their response to him, even implicitly guilty with him by their approval (v. 2). Another evidence that Paul considers him saved is in verse 5: the purpose of Paul's instructions about dealing with the man is so that "his spirit may be saved in the day of the Lord Jesus." This is not saying that his punishment will save him, but that his assessment at the Judgment Seat of Christ ("the day of the Lord Jesus") will not be a total disaster. The man's spirit will be delivered from a total loss of reward. One more clue that shows the man was saved is from verse 11 where there is an oblique reference to him as "anyone named a brother" (The NASB uses the term "so-called brother" implying he is a false professor, but that translation is interpretive and does not accurately translate the original language). That Paul would use such a term for a Christian is clear in verse 12 when he categorizes him as one "inside" the church, as opposed to those who are clearly unsaved "outside" the church.

The resolution of this problem in the Corinthian church is found in 2 Corinthians 2:1-11. There, we see that the church discipline worked; the man was repentant and even overly sorrowful. Paul encourages the church to forgive him so that Satan does not overwhelm him with guilt. There is no indication here that the man was saved through this punishment; he was restored, which is always the purpose of church discipline.

Having noted these things, what do we do with the idea of delivering a sinner over to Satan for the destruction of the flesh? This speaks of the church excluding the man from the safety of their church fellowship (and maybe even their prayers). In the spirit of Matthew 18:17-20, the church is treating the unrepentant man as an unbeliever. That does not mean they think he is an unbeliever, but it does mean that he can no longer associate with the church as a Christian in good standing. The destruction of the flesh probably refers to some physical consequence, which we know Satan is capable of inflicting (cf. Job chapters 1-2), though some think it could refer to the destruction of the man's sinful fleshly tendencies. One thing is certain, no person or church has the power to consign an unbeliever to hell; that is God's prerogative alone.

For church discipline to make sense, this man has to be considered a Christian. Otherwise, Paul's instructions would have been not only to exclude him from fellowship, but also to share the gospel with him so that he is saved. The purpose of church discipline is not to get unsaved sinners saved, but to get saved sinners restored.

We probably take for granted the power and benefits of our fellowship with our local church. In places where there really are no other churches (such as at Corinth), exclusion from fellowship is a severe discipline. The sinning Christian has nowhere to go for help, for prayers, and for the comforting ministry of the Word. Though few churches practice discipline today, perhaps more should. Sure, the sinner may simply find another church (easy to do in our American culture), but that should not absolve the biblical responsibility of the church to discourage sin and promote holiness by loving, gentle, restorative, and spiritual discipline.

Will not inherit the kingdom of heaven. 1 Corinthians 6:9-11 (cf. Galatians 5:19-21; Ephesians 5:3-5)

> [9] *Do you not know that the unrighteous will not inherit the kingdom of God? Do not be deceived. Neither fornicators, nor idolaters, nor adulterers, nor homosexuals, nor sodomites,* [10] *nor thieves, nor covetous, nor drunkards, nor revilers, nor extortioners will inherit the kingdom of God.* [11] *And such were some of you. But you were washed, but you were sanctified, but you were justified in the name of the Lord Jesus and by the Spirit of our God.*

A Truth Interpretation: Those who are characteristically sinful will not enter heaven.

B Truth Interpretation: Believers who sin will not enjoy rewards in the kingdom.

> Second B Truth Interpretation: Believers should not sin like those
> who are unsaved.

These three passages are treated together because the message seems the
same. Those who practice these sins will not "inherit the kingdom of God."
The lists of sins are different in each passage, and the severity of the sins
varies from murder to envy. Those who hold an A Truth interpretation take
these passages to mean that Christians who do these things will lose their
salvation or that people who do these things prove they were never saved in
the first place. In either case, they are excluded from heaven or the kingdom
of God based on their sinful behavior. This interpretation is contrary to
salvation by grace, which by definition, is not by human performance.

The most important interpretive questions are: what does it mean to
"inherit the kingdom of God," and who is Paul talking to? In the first B Truth
interpretation, some have argued that the idea of inheriting the kingdom
of God is more than just entering the kingdom; after all, the author doesn't
say, "*enter* the kingdom of God." They would say that inheriting speaks of
enjoying a reward in the kingdom, such as ruling with Jesus Christ. In this
understanding, believers who sin like unbelievers will forfeit their reward
in the kingdom of God. At least that view sees the obvious, that Paul is
writing to believers. However, the idea of inheriting the kingdom of God
is best understood here as entering the kingdom. We can see how the idea
of obtaining eternal life is used synonymously with inheriting the kingdom
when we compare Matthew 19:16 with its parallel accounts in Mark 10:17
and Luke 18:18. The concept of inheriting the kingdom included not only
entering the kingdom, but also enjoying the rewards of it, for no one would
conceive of entering the kingdom without enjoying its benefits to some
degree.

The second B Truth interpretation also considers these passages as
truth relevant to believers. In the 1 Corinthians 6 passage, it is easy to see
the spiritual state of the readers. They are clearly believers because Paul
tells them they should judge matters in the church and rebukes them for
taking a "brother" before "unbelievers" in the court system (1 Cor. 6:1-8).
The "unrighteous" in verse 9 would be the same "unrighteous" unbelievers
named in verses 1 and 6, so the contrast is between believers and unbelievers.
After listing the sins of these unbelievers who will not inherit the kingdom
of God, he says "And such were some of you. But you were washed . . .
sanctified . . . justified" (1 Cor. 6:11). This strongly worded contrast makes
the most sense if he is contrasting the saved position of the Corinthians

(the three verbs are in the passive tense emphasizing position) with those who are unsaved.

The Galatians 5 passage also is written obviously to Christian readers. Paul exhorts them to "walk in the Spirit" in order not to fulfill the lust of the flesh. Either option is possible for Christians (Gal. 5:16). He then lists the sins of the flesh concluding that those who do these things will not inherit the kingdom of God. We should understand the phrase "inherit the kingdom of God" the same as in 1 Corinthians 6:9.

The controlling subject of Ephesians 5 is behavior that is "fitting for saints" (Eph. 5:3). The contrast between believers and unbelievers is prominent in 5:1-18. The readers should conduct themselves like the new people that they are in Christ, not behave like those without Christ. Now that they have come out of that darkness, they should "Walk as children of light" (Eph. 5:10). So we have the same contrast of the believer's behavior with the unbeliever's behavior.

In all three passages, Paul's message to the Christian readers is simply this: Do not behave like those who are not going to enter heaven, the non-Christians. Such sinful behavior is incongruous with the believer's new position and new identity. Both of the B Truth interpretations makes more sense than the A Truth interpretation that says Christians who behave badly will lose their salvation, or that bad behavior proves these people were never saved. The readers' salvation is not in question in any of these passages, thus it fits best under B Truth. I prefer the second B Truth interpretation.

It may be hard to accept that Christians could possibly behave as murderers, fornicators, and such, but life experience and the Bible both testify that it happens. King David murdered and committed adultery, and the man in 1 Corinthians 5 had sexual relations with his stepmother. As a pastor and Christian, I have had to deal with believers who had committed horrendous sins. Christians who act like that are behaving no different than the hell-bound unbelievers around them. There ought to be a great contrast between the lifestyles of believers and non-believers.

Lest I become disqualified. I Corinthians 9:27

But I discipline my body and bring it into subjection, lest, when I have preached to others, I myself should become disqualified.

A Truth Interpretation: If a person does not have self-control, he will not go to heaven or will lose his salvation.

B Truth Interpretation: If a person does not have self-control, he will be disqualified from a reward.

One quick way to determine whether this is A Truth or B Truth is to define what it means to be "disqualified" (*adokimos*). The word means to be *disapproved*, and it is never used to mean disqualified from heaven, unsaved, or consigned to hell. Paul even indicates the possibility that he could be disqualified. Did Paul doubt whether he was going to heaven?

If this speaks of one's eternal destiny, then it makes self-discipline the condition of salvation. Salvation by grace does not allow someone to earn or keep salvation by strenuous self-control. The grace that saves us excludes self-effort, so this could not be A Truth.

The context shows why this is B Truth. Paul is writing to the believers in the Corinthian church and he applies this to himself as a Christian as well. Nowhere in the New Testament do we find Paul expressing doubts about whether he is or will stay saved, neither do we here. He uses the analogy of runners in a race who compete for a "prize" (v. 24) to "we" who compete for "an imperishable crown" (v. 25). He is identifying himself with the Christian readers as those who must discipline themselves to achieve their reward.

It would be odd and unprecedented to refer to salvation or heaven as a "prize" or an "imperishable crown." It is more natural to take this as a prize that must be won, a reward earned. Prizes and rewards are given to those who work for them, so this could not refer to salvation, which is a gift. Paul does not specify what the reward is because that is not his point. He is simply admonishing and motivating the readers to self-control.

Since a reward is in view, we can understand what it means to be "disqualified." It means to fall short of winning the prize, to be disapproved of the prize. In a race, the prize usually goes to those who work the hardest and subject themselves to strict discipline in training and obeying the rules of competition. That is Paul's point. To reinforce his point, he goes on in chapter 10 to show how the Israelites did not discipline themselves, therefore God disciplined them in the wilderness; God disqualified them from His blessings.

As Christians, we have all received the gift of salvation by grace, but we can all still work for a prize. Self-discipline will keep us from the decimating effects of sinful behavior that will disqualify us from the prize. Though this passage does not explain to us the exact nature of the prize, it is enough to know that God will reward us for our effort.

If you hold fast. 1 Corinthians 15:1-2

[1] *Moreover, brethren, I declare to you the gospel which I preached to you, which also you received and in which you stand,* [2] *by which also you are saved, if you hold fast that word which I preached to you— unless you believed in vain.*

A Truth Interpretation: A person must persevere in the faith to be saved.

B Truth Interpretation: A person must persevere in the faith to experience the full benefit of the new life provided in the gospel.

To interpret this passage properly, we need to recall that the word *salvation* or *saved* does not always refer to eternal salvation from hell. The Corinthians were saved from hell when they heard Paul's gospel and received it, their justification. Now Paul can say that they stand in its salvation, assurance, and hope. Their *position* is secure. However, their *experience* of being delivered (saved) by the provision of the same gospel is dependent on their steadfastness in the truth.

The word *saved* then, is being used to describe the experience of living out the truths of the gospel centered on the death and resurrection of Christ (1 Cor. 15:3-4), their sanctification. The death and resurrection of Christ is not only the basis of our salvation from hell, it is the basis of our position and experience as Christians. In Romans 6:3-8, Paul explains the believer's union with Christ as the basis for a life of victory over sin. As Christ died and rose, so also we who are in Him have died to sin and have been raised with Him to walk in a new life (Rom. 8:11-13).

No one can be delivered from sin who does not continue to identify with the death and resurrection of Christ taught in the gospel. This is what Paul means by "if you hold fast that word which I preached to you." This is not an assumed accomplishment or a hypothetical condition, but a real one (The Greek first class condition does not justify the translation of "if" as "since"). The verb for "hold fast" (*katechō*) is used in the New Testament in relation to the Christian's sanctification experience (see Luke 8:15; 1 Thess. 5:21; Heb. 10:23).

Any defect in the gospel or our identification with the death and resurrection of Christ will result in a defective Christian experience. In other words, if the Corinthians do not continue to hold to the gospel Paul preached, they would have "believed in vain" because their initial faith in the gospel would not produce a sanctifying experience. The term "in vain" (*eikē*) means *to no avail* and means that the gospel they believed for salvation would not produce its intended result in them--sanctification. Some think that the phrase "unless you believed in vain" refers to the possibility that the Corinthians could have believed a defective gospel, one that denied the resurrection. But Paul has just said that they believed the gospel that he delivered to them, which included the death and the resurrection of Jesus Christ.

The A Truth interpretation is weak in several respects. First, it rigidly defines "saved" as saved from hell. Second, it ignores the sequence of thought: Paul preached the gospel, the Corinthians received it, and they now stand in it. What is left is to experience that salvation in an on-going sense, thus Paul uses the present tense "you are saved." If Paul meant saved from hell, he would have spoken more naturally of their past justification as "you have been saved," and if he was speaking of salvation as a future result of their justification and perseverance in the faith, he would have said "you will be saved."

The A Truth interpretation also makes steadfastness to the truth or perseverance a condition of eternal salvation because there can be no defect or departure from the truth. With that interpretation, all hope of assurance is gone because no one knows if they will steadfastly continue in the truth of God's Word. The New Testament has quite a few examples of believers who defected or will defect (1 Tim. 4:1-3; 5:14-15; 6:20-21; 2 Tim. 1:15; 2:17-18; 24-26; 4:10, 14-16).

No wonder Paul makes the gospel his priority: "I delivered to you first of all" (1 Cor. 15:3; Some Bibles translate this as "of first importance"). We have to get the gospel right to get saved (from the penalty of sin—saved from hell), but we must also get the gospel right to keep on getting saved (from the effects of sin). The deliverance God wants for us is not only from the penalty of sin (our justification), but also from the power of sin (our sanctification). As Christians, it is crucial that we understand what it means to be united with Jesus Christ in His death and resurrection. If we keep the gospel straight, our walk will be also.

Love Jesus or be cursed. 1 Corinthians 16:22

If anyone does not love the Lord Jesus Christ, let him be accursed. O Lord, come!

A Truth Interpretation: Someone who does not love God is cursed with eternal damnation.

B Truth Interpretation: A believer who does not love God is under God's curse in this life.

If taken as A Truth, someone who does not love God cannot be saved, loses his salvation, or proves he never had it. In this view, the curse (*anathema*) refers to an eternal curse or hell.

The word *anathema* means *to be under God's curse*. As is true with so many words in the Bible, the nature of that curse must be determined by the context. The noun *anathema* is used six times in the New Testament. It may refer to an eternal curse in Romans 9:3, but it is clear there that Paul is expressing his great desire for his fellow Jews to be saved, so much so that he would be willing to be "accursed from Christ," a clear reference to forfeiting his relationship to Christ (were it possible). In 1 Corinthians 12:3, someone can call Jesus "accursed," but it is difficult to know exactly what that means. Another occurrence in Acts 23:14 uses the verb and noun form of the word to mean *bind with an oath*, which is clearly not eternal condemnation. It is used twice in Galatians 1:8-9 as a potential danger for anyone who proclaims a false gospel. Since Paul includes himself and angels as candidates, this does not seem to refer to eternal condemnation (though the NIV interprets it that way). It is possible for Christians to hold to a false gospel--the Galatians were in the process of turning away to a different gospel (Gal. 1:6), and Paul relates how Peter was at least contradicting the true gospel (Gal. 2:11-14). The Greek translation of the Old Testament uses the word *anathema* as a temporal curse of God (Num. 21:3; Josh. 6:17; 7:12; Judg. 1:17; Zech. 14:11).

Given this range of meaning and the context, the word used in 1 Corinthians 16:22 should be considered as the threat of a temporal curse of some undefined nature. Paul is, after all, writing to believers and there is no evidence in the entire epistle to the contrary. In the immediate context, Paul wishes them all the grace of the Lord Jesus Christ and says, "My love be with you all in Christ Jesus" (vv. 23-24). There could be no inclusion of unbelievers in these blessings. Paul has put a high premium on love throughout the epistle. He proclaims the virtues of love for others in chapter 13 and says in 16:14, "Let all that you do be done with love." But he indicates that love is sourced in God and is something that the readers, as believers, could neglect (see the "if" in 8:3). Yet he also had proclaimed that those who love God have an indescribable blessing awaiting them (2:9), which may explain Paul's great desire to see the Lord's return ("O Lord, come!" 16:22) and also imply that there is the lack of reward or blessing for those who do not love God.

The B Truth interpretation assumes that loving God is not the same as believing God for salvation. Neither is loving God a guarantee for all believers. Otherwise, it would not be commanded or questioned (cf. John 14:21; 21:15-17).

As Christians, we can love God because we have experienced His grace: "We love Him because He first loved us" (1 John 4:19). Unfortunately, we can neglect to love God just as much as we can neglect to love others. In that case, we would be under God's curse instead of His blessing in this life.

Examine yourselves. 2 Corinthians 13:5

Examine yourselves as to whether you are in the faith. Test yourselves. Do you not know yourselves, that Jesus Christ is in you? —unless indeed you are disqualified.

A Truth Interpretation: Professing Christians are encouraged to examine themselves to see if they really are Christians.

B Truth Interpretation: The Corinthian Christians are told to look at their own salvation as a testimony to Paul's authenticity as an apostle because he preached the message that saved them.

One of the consequences of having a performance-based salvation is that assurance of salvation is not based on faith in Jesus Christ alone but on one's commitment, works, or faithfulness. This alone invites introspection. The problem is that there is no biblical exhortation to examine our own salvation—unless we use this passage, as many do. On the contrary, the New Testament is full of claims, statements, and assumptions that the authors and their readers are undoubtedly saved.

"But doubts are good," it is claimed. "We should all question our behavior to see if we are really saved." But is that a healthy approach to the Christian life? I think we should all question our beliefs about Jesus Christ, His person, His work, and His Promise, to make sure the object of our faith is true. But others say we should focus on ourselves instead. Have we really believed? Are we behaving like a Christian should or would?

The A Truth significance of this passage is that it gives explicit permission, even directive, to question the authenticity of our salvation. Taken in isolation from the context, that is what this verse seems to say. *But context changes everything.*

We have to start with the purpose of the epistle. Paul is writing to the Corinthian church which had its moral problems, but was also questioning the authenticity of Paul's apostleship. Not that they always had doubted him, but false apostles had influenced them against Paul (10:2). So in the midst of correcting their moral issues, he also defends his apostleship (5:12-13; 10:1-11:33; 12:11-33).

In spite of their immorality and the Corinthians' doubts about him, Paul affirms their salvation. In fact, his appeals to them are based on that fact that they are believers (1:21-22; 3:2-3; 6:14; 8:9; 13:11-14). Paul had no doubt they were saved—he led them to Christ (1 Cor. 15:1-2; 2 Cor. 1:19). And that fact forms the climax of his argument for his own authenticity. He considers the saved Corinthians his credentials of authenticity (2 Cor. 3:1-3). He says in 10:7, "If you are Christ's, then we are Christ's." In other words, if Christ is in them, then he also belongs to Christ, because he brought them the gospel that saved them.

So in chapter 13, we see the Corinthians wanted proof that Paul is a genuine spokesman for Jesus Christ (v. 3). Paul resorts again to the argument that they themselves are his credentials of authenticity. After inviting them to self-examination, he asks, "Do you not know yourselves, that Jesus Christ is in you?—unless indeed you are disqualified." It is a rhetorical question tinged with irony. Rhetorical because they know the answer—Yes, they are in the faith (the truth of Christ, not personal faith) and Christ is in them. Ironical because they want to examine Paul but he turns it around telling them the answer is in them, not him. Since they are saved, he is an authentic apostle of Jesus Christ, because he is the one who preached Christ to them! Only if they failed the test (from *adokimos*, "are disqualified"), would he also. What are they disqualified from or what test might they fail? It may be that Paul is not referring to their (or his) eternal salvation per se, but the failure to live up to the truthfulness of the faith in Christ that they claim. In other words, they would fail to live faithfully as the gospel demands. This ethical concern is certainly prevalent in the context (vv. 4, 7, 8). Just as Paul has been consistent with his claim to be an apostle (vv. 7-8), they should pass the same test of living up to what they claim they are.

In my opinion, never has a passage been so carelessly yanked out of context and used to do immeasurable damage to God's people. Doubt does not grow disciples of Jesus Christ. You can't go forward if you are always looking backward. Did I believe enough? Do I behave good enough? These questions are subjective and slippery. The only legitimate question is an objective one: Do I believe in Jesus Christ as the Son of God who died and rose for me and guarantees me eternal salvation? This passage does not invite examination of behavior anyway—it invites them to look at what they believe; "as to whether you are in the faith" refers to objective Christian truth.

Self-examination would produce doubts in any honest person who is less than perfect. But God does not want us to doubt His acceptance of us in His family. On the contrary, the assurance of His love and acceptance is His main motivation for us to love and serve Him in return.

To know if you are saved, keep your eyes off yourself and keep them on Christ!

Let him be accursed. Galatians 1:8-9

> [8] *But even if we, or an angel from heaven, preach any other gospel to you than what we have preached to you, let him be accursed.* [9] *As we have said before, so now I say again, if anyone preaches any other gospel to you than what you have received, let him be accursed.*

A Truth Interpretation: Anyone who preaches a false gospel is cursed with eternal condemnation.

B Truth Interpretation: Anyone who preaches a false gospel is under God's curse.

The word used for "accursed" is the Greek *anathema*, which we have already seen (see the discussion of 1 Cor. 16:22) does not necessarily mean *eternal condemnation*. Yet that is the A Truth interpretation used in the NIV translation of verses 8 and 9.

We showed earlier that some kind of temporal curse is probably intended. As we argued, Paul is writing to Christians in the Galatian church who had received from him the true gospel but were turning away from it to follow a false one (1:6-9). The curse of God would be upon anyone who taught a false gospel. This would include the Galatian believers, angels, and Paul himself, as well as the false teachers who were corrupting them (we don't know if those teachers were saved). In 2:11-14, we see that Peter and Barnabas were capable of distorting the true gospel.

The A Truth interpretation would eternally condemn those who taught a false gospel and perhaps even those who turned away from the true gospel. Some might even claim that the Galatians lost their salvation when they turned away to follow a different gospel. The B Truth interpretation makes more sense because the warning of the curse is applied to the Galatians as believers and includes Paul, all of whom are obviously saved and cannot lose their salvation. The exact nature of the curse is undefined, but the impression is left that it is very serious.

Every Christian should take great care to understand and communicate the gospel clearly lest a false gospel is presented. God will not bless, perhaps even curse, any misguided effort or information about the gospel. This is understandable—people's eternal destinies are at stake.

Falling from grace. Galatians 5:4

You have become estranged from Christ, you who attempt to be justified by law; you have fallen from grace.

A Truth Interpretation: A person who tries to be saved by the law will not be saved.

Second A Truth Interpretation: A believer can lose his salvation.

B Truth Interpretation: A believer can choose to ignore the benefits of grace.

The first A Truth interpretation assumes the apostle Paul is addressing an unsaved group within the Galatian church. However, we see no indication that Paul is altering his message back and forth between believers and unbelievers. It is clear that he considers the Galatians saved. He reminds them that they had received the Holy Spirit (3:1-5), they are sons of Abraham (3:26; 4:6-7), they know God (4:9), and in the immediate context, they are standing in the liberty of Christ who made them free (5:1). To be "estranged from Christ" implies that they were *not* estranged at one point, which could not describe unbelievers. The phrase "fallen from grace" would be an odd term to indicate unbelief. Rather, it implies that they were in a position of grace, but left it. The context of Paul's discussion in this epistle is the problem of believers who return to the law for either salvation or sanctification.

At least the second A Truth interpretation assumes the readers are saved. But the view that they have lost their salvation should be rejected. As seen, Paul appeals to them as Christians. He simply wants the Galatians to live in the benefits of grace, which would be impossible if they returned to the law.

Paul's teaching on grace is the key to this passage and indeed, the whole book of Galatians. The Galatians were called "in the grace of Jesus Christ" (1:6). But false teachers were trying to sabotage Paul's teaching and seduce the Galatians to go back under the Mosaic Law (1:6-9; 3:1; 4:7; 5:7, 12). Paul writes to show them the folly of trusting in the Law to either save them or sanctify them. Part of his strategy was to show how Peter was being inconsistent with grace (2:11-14). In response, Paul affirms, "I do not set aside the grace of God" (2:21). Just as the Galatians began in the Spirit, he wants them to continue in the Spirit rather than revert to their own efforts to keep the Law (3:2-3). He exhorts them to "stand fast" in their liberty under grace and not go back to the bondage of the Law (5:1). They cannot please God or grow under the Law because fleshly efforts do not bring anyone closer to God, nor could they keep the law perfectly.

In verse 4, Paul explains that if the Galatian Christians go back to the law as a means of sanctification, they will become "estranged" (from *katargeō*) from Christ. The word means to be *separated* or to render something *ineffective* or *powerless*. If the Galatians trust in their own efforts to keep the law, they will not be trusting in the power of God's grace through faith. To be "fallen" (from *ekpiptō*) has the idea of *losing one's grasp* of or *drifting from* something. They will lose their grip on grace, not their salvation, which is sure and irreversible. Paul is talking about their practice, not their position. They will be operating in contrast to God's grace as a gift to help them grow. They will be cut off from the benefits of His power and provision. Any Christian can live contradictory to who he really is. The thrust of Paul's argument to the Galatians supports the B Truth interpretation.

To be saved by grace as a gift but then try to please God afterward by our own effort is to fall from grace. The grace that saves us is the same grace that keeps us saved and helps us grow. God's grace is everything we don't deserve and more for anything we need, from salvation to ultimate glorification. We can access his grace through faith (Rom. 5:2) for any and every need.

Faith working through love. Galatians 5:6

For in Christ Jesus neither circumcision nor uncircumcision avails anything, but faith working through love.

A Truth Interpretation: Genuine saving faith must demonstrate love.

B Truth Interpretation: Christians are not sanctified by keeping the law, but by allowing their faith to demonstrate love.

An important question to answer here is what "avails anything" refers to. The word "avails" (*ischuō*) means *is able to do* or *accomplish* something. Paul is asserting that faith and love do accomplish something. Is "faith working through love" able to accomplish or prove salvation for someone? If so, salvation would be on a performance basis.

Salvation or proving salvation can't be the issue, because in this section, Paul is talking about the Galatians' sanctification experience, not their justification (that discussion was in 3:1-9). Besides, his statement is about those "in Christ," a clear reference to believers. The issue is whether Christians can be sanctified by the law (represented by circumcision) or by grace. But it is not whether a Christian is circumcised or not circumcised that accomplishes sanctification, only whether he is exercising his faith by loving others. Those who think that keeping the law (getting circumcised) will produce righteousness in their lives are not trusting in Christ; they have departed from grace and its powerful benefits (Gal. 5:2-4; see above). Righteousness in the Christian life is only produced through faith (5:5), and the chief way that faith can be exercised is in loving others (5:6; cf. 5:13-14).

The A Truth perspective on this passage is confusing and wrong about how a person is saved. The B Truth perspective is a powerful principle for believers: When our faith expresses itself in love, we grow in righteousness to be more like Jesus Christ, the Righteous One.

Reap what you sow. Galatians 6:7-8

> [7] *Do not be deceived, God is not mocked; for whatever a man sows, that he will also reap.* [8] *For he who sows to his flesh will of the flesh reap corruption, but he who sows to the Spirit will of the Spirit reap everlasting life.*

A Truth Interpretation: Bad deeds bring eternal condemnation or prove a person is going to hell, but good deeds bring or prove eternal salvation.

B Truth Interpretation: Christians who live by the flesh will waste their lives, but those who do good will experience the fullness of God's life.

The immediate context is enough to provide a good interpretation of this passage. The first thing we notice is that Paul is addressing the believing readers (see the previous arguments about their saved status) as those who have been "taught the word" (v. 6). They are told to "share in all good things" with those who taught them, an obvious reference to at least assisting their teachers (who were probably traveling missionaries like Paul) financially and in other ways in their ministry. Paul repeats the thought of sharing in the "bookend" verse 10 but expands his exhortation to do good not just to their teachers, but to all people, especially to those in the church.

With bookends of verses 6 and 10 addressing Christians giving to Christians, who are those we expect to be the focus of Paul's words in verses 7-9? It could only be believers, and it is! The basic thought is this: If believers think they will gain more by holding back from sharing their resources, they are simply deceiving themselves. The principle is that one gains by what he gives, just as a farmer can only reap according to the amount and kind of seed that he sows. When believers sow selfishly (implying they withhold sharing with others), they reap "corruption," but if they sow in a way led by the Holy Spirit, they reap "everlasting life."

We have been arguing here for the B Truth interpretation. It is largely because of the terms "corruption" and "everlasting life" that some will interpret this as A Truth. But these terms do not speak of eternal damnation and eternal salvation. Not only does that interpretation ignore the context, but it assumes definitions that cannot be supported. In the New Testament, the word *corruption* (*phthora*) is never used for eternal damnation, but has the meaning of *deterioration, decay,* or *ruin*. We have already seen that the term "everlasting life" is used not only for eternal deliverance from hell, but as a present quality of life, an abundant life that reaches into eternity (John 4:14; 10:10; 17:3).

Given those definitions, Paul's words are a good exhortation to Christians. If we withhold our resources from helping others or use them to please our sinful desires, we will experience the waste and ruin of the very life we are trying to enhance (see the previous discussion of Matt. 10:39; 16:25-26). If, however, we use our resources unselfishly as led by the Holy Spirit for His purposes, we will experience more of God and His life flowing in and through us now and in eternity. That is why Paul says in verse 9 that we should never be discouraged from doing good to others or giving to others. We will be rewarded. It will be worth it!

Faith and the gift of God. Ephesians 2:8-10

> [8] *For by grace you have been saved through faith, and that not of yourselves; it is the gift of God,* [9] *not of works, lest anyone should boast.* [10] *For we are His workmanship, created in Christ Jesus for good works, which God prepared beforehand that we should walk in them.*

A Truth Interpretation: People are not saved by works, but by a faith that is given by God, which guarantees good works.

B Truth Interpretation: People are not saved by works, but through faith, so that they will fulfill God's purpose of doing good works.

There are two issues that need to be addressed here. The first has to do with the nature of the faith through which we are saved. Does God give the faith we need to be saved? The second issue has to do with the role of works in relation to our salvation.

There are many who understand verse 8 to mean that in salvation, God's grace can only be accessed by a faith that God gives to an unbeliever. They see faith as a gift of God. Some even call it a divine empowerment. This fits the theological position that teaches human beings are so totally corrupted by sin that they have no capacity to respond to God, even to believe. In their view, not only must an unbeliever be regenerated to believe, but after regeneration must then be given faith to place in the Lord Jesus Christ for salvation.

Let's lay aside the theological problems with such a view and just deal with the text. That interpretation assumes that the word "that" (*touto*) in verse 8 refers to "faith" as the gift of God (the words "it is" in v. 8 are not in the Greek text but are supplied by translators). However, if "that" refers to "faith," it would have to be in the feminine gender, as is true of abstract nouns like *faith*. But it is in the neuter gender. So what does "that" refer to? Obviously, it refers to *salvation by grace*. A survey of the commentary tradition on this verse will find that many, and maybe most, agree with the view that "that" does not refer to "faith." This fits the context perfectly from chapter 1 through 2:1-10, which is about how God has saved us by His grace. The neuter pronoun translated "that" is used elsewhere in Ephesians to refer to a phrase or clause that immediately precedes it (cf. 1:15; 3:1). The parallelism of "not of yourselves" in verse 8 and "not of works" in verse 9 seals the argument that salvation by grace is in view as the gift of God.

Faith is not a gift of God, because it is a human response. Neither is it a divine power or enablement. That confuses the work of the Holy Spirit with human responsibility. The Holy Spirit may prompt faith in an unbeliever by drawing him (John 6:44), convicting him of the truth of the gospel (John 16:8-11), and opening his eyes to the gospel (2 Cor. 4:6). But the power of God and the faith of a person are two different things. The Holy Spirit is the agent or effective power of our salvation, and faith is the instrument by which we have access to God's Spirit and power that saves. That is why it is most accurate to say we are saved *by* grace, but *through* faith.

We will discuss a second issue because verse 10 is so integral to verses 8-9. The issue is the role of works as proof of our salvation. Verse 10 says that we who are saved are made new creatures in Christ "for good works" with the intent "that we should walk in them." The A Truth interpretation believes that verse 10 guarantees every believer will have good works, and if they don't, they are not really saved. Their view is related to the idea that faith is a divine gift or empowerment. As such, it will not fail to produce a godly life with good works. But that view reads into verse 10 more than it says. The clause "for good works" expresses a purpose, not a promise. While it may imply or infer that a believer will have good works, this verse says nothing about the fulfillment of that purpose. God created good works before our salvation with the intent "that" we should walk in them. The word "that" in the original Greek (*hina*) along with form of verb used in "should walk" (subjunctive mood) has the force of potentiality and probability, but not certainty. Good works are God's desire for every believer, but they are not forced upon a believer. If a believer has no responsibility or choice in his conduct, how can his works be qualified as *good*, and how would they deserve a future reward?

One need not think too far to see that if good works are guaranteed in every believer, then the admonitions of the New Testament are unnecessary or superfluous. In that case, this A Truth interpretation would be "antinomian" (which means *against the keeping of laws or commandments*) because the commands of chapters 4-6 would be unnecessary. But such a view of guaranteed good works is absurd, especially since the New Testament has many admonitions and exhortations to do various good works.

Every believer should do good works. It is God's purpose for every

Christian, it is the expectation for every Christian, and it is God's command for every Christian. Justification anticipates progressive sanctification, but justification does not guarantee progressive sanctification. Faith is the condition, works a consequence. Faith is the requirement, works a result. Salvation by grace through faith is A Truth; the resulting good works is B Truth.

God will complete His work. Philippians 1:6

Being confident of this very thing, that He who has begun a good work in you will complete it until the day of Jesus Christ.

A Truth Interpretation: God will complete His work in Christians of persevering in faith and good works to the end of their lives.

B Truth Interpretation: God will work to see that the Philippians' good work of giving will be completed.

The A Truth version of this passage takes it as a promise that all true believers will persevere in faith and good works until the end of their lives. This is sometimes rooted in the doctrine called the Perseverance of the Saints. The reasoning is related to their belief that a person becomes a Christian when God elects them, regenerates them, then gives them the faith to believe. Such faith, they conclude, cannot fail because it is God's "good work" in the Christian.

But what does Paul mean by "good work?" He does not say "good works," but seems to refer to a single issue. The meaning of their good work is found in the context. In the previous verse, Paul is recognizing their "fellowship in the gospel" (v. 5). The word *fellowship (koinonia)* has the basic meaning of *communion* or *something shared in common*. What was it the Philippian believers shared with Paul? While it could refer in general to their partnership in the gospel, foremost in Paul's mind, and really the occasion for his writing, is their financial sharing, which is mentioned here in the introductory remarks as well as in the closing remarks (1:5-6; 4:15-18). Epaphroditus had delivered the Philippians' gift and now Paul is sending him back with a "thank you note" and some information about his circumstances. In fact, in 4:15, Paul uses the verbal form of *koinonia* when he says, "no church *shared* with me concerning giving and receiving except you only." The noun *koinonia* is actually translated "contribution" in other New Testament passages (Rom. 15:26; 2 Cor. 8:4; 9:13; Heb. 13:6).

The Philippians' financial support is described in verse 5 as "from the first day until now." This could not refer to the first day of their salvation because he is not speaking to one person but many who would have been saved at various times. It most obviously refers to when they began to share financially as a church as noted in 4:15. The reference to "now" would then refer to their contribution that Paul has just received in prison (4:10, 14, 18). One finds echoes of Philippians 1:3-7 and 4:10-20 in Paul's description of the generosity of those in Macedonia (where the Philippian church was located) in 2 Corinthians chapters 8-9.

This is B Truth. The "good work" of which Paul speaks is not good works or sanctification in general that proves one is saved. It is the Philippians' fellowship in the Gospel through giving. To consider this verse a promise that all Christians will persevere in a godly lifestyle ignores the occasion, the context, and Paul's point. First, he is not addressing all Christians, but the Philippian believers specifically. Second, Paul is not speaking about lifestyle, but about the Philippians' support of his ministry. Third, he is not making a promise, but is only expressing his confident feelings. Paul is confident that God will "complete" or carry through the impact of their support as its effects are multiplied in ministry to others until the return of Christ. Certainly, the Philippians would not live until the return of Christ, but through Paul's ministry, they have given a gift that will keep on giving to advance the gospel to others who will do the same. The reference to the day of Jesus Christ may also imply that their generosity will be rewarded at the Judgment Seat of Christ.

Contrary to the A Truth interpretation, Paul knew that all Christians do not persevere in godliness and righteous behavior until the end. He reminds the Corinthians that there were some in their church who had died from abusing the Lord's Supper (1 Cor. 11:30). Elsewhere in the Bible we find that a believer can persist in sin such that it leads to his or her death (Jas.5:20; 1 John 5:16). God works in believers to produce good works and progressively sanctify them, but the results are not always measurable and observable. Furthermore, His work is only carried out in concurrence and cooperation with the individual's will (cf. 1 Cor. 15:10; Gal. 2:20; Phil. 2:11-12), which makes disobedience a possibility.

Perhaps we could learn from this passage that God will use our generous giving to help others and accomplish His will. Knowing that our giving will have eternal impact on others and possibly be rewarded at Christ's return should motivate us to give toward the spread of the gospel. But since this passage does not guarantee perseverance in faith and good works, let us be careful not to use it to condemn those who may genuinely be God's children, yet struggle with lifelong bad habits and weaknesses of will and discipline.

Turn out for deliverance. Philippians 1:27-28

> [27] *Only let your conduct be worthy of the gospel of Christ, so that whether I come and see you or am absent, I may hear of your affairs, that you stand fast in one spirit, with one mind striving together for the faith of the gospel,* [28] *and not in any way terrified by your adversaries, which is to them a proof of perdition, but to you of salvation, and that from God.*

A Truth Interpretation: The Philippians' bold unity in the gospel proves their eternal salvation.

B Truth Interpretation: The Philippians' bold unity in the gospel indicates their expectation that God will deliver them through their suffering.

The key issue that distinguishes this passage as A Truth or B Truth is how "salvation" is defined. If Paul is talking about eternal salvation from hell, then this passage is saying that the Philippians' conduct is proof that they have it. We have argued elsewhere that using one's conduct to prove salvation is not possible much less Biblical. But we have also argued elsewhere that it is important to understand that the word *salvation* does not always refer to eternal salvation from hell, but can also mean deliverance from trouble.

The word *salvation* (*sotēria*) is used three times in the opening chapters of Philippians: 1:19, 28, and 2:12. The discussion in this section is dominated by the circumstances of Paul's imprisonment, the activity of his and the Philippians' adversaries, and the Philippians' response in suffering through this adversity. In 1:19, he expresses confidence that he will be saved (delivered) from the trouble his adversaries are causing because the Philippians are praying for him and the Holy Spirit is ministering to him. Certainly, Paul is not speaking of his eternal salvation. Some think he could be referring to deliverance from prison or vindication by the Roman courts, but the following verses 20-26 show that he considers the possibility he may die in prison. It is more probable he is speaking of deliverance by a victorious attitude that magnifies Christ in his suffering (1:20).

The second use of *salvation* in 1:28 should be interpreted in the same way as 1:19, but applied to the Philippians. By their bold unity in the gospel, they will indicate to their adversaries their expectation of deliverance by God through their suffering, just like Paul. (The word "proof" may be too strong in force since *endeiksis* can also have the meaning of something that is *an indication* or *sign* of something else). In the next verses, 29-30, Paul ties their suffering together, which indicates the deliverance they all experience is of the same nature—a victorious attitude that magnifies Christ in suffering. Such an attitude will indicate to their adversaries that they will be defeated and destroyed (not necessarily eternally, but that could be implied).

We will find that the third use of *salvation* in 2:12 continues the themes developed in chapter 1, but that is discussed separately below.

What is clear from the context and the use of the word *sotēria* in both 1:19 and 1:28 is that eternal salvation is not in view like the A Truth interpretation asserts. Paul is not talking about proving eternal salvation, but about being delivered through suffering by confidence in the victory God brings so that Christ is glorified.

The B Truth interpretation is an encouragement for us as believers to endure suffering and adversity with the confidence that God will deliver us through them, in such a way that Jesus Christ will be magnified in us. God may not deliver us *out of* our suffering, but *through* our suffering (cf. 1 Pet. 5:10). It may be difficult to identify with Paul's suffering—imprisoned and facing possible death—yet his example of confidence in God shows that we, like him, can be victorious and continue to glorify God whatever our circumstances.

Work out your own salvation. Philippians 2:12-13

> [12] *Therefore, my beloved, as you have always obeyed, not as in my presence only, but now much more in my absence, work out your own salvation with fear and trembling;* [13] *for it is God who works in you both to will and to do for His good pleasure.*

A Truth Interpretation: People must work for salvation, or Christians must work to prove their salvation.

B Truth Interpretation: Once saved, Christians must cooperate with God to live out their new lives.

Second B Truth Interpretation: Christians must endure suffering in such a way that they experience deliverance by God.

As you can see, the A Truth interpretation injects works into salvation either at the front end or the rear. It is not so common to hear Christians insist on works as a condition at the front end of salvation. However, it is very common to hear Christians insist on works to prove they are genuinely saved. All this comes from the assumption that the salvation spoken of is soteriological, or eternal deliverance from hell.

One B Truth interpretation also assumes this passage speaks of eternal salvation, but does not insist on works as a condition or proof of salvation. This view would note that the text says "work out" not "work for" this salvation. In other words, those who are saved should allow their salvation to have its intended effect in sanctification. This happens, this view would say, as believers cooperate with God who is working in us (v. 13). I am sympathetic to this view because it is at least consistent with the gospel of grace by removing works as a condition for eternal life.

When we look at how the word "salvation" is used in 1:19 and 28, the second B Truth interpretation seems more consistent with this context. In 2:12, Paul draws a conclusion ("Therefore") from what has been said previously. Going back to 1:12, the flow of Paul's thought goes like this:

- Though I am suffering in prison, I have confidence that I will experience deliverance from dishonoring God to victory through these circumstances so that Christ will be magnified. (1:12-20)

- This deliverance gives me victory whether I die or live, though I expect to live. (1:21-26)

- You who are also suffering can experience the same victory of deliverance as you trust in God and stay fearlessly united in the gospel. (1:27-30)

- Because you will be delivered through these circumstances, you can therefore continue being selflessly united and encouraged by the example of Christ's selflessness and victorious exaltation. (2:1-11)

- You should therefore continue to cooperate with God as you live out the benefits of your deliverance in your troubles. (2:12-13)

- Your perseverance in unity will triumph over the evil world and bring me joy now and at the Judgment Seat of Christ. (2:14-18)

This shows a consistent meaning of *salvation* as a deliverance from dishonoring God in the midst of the adversaries and the suffering they are causing. It is not only deliverance *from* this, it is also deliverance *to* a victorious attitude that endures in faith toward God and selfless behavior toward others. It is a sanctifying deliverance, not a soteriological one. Some have taken the deliverance (also in 1:19 and 28) to mean a vindication at the Judgment Seat of Christ, a deliverance from the shame of an improper attitude and conduct. This would imply future rewards as well. While a good assessment at the Judgment Seat of Christ would certainly result from good attitudes and conduct in suffering, the passage seems to focus on the Philippians' present experience.

A victorious sanctification experience is not guaranteed to Christians. It can be difficult to maintain a God-honoring life when persecuted by enemies or suffering difficult circumstances. By trusting God and the supply of His Spirit to serve others selflessly, we can be delivered from defeat by our enemies and our circumstances and delivered to a victorious attitude that witnesses to the world the truth we proclaim.

Press on for the prize. Philippians 3:12-14

[12] Not that I have already attained, or am already perfected; but I press on, that I may lay hold of that for which Christ Jesus has also laid hold of me. [13] Brethren, I do not count myself to have apprehended; but one thing I do, forgetting those things which are behind and reaching forward to those things which are ahead, [14] I press toward the goal for the prize of the upward call of God in Christ Jesus.

A Truth Interpretation: Salvation is the prize for those who persevere.

B Truth Interpretation: The deeper experience of Christ's suffering and power is the prize for those who persevere.

It is good to remind ourselves of something we have already discussed: there is a gift and there is a prize. Eternal salvation is a free gift to the unbeliever, but rewards for faithfulness are a prize to be earned by the believer. Which is the apostle Paul addressing here?

It does not appear to be eternal salvation, because it is clear that Paul does not question his salvation in this epistle or elsewhere. Should he do that, he would contradict his bold exhortations to the readers of his epistles, undermine his authority as an apostle, and make vapid his exposition of the gospel as a sure promise of salvation. This passage shows that Paul was pursuing something else—a prize. His testimony is that "Christ Jesus has also laid hold of me" (3:12) and on that basis, he now seeks to possess fully what Christ has intended for him. That purpose is explained in verse 14 as "the prize of the upward call of God in Christ Jesus" which is most likely a reference to what he described earlier as his desire in verses 10-11: to know Christ (in the sense of a deeper experiential knowledge), to experience the same power that raised Christ from the dead, and experience the fellowship of Christ's sufferings (not for sin, but for doing right). Paul sought to enter into a complete identification with Jesus Christ in His experience of suffering and resurrection power (cf. Rom. 6:4-5). Life experience shows us that those who suffer a trial together enjoy a special fellowship in a way that others cannot. Consider, for example, the common bond between women who have suffered through pregnancy, or between those who have suffered with cancer.

Paul also proclaims his desire to "attain to the resurrection from the dead" (3:11). Of what does Paul speak? There are many interpretations, but the key seems to be in the unique word used for resurrection, which would be translated literally as "out-resurrection" (*exanastasin*). It seems Paul is referring to the imminent Rapture event in which dead believers are raised from the grave (that is, from among the dead) and living believers are transformed as both groups meet the Lord Jesus in the air. Paul is saying that he hopes to live until that event. He is not doubting his rapture or resurrection—"if, by any means" (*ei pōs* with the subjunctive voice in the verb) is well translated by the NIV "and so, somehow" reflecting more of a desired outcome, and "attain" (from *katantaō*) can have the meaning "to arrive at."

So the B Truth interpretation of this passage does not make Paul doubtful of his salvation or resurrection, but expresses his desire to fully experience the suffering and power of Jesus Christ until, should he live so long, he is raptured from this life.

Besides the exegetical and theological problems of an A Truth interpretation which makes Paul doubting his salvation and seeking to earn it, there are sad practical consequences to such a view because it misses what should be every Christian's goal. Like Paul, we should seek to experience a deeper fellowship with Christ through suffering for righteousness like He did, and we should want to experience the greatness of God's resurrecting power like Christ did. But this deeper experience does not come as a gift; believers must "press on" or persevere in faithfulness towards that goal and this resulting prize that God desires for every believer. Unfortunately, an A Truth interpretation does not offer this blessed prospect.

If you continue. Colossians 1:21-23

> [21] *And you, who once were alienated and enemies in your mind by wicked works, yet now He has reconciled* [22] *in the body of His flesh through death, to present you holy, and blameless, and above reproach in His sight—* [23] *if indeed you continue in the faith, grounded and steadfast, and are not moved away from the hope of the gospel which you heard, which was preached to every creature under heaven, of which I, Paul, became a minister.*

A Truth Interpretation: People are reconciled to God in salvation if they continue to believe or adhere to the Christian faith.

B Truth Interpretation: Christians will have a good presentation to the Lord at the Judgment Seat of Christ if they continue in the faith.

This passage is very often understood as A Truth, but in several differing ways. Some think it teaches that people will only be saved if they continue toward Christian truth. Others think it teaches that only those who persevere in their faith to the end of their lives are truly saved. Still others interpret this as a warning that if Christians do not continue steadfastly in their faith, they will lose their salvation, a position we have dismissed as contrary to clear biblical teaching.

First, we should establish whether the warning is written from the perspective that salvation is a future possibility or a past event for these readers. The evidence shows that the readers had an unquestionable salvation experience. Paul calls them "saints and faithful brethren in Christ"

(1:2) who have a reputation for faith and love (v. 3). Positionally, they have been transferred into the kingdom of Christ (v. 13), are redeemed (v. 14), and are reconciled to God (v. 21). Their present position of reconciliation is contrasted to their previous position as those alienated from God and His enemies (v. 21).

So at the outset, it contradicts Paul's statements about the readers' saved position if their reconciliation is made conditional by what he says in verse 23: "if you continue in the faith." These readers are not *on their way to* faith, but are "in" the faith. If they are not yet saved, then "in the faith" cannot refer to their personal faith, nor can it refer to objective Christian truth because the starting point for that is a saving knowledge of Jesus Christ.

Some who take this warning as B Truth think that reconciliation with God is in view in the conditional warning, but argue that the construction of the conditional clause has the meaning "since" as in "If you continue, and you certainly will." But this construction (first class condition in the Greek) does not necessarily express certainty of fact, only certainty for the sake of argument. Statements of first class condition can be purely hypothetical and even contrary to fact (see Gal. 3:4).

There is a better B Truth interpretation. To continue in "the faith" (note that Paul doesn't say "your faith") must mean to continue on the path of Christian truth first encountered by coming to know Jesus Christ as their Savior. This is foundational truth for Christian living and sanctification. Since reconciliation is a present reality to the readers, the conditional "if you continue in the faith" must look forward to something in the future. In the text, that would be the prospect of the readers' presentation in holiness and blamelessness in God's sight (1:22). This presentation to God is found elsewhere in the New Testament (2 Cor. 4:14; 11:2; Eph. 5:27; 1 Thess. 5:23; Jude 24) and as used in Romans 14:10, is a clear reference to the believer's appearance before the Lord at the Judgment Seat of Christ where one's life, not one's salvation, is judged (cf. 1 Cor. 3:13; 2 Cor. 5:10). The terms "holy, blameless, and irreproachable" are not used positionally but qualitatively for the degree of sanctification attained by the believer (cf. Eph. 5:27; 1 Tim 3:2; Tit. 1:6-7). It was Paul's goal to "present every man perfect in Christ Jesus" (1:28). Every believer will be presented to the Lord in that Day, but not all will be presented with equal honor.

The attainment of these qualities and a favorable presentation are conditioned on their steadfast continuance in the faith that they had learned and experienced in the gospel, but it is also conditioned on them not moving "away from the hope of the gospel" which they had heard. *Hope* is similar to faith because it is the expectation of a future event. Paul reminds these readers of "the hope which is laid up for you in heaven" which they heard through the gospel of grace he preached to them (1:5-6). A key to interpreting 1:21-23 is the relationship between hope and its fruit as described by Paul in 1:4-6. Their hope resulted in an on-going faith in Jesus Christ and love for other believers (1:4). In other words, the confidence they had in their future because of the gospel (their hope), had a sanctifying effect on their lives (the sanctifying effect of hope is seen in other New Testament passages as well: Rom. 5:2; 12:12; 2 Cor. 3:12; Heb. 7:19; 1 John 3:3). If the readers move away from this confident hope, the fruit of hope will be impaired and consequently their favorable presentation to the Lord compromised.

The difference between the A Truth Interpretation and the B Truth Interpretation is quite profound. If salvation depends on perseverance in faith or faithfulness, assurance of salvation is lost. Without the sure hope of eternal life, motives to trust God and love others are subverted. Without these sanctifying qualities, a favorable evaluation at the Judgment Seat of Christ is jeopardized or lost. In short, believers cannot grow fully in an environment of doubt and uncertainty. Confident hope and assurance of salvation give both the motive and the freedom to trust God and love others. Such hope and assurance must be based on the gospel of God's grace, not human performance.

Work of faith. 1 Thessalonians 1:3

Remembering without ceasing your work of faith, labor of love, and patience of hope in our Lord Jesus Christ in the sight of our God and Father.

A Truth Interpretation: Justifying faith must include works.

B Truth Interpretation: Sanctifying faith produces works.

The introductory thanksgiving given in this epistle is motivated by Paul's memory of three things which he states in parallel construction. When considered as parallel qualities, they refer to the Thessalonians' post-salvation demonstrations of good works prompted by faith, labor prompted by love, and patience prompted by hope. These things are the results of their election by God, their reception of the gospel, and their subsequent following of the apostles (1:4-6). Paul is not stating that these virtues prove their faith (which would be A Truth), but only that he observed these things after their reception of the gospel. The faith of which he speaks in verse 3 is best taken as sanctifying faith (B Truth), just as love and hope are sanctifying virtues. He doesn't allude to their justifying faith until verses 4-11. In his similar introduction in 2 Thessalonians, Paul mentions sanctifying faith as faith that grows and helps them endure persecutions and tribulations (2 Thess. 1:3-4). Also, we see the same term, "work of faith," used clearly of the sanctification experience in 2 Thessalonians 1:11.

It is overreaching to use this verse to say that saving faith must include works. Such an interpretation is not derived from the text, so it must come from one's theological persuasion. We are saved through initial faith in Christ for good works which come from our on-going exercise of faith in the Lord.

Those who reject the faith. 1 Timothy 1:19-20

[19] *having faith and a good conscience, which some having rejected, concerning the faith have suffered shipwreck,* [20] *of whom are Hymenaeus and Alexander, whom I delivered to Satan that they may learn not to blaspheme.*

A Truth Interpretation: Hymenaeus and Alexander rejected the Christian faith and lost their salvation, or they proved they were never saved.

B Truth Interpretation: Hymenaeus and Alexander rejected the Christian faith and suffered severe temporal consequences.

The evidence in the text weighs heavily toward a B Truth interpretation. Hymenaeus and Alexander are mentioned as a contrast to Timothy's faithfulness. It is implied by verse 5 that Timothy has faith and a good conscience and he is commended in verse 18 for waging a good warfare. These are all Christian life issues, not salvation issues. Instead of waging a good warfare with faith and a good conscience, Hymenaeus and Alexander have shipwrecked their Christian lives.

The term "shipwreck" (from *nauageō*) can, of course, refer to a literal shipwreck (2 Cor. 11:25), or refer figuratively to suffering ruin, loss, or disaster as it does here. There is nothing about the term that automatically denotes the loss of salvation or an unsaved state. Christians can meet with disaster. The disaster that Hymenaeus and Alexander faced concerned "the faith," most likely a reference to their Christian faith not their personal faith since the article "the" is used, although it certainly implies a crisis of personal faith as well.

Those who would lean toward an A Truth interpretation might argue that these men could not be saved because they rejected the Christian faith. However, the text indicates that what they had rejected was faith and a good conscience, the Christian virtues Timothy was commended for. Even so, if they rejected the Christian faith itself, this does not demand the loss of salvation or prove they were never saved. Christians can turn their back on the truth (the word "reject" [from *apotheō*] can mean *to push aside or repudiate*) in varying degrees. One need only consider the whole point of the letter to the Hebrews, as well as other evidence in the New Testament:

- Peter denied the Lord (Luke 22:34, 54-62).
- The apostle Paul predicts apostasy in later times (1 Tim. 4:1-3).
- The warning of 1 Timothy 4:16 implies a Christian can depart from the faith.
- There were widows in the church who "turned aside to follow Satan" (1 Tim. 5:14-15).
- The apostle Paul says that some have strayed from the faith (1 Tim. 6:20-21).
- Those who deserted the apostle Paul and opposed him (2 Tim. 1:15; 4:9-10, 14-16) are to be gently instructed so that they can escape the snares of Satan (2 Tim. 2:24-26).
- Those who stray from the truth can overthrow the faith of others (2 Tim. 2:18).

Also, the clear statement of 2 Timothy 2:13 is "If we are faithless, [literally, *unbelieving* from *apisteuō*], He [God] remains faithful; He cannot deny Himself." Our salvation depends on our initial faith for justification, not our continuing faith, which can fail in our Christian experience.

What may push some toward an A Truth interpretation is the statement by Paul that he delivered Hymenaeus and Alexander to Satan. But even here, the text does not say they were delivered to Satan in hell or into his kingdom of darkness. The purpose for Paul's action was so that these men would "learn not to blaspheme." It would not make sense for Paul to teach unbelievers not to blaspheme. His action is ultimately restorative discipline for these seriously erring believers. This truth reminds us of Paul's prescription for the sinning brother in the Corinthian church (1 Cor. 5:3-5; 2 Cor. 2:1-11), which was most likely forced disassociation from the church that put him in danger of Satan's devices in this world.

Christians are capable of the most serious sins, including rejecting the beliefs that saved them. But we see that the consequences are just as serious. Though it may not be by apostolic action, apostate Christians today who forsake the safety of God's truth and His church place themselves in the dangerous domain of the Evil One.

Laying hold on eternal life. 1 Timothy 6:17-19

> [17] Command those who are rich in this present age not to be haughty, nor to trust in uncertain riches but in the living God, who gives us richly all things to enjoy. [18] Let them do good, that they be rich in good works, ready to give, willing to share, [19] storing up for themselves a good foundation for the time to come, that they may lay hold on eternal life.

A Truth Interpretation: Those who are rich in good works will earn eternal life.

B Truth Interpretation: Those who are rich in good works will enjoy a divine quality of life.

This is a word to those who are under Timothy's care who are rich. It is not a word about how Timothy should treat all unbelievers or all believers. Evidently, these rich people are believers because 1) They are associated with Timothy, 2) Doing good works, giving, and sharing are Christian virtues, 3) The "time to come" is mentioned in a positive way as a certainty.

Some may view this as A Truth because of the last phrase "that they may lay hold on eternal life," as it is translated in the NKJV. However, the word "eternal" is not in the Greek text. Most of the major translations agree in meaning with the ESV, "that which is truly life" (cf. the NET Bible, NASB, NIV). In 6:12, the word "eternal" is used when Paul says, "Fight the good fight of faith, lay hold on eternal life." But the point of both passages is similar. Paul's exhortation to Timothy in 6:19 is that wealthy believers should not find their significance in uncertain riches, but in God and in serving him. To make God the focus of one's life is truly life. It is enjoying one's relationship with God obtained in salvation, an abundant life (John 10:10; 17:3).

Storing up a good foundation speaks of rewards in the future, or as Jesus puts it, laying up treasures in heaven (Matt. 6:20). It would be odd to refer to obtaining eternal life by this language. "Foundation" (*themelios*) has the idea of something that gives stability like a reserve or a treasure. The "time to come" is not spoken of in verse 19 as a possibility, but a certainty. What is conditional (expressed by the subjunctive mood) is the laying hold of "that which is truly life."

This important B Truth teaches us that all believers face a future in heaven and the kingdom of God, but some believers will have a better treasure waiting for them. We might say that those believers "send their riches ahead." They are the ones who also have learned to focus their present lives on God, not their riches, and enjoy a richer experience of life with Him.

If we deny Him. 2 Timothy 2:10-13

> [10] *Therefore I endure all things for the sake of the elect, that they also may obtain the salvation which is in Christ Jesus with eternal glory.* [11] *This is a faithful saying: For if we died with Him, We shall also live with Him.* [12] *If we endure, We shall also reign with Him. If we deny Him, He also will deny us.* [13] *If we are faithless, He remains faithful; He cannot deny Himself.*

A Truth Interpretation: Those who are elect will endure in faithfulness to obtain salvation, but those who deny Christ will be denied salvation.

B Truth Interpretation: Believers are guaranteed salvation and faithful believers will also reign with Christ, while believers who deny Christ will be denied the reward of reigning with Him.

The passage begins with a statement from the apostle Paul that he is enduring (v. 10), which is obviously a reference to his suffering (v. 9). But he endures not for his own sake, but for the sake of others. So the word "endure" is a condition not of his eternal salvation, but in order that others "may obtain the salvation which is in Christ Jesus" (v. 10). Paul's endurance certainly cannot save others eternally, so how do we interpret this? Some could argue that Paul suffered to bring the gospel to the elect so that they would be saved. However, the next use of the word "endure" in verse 12 speaks of believers enduring for the future reward of reigning with Christ. With this in mind, the salvation of verse 10 would be the final consummation of salvation when believers are with Christ and in His glory. In other words, Paul is laying down an example of enduring in hardships so that believers will follow him and endure hardships, and thus secure their future reward, the final goal of their salvation.

Paul then recites what many think is a hymn because of its structured parallelism and couplets. Verse 11 is a confident statement of our salvation because we are united with Christ and will live with Him forever (Rom. 6:3-5; Gal. 2:20). We should note preemptively that this argues against the possibility of someone losing salvation, which has implications for verse 12.

In verse 12, there is a different condition and a different consequence. The condition is endurance; which Paul has already mentioned in relation to suffering through hardships. Endurance is a key virtue in the Christian life (e.g., 2 Tim. 2:3; Heb. 10:23, 36; 12:1; Jas. 1:2-4, 12). As noted above, the consequence of reigning does not refer to salvation, but to the reward for faithfulness—reigning with Christ in His kingdom, as is taught in many other passages (Luke 19:11-19; Rev. 2:26-27; 3:21; Rev. 22:3-5). If we deny Christ, He denies us His approval and reward (see the discussions on Matt. 10:32-33). Denying Christ may have in mind denying Christ's ability to help us endure in trials, but could also include verbal denials of our association with Him (such as Peter's famous three-fold blunder), or a denial of Him by our actions (see 1 Tim. 5:8).

Verse 13 then speaks of another circumstance altogether. If we are "faithless" (from *apisteuō, without faith, unbelieving*; cf. Rom. 3:3), God remains "faithful" (*pistos*). What is God faithful to? Some believe this means that God is faithful to Himself in that He will judge those who are unfaithful to Him or deny Him, as addressed in verse 12. However, it is unimaginable that a threat of judgment would be based on God's positive attribute of faithfulness. This is more likely an encouraging promise that follows the negative threat mentioned in verse 12. The sense is that even though we may deny Him and He may have to deny us rewards, God is faithful to His promise that we will live with Him forever, as stated in verse 11. This is intended to comfort believers.

If this is indeed a hymn or recitation, then the structure flows poetically in what is called a chiasm—an inverted relationship in parallel phrases. If we apply the categories of A Truth B Truth, we get this:

Verse	Couplet	Chiastic Structure	A/B Category
2:11	For if we died with Him, We shall also live with Him.	X-1	**A Truth** Salvation is guaranteed based on our union with Christ.
2:12a	If we endure, We shall also reign with Him.	Y-1	**B Truth** Reward is promised for those who endure hardship.
2:12b	If we deny Him, He also will deny us.	Y-2	**B Truth** Denial of reward is threatened for those who deny Christ.
2:13	If we are faithless, He remains faithful; He cannot deny Himself.	X-2	**A Truth** Salvation is guaranteed based on God's faithfulness to His promise that we will live with Him.

This passage is a comforting affirmation of our eternal salvation that cannot be lost and a sobering threat that rewards can be denied. God's disposition toward Israel illustrates this truth. Though Israel now rejects Christ and is under God's discipline, they will one day be restored because God is faithful to the promises He made to their patriarchs (Rom. 3:3-4; 11:25-32). His gifts are irrevocable (Rom. 11:29). So it is also for us Christians today. Even if we stop believing or become unfaithful, God will be faithful to His promise to save us eternally, though He may deny us the reward of reigning with Him.

Keeping the faith. 2 Timothy 4:7-8

> [7] I have fought the good fight, I have finished the race, I have kept the faith. [8] Finally, there is laid up for me the crown of righteousness, which the Lord, the righteous Judge, will give to me on that Day, and not to me only but also to all who have loved His appearing.

A Truth Interpretation: By perseverance in faith and loving the Lord's appearing, Paul expects God's righteousness for salvation at the final judgment.

B Truth Interpretation: By perseverance in faith and loving the Lord's appearing, Paul expects a reward at the Judgment Seat of Christ.

Those who teach that someone must persevere in faith and good works until the end of life would use this passage to say that Paul stayed faithful and thus he expects to be considered righteous by the Lord when he enters eternity (A Truth). That Paul persevered in faith and good works is not in question. But did that earn him salvation? That understanding assumes the "crown of righteousness" is the judicial righteousness granted at justification (Rom. 3:21-24; 2 Cor. 5:21). In total, this passage would then teach that eternal salvation comes by fighting for the faith, finishing one's ministry faithfully, staying faithful to Christian doctrine, and looking forward lovingly to Christ's appearing. This is in total contradiction to Paul's teaching that righteousness is through faith alone in Jesus Christ alone (Rom. 3:21-24; Gal. 2:16). We must interpret the less clear passage of 2 Timothy 4 in light of the very clear teaching in Romans and Galatians.

The context nowhere indicates Paul is speaking of earning salvation. Elsewhere, he repudiated good works, even his own, as a basis for obtaining eternal salvation (Eph. 2:8-9; Phil. 3:3-9). Here, he is simply summarizing his ministry knowing that his life is nearly over (v. 6). The crown of righteousness is not judicial righteousness. He had earlier spoken of a crown earned by an athlete who competes according to the rules (2:5). This was spoken as an exhortation for Timothy to be strong in Christ (2:1-3). A crown is an earned reward, the reward that Paul anticipated if he disciplined his body and was not disqualified (1 Cor. 9:25-27). James 1:12 speaks of a "crown of life" given to those Christians who endure suffering faithfully. Church elders who rule faithfully will receive the "crown of glory" (1 Pet. 5:4). Crowns are B Truth rewards given to believers. It is not always clear what these crowns represent, but it is clear that they are rewards for faithful believers.

Paul's example of persevering faithful ministry should inspire us to do the same and anticipate the same rewards. The ministry is not a skirmish but a fifteen-round prize fight, not a sprint but a marathon. Are you serving God with a long view? We may not know the details of our rewards, but it will all be worth it.

The Epistle to the Hebrews

THE BOOK OF Hebrews deserves some introductory comments about its interpretation that will apply to the passages discussed below. These passages, which many find difficult to interpret, sort themselves out quickly once we understand who the author is addressing, why he has written them, and the nature of the judgments threatened in the five warning passages (2:1-4; 3:7-4:13; 6:1-8; 10:26-39; 12:25-29). Essentially, what we must determine in interpreting Hebrews is whether it is written to unbelievers as A Truth, to believers as B Truth, or to a mixed group of both.

Were it not for the severe language and threats of the warning passages, it would be readily apparent that Hebrews was written to believers in Christ. Outside the warnings, the readers are called "brethren" (3:1; 10:19; 13:22). Various things said to them can only be applied to Christians (3:1; 6:9; 5:12; 10:24-25), especially the exhortations of chapter 13. If taken for the whole epistle, as it should, the author explains that the purpose of his writing to his "brethren" is to exhort them (13:22).

The Readers' Spiritual State

When we consider who is addressed in the warning passages, we observe that there is never any transition that shows the author is addressing a different group (i.e., unbelievers) from among the larger readership. If anything, close examination of the author's language *in the warnings* confirms that those addressed are Christians.

- He identifies with them as believers using the first person plural. (2:13; 3:14; 4:1-3, 11; 6:1, 3; 10:26, 30, 39; 12:28)
- They also are called "brethren." (3:12)

- The author says they have believed (4:3) or are believing. (10:39)

- They have Christian confidence or assurance of the benefits of Christ's provisions and are told to hold fast and endure in that confidence. (3:14; 4:14; 10:23, 35)

- Though they have not, they are in danger of falling away from their faith, which assumes the point of departure is their experience of salvation in Christ. (2:1; 3:12; 6:6; 10:39; 12:25)

- They are encouraged to enter into God's rest (4:11) and go on to maturity (6:1), both privileges of believers only.

- They suffered for their faith after they were "illuminated." (10:32-34)

- No one is ever told to believe in Christ as Savior, a serious omission if this is written to unbelievers.

- Their experience of the blessings that go with salvation is described in explicitly Christian terms. (6:4-5; 10:26, 29-30, 32, 38)

- Old Testament examples of God chastening His people are applied to the readers as God's people. (3:16; 10:30)

- They are exhorted to serve God with reverence (12:28), which would only apply to believers.

- The promises of various rewards to the readers for faithful perseverance and obedience apply to believers only. (3:14; 4:9, 11; 10:34-35; 12:28)

The inevitable and obvious conclusion about the readers in Hebrews is that they are believers.

The Author's Purpose

A second interpretive key to Hebrews is to understand the author's purpose for writing. In other words, what is he trying to accomplish with his readers? Besides the warnings, we notice an elaboration of the superiority of Jesus Christ and the New Covenant over Moses, the priesthood, and the Old Covenant of Mosaic Law. Taken together with the warnings, we conclude that the readers had stopped progressing in their Christian faith and were contemplating a return to Judaism (2:1; 3:12; 6:6; 10:39; 12:25), perhaps to escape persecution (10:32-34; 12:4). The author is showing them the superiority of Christ, the weakness of the Mosaic system, and the consequences that await them should they forsake their Christian faith and go back under the Law. There is also a positive purpose; the author encourages them to hold fast and keep progressing in their Christian faith and maturity (3:6; 4:14; 5:11-6:1, 11-12; 10:23; 12:1-3) so that they can enjoy the fullness of their destiny in this life and in the kingdom (see the discussion on Hebrews 3:18-19).

The Nature of the Warnings' Threats

The third interpretive key is the nature of the threats in the warnings. Severe consequences are threatened, but does that mean they refer to the threat of hell? The mere mention of fire is enough for many to conclude that hell is in view. Keeping in mind a Christian readership, we make these observations about the Bible's use of fire:

- Fire is an expression of God's wrath that disciplines His people in the Old Testament. (Num. 11:1-3; Isa. 9:19; Jer. 11:16; Lam. 2:3-4; Exod. 22:20-22; Amos 2:5; Ps. 78:21)

- Fire is an aspect of the Judgment Seat of Christ for believers in the New Testament. (1 Cor. 3:13-15)

- Fire can also signify God's cleansing (Ps. 66:12; Mal. 3:2; 1 Pet. 1:7) or jealousy. (Deut. 4:24; Ps. 79:5; Zeph. 1:18)

- Hell, eternal fire, eternal torment, and Gehenna are never mentioned in the warnings of Hebrews.

The absence of any explicit threat of hellfire in Hebrews does not diminish the seriousness of the judgments threatened in the warning passages to believers. They remain a "fearful expectation of judgment" and express the "fiery indignation" of God.

The saved status of the readers, the author's purpose of motivating the readers to press on in their faith, and the possibility of a severe judgment for God's disobedient people lead us to interpret the book of Hebrews as B Truth pertaining to Christians. Though A Truth is present in the reminders of their initial salvation, the exhortations, warnings, and applications are B Truths. With this perspective, we discuss some particular passages that are often misunderstood.

How shall we escape? Hebrews 2:1-4

> [1] *Therefore we must give the more earnest heed to the things we have heard, lest we drift away.* [2] *For if the word spoken through angels proved steadfast, and every transgression and disobedience received a just reward,* [3] *how shall we escape if we neglect so great a salvation, which at the first began to be spoken by the Lord, and was confirmed to us by those who heard Him,* [4] *God also bearing witness both with signs and wonders, with various miracles, and gifts of the Holy Spirit, according to His own will?*

A Truth Interpretation: Those who depart from the faith or from professing the faith will not escape the judgment of hell.

B Truth Interpretation: Those who depart from the faith will not escape God's disciplinary judgment.

Escape what? That is the key question. Hell is not mentioned. In fact, no specific judgment is mentioned, which serves to make this threat all the more ominous, as when a parent tells a child, "You don't want to find out what I will do if you disobey me!"

The author includes himself with his use of "we" showing that this is B Truth. The warning is against drifting away from something. One cannot drift away from something he was not once associated with, so this must refer to the Christian faith which they had heard (v. 1) and which was so well attested to by the Lord, confirmed by the apostles (v. 3), and authenticated by the miraculous (v. 4). The nature of this sin is expanded in the other warning passages.

Christians who neglect their faith or turn away from it will not escape God's disciplinary judgment. We should be diligent to progress and grow in our Christian faith.

Entering His rest. Hebrews 3:18-19

> [18] *And to whom did He swear that they would not enter His rest, but to those who did not obey?* [19] *So we see that they could not enter in because of unbelief.*

A Truth Interpretation: Those who disobey do not believe and do not hold fast to their confession of faith in Christ, so they will not go to heaven.

B Truth Interpretation: Those who disobey do not believe and do not hold fast to their confession of faith in Christ, so they will not experience God's reward of rest.

In the description of the Israelites' rebellion against God in the wilderness and their failure to enter the Promised Land in Hebrews 3, disobedience in 3:18 seems to be used synonymously with unbelief in 3:19. This unbelief is equated with the readers not holding fast their confidence in Christ (3:12, 14) and departing from the living God (3:12), and is what kept the Israelites from entering into their promised "rest" (4:6). Put all together, some have come to the conclusion that faith is obedience, and that rest (which they interpret here as the Promised Land) is heaven or the kingdom of God. Thus, those who do not obey Christ will not be saved—an A Truth.

Clearly, there is a close relationship between unbelief and disobedience, and faith and obedience. The relationship is one of cause and effect, but that does not make unbelief and disobedience or faith and obedience the same thing. Disobedience is evidence of unbelief and obedience is evidence of belief. In this account, unbelief is described as disobedience because when the Israelites' did not believe God's promise concerning the Promised Land, they consequently refused to obey His command to possess it.

But since the readers are believers (3:1, 12, and the use of "we" in 3:6, 14, 19), the conditional and still future experience of rest is not salvation from hell. Rest can refer to the experience of blessings by faithful believers today (4:1, 6, 9, 11), but also to the experience of kingdom rest in the millennium. For the Israelites, rest was not just entering the Land, but enjoying the benefits of it, such as a cessation of strife with their enemies (Josh. 11:23; Judg. 3:11, 30; 5:31). So believers who live by faith and persevere in their Christian faith enjoy peace as they rest in the promises, provisions, and power of God. This is a blessing that can be forfeited now and in the kingdom by disobedience born of unbelief, unbelief in the superiority of Christ over Judaism, and His promise of future blessings in the kingdom.

The future aspect of the believers' rest is a major theme of Hebrews. The author is concerned with their experience in the kingdom, not their entrance. He is writing to saved people whom he calls "partakers" (*metachoi*, 3:1). We first see the word used in 1:9 in a quote from Psalm 45:7, but translated "companions" (NKJV). The point from the Psalm is that the Son of God will rule in His kingdom with his "companions." Angels will not have this privilege, but will minister to these companions "who will inherit salvation" (1:13-14; 2:5). The future tense "will inherit" does not refer to their past justification, but their future reward in the kingdom. After chapter 2 introduces Christ's high priesthood, chapter 3 explains that He is a priest over His "house" like Moses was a priest over the tabernacle (3:2-5; cf. Num. 12:7). Christ's house is sometimes misunderstood as the church or the body of Christ, but the condition for being in Christ's house is not faith in Him as Savior; it is holding fast to their faith (3:6; 14). The word "companions" is used for those who are faithful to the end of their lives (3:14) and will inherit the reward of sharing in Christ's dominion over the world (6:12, 17; cf. 2 Tim. 2:12). This is important because the discussion of this role leads up to the discussion of rest. To enter into one's future rest is dependent on the believer's performance, that is, holding fast to their profession of faith (not turning back to Judaism). This is B Truth.

The B Truth interpretation leaves us with a sobering application. We must hold fast to our hope in Christ lest we lose the blessings of God's rest in this life and the reward of His rest in the kingdom. It would be the worst kind of unbelief and disobedience to turn aside from Christ to something else, because no other religion, person, or system can give us these blessings.

Salvation to all who obey. Hebrews 5:9

And having been perfected, He became the author of eternal salvation to all who obey Him.

A Truth Interpretation: Obedience brings the unbeliever Christ's eternal salvation.

B Truth Interpretation: Living obediently brings the believer all the benefits of Christ's salvation in this life and in the future.

In the context immediately preceding this passage, the readers are told that Jesus Christ obtained His office of High Priest through His obedience (4:15; 5:7-8), which also qualified him to be the "author" (*aitios*, or *cause, source*) of salvation to others who are obedient. Thus in the same way, Christians obtain their blessings through obedience. The salvation in view here is not justification (nor is it used clearly in the sense of justification in its other uses in Hebrews: 1:14; 2:3, 10; 6:9; 9:28; 11:7), but looks forward to their future experience of living in the blessings of the kingdom. The obedient act of initially believing in Christ is the first act of obedience that places sinners under the benefits of Christ's priestly sacrifice and ministry. But it is by continued obedience that believers avail themselves of the benefits of His High Priestly ministry, a privilege that can be forfeited (unlike salvation from hell).

That this does not refer to salvation from hell is also apparent from the use of the present tense of "obey," not the past tense "obeyed." It is not continual obedience that saves one from hell; it is the initial obedience of believing in Jesus Christ as Savior. Again, the concept of salvation in Hebrews has a distinct sense of not only a final deliverance from hell, but a present and future aspect (1:14; 9:28). Continual obedience allows the Christian to enjoy the present aspects of salvation relating to the believer's rest (4:1, 3, 6, 9-11) and the benefits of Christ's priestly ministry (4:14-16; chs. 7-10), as well as the future aspect as something to inherit in the kingdom (1:14; 6:12, 17; 7:25; 9:15, 28; 12:28). Since the argument of the book is concerned with keeping Christians from falling away and keeping them in the full benefits of Christ's ministry, obedience for salvation is used in the sense of B Truth for believers.

We who are Christians should rest in the fact that Christ's present priestly ministry provides us all the benefits of deliverance from sin, confidence in drawing near to God, and an inheritance in the kingdom of God if we live obediently.

If they fall away. Hebrews 6:1-10

[1] *Therefore, leaving the discussion of the elementary principles of Christ, let us go on to perfection, not laying again the foundation of repentance from dead works and of faith toward God,* [2] *of the doctrine of baptisms, of laying on of hands, of resurrection of the dead, and of eternal judgment.* [3] *And this we will do if God permits.* [4] *For it is impossible for those who were once enlightened, and have tasted the heavenly gift, and have become partakers of the Holy Spirit,* [5] *and have tasted the good word of God and the powers of the age to come,* [6] *if they fall away, to renew them again to repentance, since they crucify again for themselves the Son of God, and put Him to an open shame.* [7] *For the earth which drinks in the rain that often comes upon it, and*

bears herbs useful for those by whom it is cultivated, receives blessing from God; [8] *but if it bears thorns and briers, it is rejected and near to being cursed, whose end is to be burned.* [9] *But, beloved, we are confident of better things concerning you, yes, things that accompany salvation, though we speak in this manner.* [10] *For God is not unjust to forget your work and labor of love which you have shown toward His name, in that you have ministered to the saints, and do minister.*

A Truth Interpretation: Those who depart from the Christian faith either lose their salvation or prove they were never really saved and go to hell.

B Truth Interpretation: Those who depart from the Christian faith have no other plea before God and will be disciplined severely.

We have already asserted that those addressed in the warning passages are believers. The careful description of these readers in the immediate context demands this conclusion (vv. 4-5). Some would argue for an A Truth interpretation of this passage, but their arguments vary. Some claim that falling away only proves that the apostates were never saved to begin with, but that is untenable in view of the descriptions in 6:4-5. Others say that this passage speaks of believers who lose their salvation. Believers cannot lose their salvation, but if that is being taught here, then verses 4 and 6 also teach that they can never be saved again. Neither is the author speaking hypothetically about the possibility of believers falling away from the faith, as some claim. In verse 6, the conditional statement is not treated as hypothetical in the original language. A similar word for falling away is seen in 4:11, which refers to the example of the sin of rebellion against the Lord that happened at Kadesh Barnea (cf. 3:12; Num. 14). Surely a comparison is intended.

What concerns the author of this warning is the spiritual progress of the readers, which he addresses in the passages that bracket the warning (5:12-14; 6:11-12). If they fall away from their faith in Christ, they will not advance in maturity or inherit the promises of rest and blessing in the present and future. Moreover, if they fall away from Christ by going back to the Mosaic Law, they have no other appeal before the Lord. They already repented of the "dead works" of the Mosaic system (6:1; cf. 9:14) and cannot do it again, because now they know better. In the past, they had rejected the Jewish sacrifices and accepted the eternal sacrifice of Jesus Christ. To go back and identify with Judaism is to publicly deny the benefits of Christ's sacrifice and even show implicit agreement that Christ deserved to die, thus, the statement in 6:6: "since they crucify again for themselves the Son of God, and put Him to an open shame." With such an attitude, it is impossible to bring them back to repentance. These believing readers could make a pivotal decision not to press forward but to deny the provision of Christ's sacrifice and thus forfeit the benefits of professing and growing in Christ. If they do, they cannot claim ignorance and start over. Again, this alludes to the pivotal incident at Kadesh Barnea mentioned in 3:7-19 in which those Israelites who decided to turn back were not allowed to enter the Promised Land, though they tried (cf. Num. 14). The author later uses Esau as an example of one who could not have another chance though he "sought it diligently with tears" (12:15-17).

The consequence for falling away is a negative judgment described in 6:7-8. If God cuts off the opportunity to press on (6:3), the believer will suffer severe consequences. A believer who turns back would be like scorched earth. The imagery of fire unnecessarily leads some to interpret this as hell, but we have already shown that fire is often used to picture God's judgment on His people. The believer is compared to the earth, which can bear either useful fruit or useless thorns; if useless thorns, the earth is "rejected" because of its uselessness (so the NKJV; but *adokimos* is better translated *not standing the test* and thus *unqualified, worthless*). It is also "near to being cursed," but is not actually cursed. According to common agricultural practice, earth that bears useless thorns is set on fire to burn the thorns so that the earth might become productive in the future. It is important to note that in the original language there is only one earth, not two, and it (the believer) is not burned, but the thorns (what the believer produces).

This B Truth interpretation yields a good exhortation and warning to Christians today. God wants us to faithfully press forward in our Christian faith. Though our eternal salvation is secure, there are severe consequences if we intentionally turn away from Him and do not go on to maturity. We will not only forfeit the progress we could have made, but face God's fiery chastisement intended to make us more useful in the future.

The willful sin. Hebrews 10:26-31

> [26] *For if we sin willfully after we have received the knowledge of the truth, there no longer remains a sacrifice for sins,* [27] *but a certain fearful expectation of judgment, and fiery indignation which will*

devour the adversaries. ²⁸ Anyone who has rejected Moses' law dies without mercy on the testimony of two or three witnesses. ²⁹ Of how much worse punishment, do you suppose, will he be thought worthy who has trampled the Son of God underfoot, counted the blood of the covenant by which he was sanctified a common thing, and insulted the Spirit of grace? ³⁰ For we know Him who said, "Vengeance is Mine, I will repay," says the Lord. And again, "The Lord will judge His people." ³¹ It is a fearful thing to fall into the hands of the living God.

A Truth Interpretation: Those who sin willfully cannot be forgiven and lose their salvation or prove they are not saved and will suffer in hell.

B Truth Interpretation: Those who sin willfully by departing from the Christian faith will be severely disciplined by God.

The immediate context reminds us again that this warning is written to Christians, among whom the author includes himself in verse 26. Interpreting the passage as B Truth is unavoidable. These readers "have received the knowledge of the truth" (v. 26), are sanctified (v. 29), know God and are "His people" (v. 30), "were illuminated" and suffered for their faith (v. 32), and have "an enduring possession" in heaven (v. 34).

What is the willful sin and its consequences? Since the Bible uniformly teaches that a person once saved cannot lose his or her salvation, the loss of salvation cannot be in view here. Besides, most sins are intentional or willful to some degree. However, the Bible recognizes some sins that are unintentional (Num. 15:22-29). Perhaps neglecting to pray for someone, like you promised, would be an example of an unintentional sin. But in most cases, the perpetrator knows that he or she is committing a sin.

Some interpret the willful sin as continual sin (e.g., NIV: "If we deliberately keep on sinning"), but this is reading too much into the present participle used for "to sin." The author of Hebrews apparently has a particular sin in mind, which becomes evident as we consult the context and remember previous passages. He had exhorted his readers previously to hold fast to their confession (3:6; 4:14) and has warned them about the dangers of not pressing on in their faith (6:1-8). He reinforces this concern in the verses just before this warning about the willful sin (10:23-25). The readers were on the verge of abandoning their confession of faith in Christ and returning to the Mosaic Law and its sacrifices.

Similar to 6:1-8, the willful sin would be a deliberate abandonment of their confession of the sufficiency of Christ's sacrifice for a return to insufficient Jewish sacrifices. The author had argued that "Christ was offered once to bear the sins of many" (9:28), that "by one offering, He has perfected forever those who are being sanctified" (10:14), and that once forgiven, "there is no longer an offering for sin" (10:18). The Law offered them nothing since it looked forward to the ultimate sacrifice of Jesus Christ (10:1-10). Should they turn back to the Law, Christ's perfect and eternal sacrifice would be sufficient to cover even that great and willful sin soteriologically, but they would still face a severe non-soteriological judgment. The author had just referred to an approaching "Day" (v. 25) implying that there will be an accounting, which we know is the Judgment Seat of Christ taught in so many other places in the New Testament (e.g. Rom. 14:10-12; 1 Cor. 3:11-15; 2 Cor. 5:10).

The background for understanding this passage is very likely Numbers 15:30-31. There we see that for certain serious (or presumptuous) sins, no sacrifices were stipulated. Therefore, those who committed those sins were "cut off" from their people (put to death). The author is saying that if the readers of Hebrews abandon the only sufficient sacrifice for their sins, they too will be judged severely. Turning back to Judaism and its sacrificial system would be tantamount to giving one's approval to the crucifixion of Jesus Christ, or trampling underfoot the Son of God, counting the blood of His covenant a common thing, and insulting the Spirit of grace (v. 29).

Again, we see that because the author uses strong language ("fearful expectation of judgment and fiery indignation") and speaks of a punishment worse than death (v. 30), many conclude he is threatening them with eternal hell fire. But because they are Christians who cannot lose their salvation and because he has in view the Judgment Seat of Christ, this cannot be. The exact judgment is not specified, only its severity.

The possibility of a negative assessment at the Judgment Seat of Christ is a fearful prospect for those who have not done good (cf. 2 Cor. 5:9-11). The "fiery indignation which will devour the adversaries" (literally "fiery zeal") refers to the zeal of God's judgment toward sin. Believers can experience the same *zeal* of judgment toward their sin as God's enemies experience toward theirs, though the results are different. As Hebrew Christians, the readers might also understand this as a warning about the impending national judgment of a fiery destruction of Jerusalem which occurred only a short time later (A.D. 70), something they would know about from Jesus' warnings (Matt. 23:27-24:2; Mark 13:1-2; Luke 21:5-6; cf. Acts 2:40). It is possible the readers could suffer both judgments.

The author speaks of a "worse punishment" than that under the Mosaic Law (v. 29). It is hard to imagine a judgment worse than death, but human experience does testify that there are occasions when death is more enticing than severe suffering (Jonah is an example; Jonah 4:3). The author is comparing this judgment to the death penalty for the presumptuous sin of Numbers 15:30-31, which was the severest penalty dictated at that time. But in light of New Testament revelation about the Judgment Seat of Christ, we know that a more severe judgment would be a negative assessment there because of the eternal implications.

In the end, these readers who would be judged are still "His people" (v. 30; a quote from Deut. 32:35-36). They will not fall into hell, but "into the hands of the living God" (v. 31). This warning is for God's children and therefore B Truth.

Some Christians think they have committed an unforgivable sin and have lost their salvation, or at least they worry that they might. But Jesus Christ died for all sins, even willful sins. There is no other refuge from sin's penalty than the sacrificial blood of Jesus Christ shed on behalf of undeserving sinners. This should be a warning to us also to look only to Jesus Christ for forgiveness because of His fully efficacious death and resurrection. We can add nothing to that, nor can we improve what He has accomplished. Should we deny or spurn this grace, we will be judged severely at the Judgment Seat of Christ. Nevertheless, there is comfort in the truth that where sin abounds, grace abounds even more (Rom. 5:20).

Holiness to see the Lord. Hebrews 12:14

Pursue peace with all people, and holiness, without which no one will see the Lord.

A Truth Interpretation: Those who do not live holy lives will not be saved.

B Truth Interpretation: Christians who do not live holy lives will not enjoy the intimate presence of God.

The word "holiness" is the same word sometimes translated sanctification (*hagiomos*), which has the meaning of "set apart" from one thing to something else. In this case, holiness denotes setting apart from sin unto God. This is not speaking of absolute holiness, just as the preceding admonition does not expect perfect peace with all people, but both are something to be pursued.

If this was A Truth, then the holiness demanded must be absolute, for nothing else would attain God's righteousness. Yet the admonition to pursue it with peace toward all makes it a process, not a one-time transaction. The A Truth view also assumes that "see the Lord" means enter into heaven or God's presence. Two immediate problems with this interpretation are the fact that the author is still addressing his readers as believers, and related to that, the context develops this exhortation to believers.

Chapter 12 sets us on the track of a B Truth interpretation by the progress of thought as the author encourages the readers as Christians:

- They are to run their race enduring opposition from sinners. (12:1-4)

- They should not be discouraged by God's chastening along the way because it shows that He loves them. (12:5-9)

- The purpose of God's chastening is that they might share in His holiness. (12:10-11)

- They should be encouraged to continue on God's path of holiness because it allows them to "see God." (12:12-14)

- On the other hand, they must not neglect their sanctification and become defiled. (12:15-17)

- They are reminded that they have come to the holiness of God revealed by the New Covenant, which is greater than the holiness revealed by the Old Covenant. (12:18-29)

At every turn, the author's exhortations only make sense for believers who should progress in their faith.

The term "see the Lord" therefore could not refer to entering heaven or God's presence. In addition to the physical sense of vision, the idea of seeing something can also mean to know it intimately. Most lexicons recognize that "see" (*horaō*) can refer to one's perception and experience of something (cf. Luke 3:6; John 6:36; 12:45; 14:9; 15:24; 3 John 11). The contrast with the Old Covenant in 12:18-29 reminds us that under Moses, no one could see the Lord (Exod. 33:20), but in Jesus Christ, we see the Father (John 1:18; 12:45; 14:9). It follows then that the more we grow in our knowledge and experience of Christ, the more we will see God until we see Him face to face in our glorification (1 Cor. 13:12; 1 John 3:2; Rev.

22:4). The prospect of a more intimate experience of God should motivate us all to pursue holiness.

A consuming fire. Hebrews 12:25-29

> [25] *See that you do not refuse Him who speaks. For if they did not escape who refused Him who spoke on earth, much more shall we not escape if we turn away from Him who speaks from heaven,* [26] *whose voice then shook the earth; but now He has promised, saying, "Yet once more I shake not only the earth, but also heaven." * [27] *Now this, "Yet once more," indicates the removal of those things that are being shaken, as of things that are made, that the things which cannot be shaken may remain.* [28] *Therefore, since we are receiving a kingdom which cannot be shaken, let us have grace, by which we may serve God acceptably with reverence and godly fear.* [29] *For our God is a consuming fire.*

A Truth Interpretation: Those who disobey God will not escape his punishment of hell.

B Truth Interpretation: Those who disobey God will not escape His severe discipline.

The author's use of "we," the assurance of "receiving a kingdom," and the exhortation to serve God indicate this is B Truth intended for believers in Christ. There is no escape from God's judgment for believers who refuse (from *paraiteomai*, to *refuse* or *reject*) what God has spoken as warnings to those who fall away, or as promises to those who persevere in faith.

That "our God is a consuming fire" (v. 29) is a motivation not to reject God's words, but to practice godly reverence in God's service, which was mentioned in the previous verse (v. 28). It is not meant to be a threat of hell, because verse 28 speaks confidently of the readers "receiving a kingdom" in the future. This metaphor of God as a consuming fire comes from Deuteronomy 4:24 where it speaks of God's jealousy.

Christians must take God's words seriously. As B Truth, Hebrews provides us with brilliant truth about the superiority of Jesus Christ and His work, exhortations to grow and persevere in faith, and warnings about neglecting or denying our faith. Our response determines our reward or our punishment.

The Epistles of James, Peter, John, and Jude

10

INTERPRETING THE VARIOUS passages from these four authors demands careful attention to their audiences and the respective purposes of each letter. Each author has a unique style to convey his distinct message in a particular setting. In general, we observe that these epistles are uniformly written to believers.

Sin brings death. James 1:15

Then, when desire has conceived, it gives birth to sin; and sin, when it is full-grown, brings forth death.

A Truth Interpretation: Sin results in a person going to hell.

B Truth Interpretation: Sin produces separation from God or physical death.

In this passage, James is explaining the process of temptation that results in sin and ultimately death. Is death a reference to hell, or some consequence experienced by the believer?

Clearly, the epistle consistently addresses believers. They are born from above (1:18), possess faith in Christ (2:1), and are called brethren (1:2, 19; 2:1, 14; 3:1; 4:11; 5:7,10, 12, 19). Indeed, verse 16 continues from verse 15 with the exhortation to "beloved brethren" to not be deceived by sinful temptations. With that in mind, it is easy to understand that in the context, there is a contrast intended with the blessed man in verse 12 who endures temptation and receives the "crown of life." If this crown refers to the eternal life procured in salvation, then it is awarded to those who endure temptation and love the Lord, a salvation that is earned. But nothing is said of faith in Jesus Christ as Savior, the condition for eternal life. Crowns are rewards; salvation is a gift. Therefore, "the crown of life" is best taken as a reward for those who earn it. While the exact nature of the crown is not specified, it could refer to a greater experience of God's life in the future.

In contrast to the blessed man in verse 12 is the one who allows his desires to succumb to temptation so that sin is born, grows, and "brings forth death" (1:13-15). This must be other than eternal condemnation because spiritual and eternal death were instantaneous consequences of the first sin of Adam, not the result of a process. Believers have been delivered forever from eternal death (John 5:24). The death of verse 15 could speak of the deadening effects of sin (as in Rom. 6:16, 23) or physical death (as in 1 Cor. 11:30 or Jas. 5:20). The two are related in that the sin which brings deadness to the Christian's experience also usually involves physically dangerous choices that lead to the deterioration of physical life and ultimately a premature death. Some Proverbs suggest the consequence of physical death for sin or foolishness (e.g., Prov. 10:27; 11:29). One could argue that experience shows us that many foolish and sinful Christians remain in the land of the living, but their status is as "the living dead;" they lack the fullness of God's life as they walk in darkness and deadness which puts them in danger of physical death.

Regardless of the exact nature of death as a consequence for sinning Christians, we would all agree it is something to avoid. Also a B Truth, James 1:21 tells Christians that they can save their lives (usually translated "souls," but *psychē* means *life*, as in 5:20) by forsaking evil conduct and humbly receiving God's Word.

Judgment without mercy. James 2:12-13

> [12] *So speak and so do as those who will be judged by the law of liberty.*
> [13] *For judgment is without mercy to the one who has shown no mercy. Mercy triumphs over judgment.*

A Truth Interpretation: Those who are not merciful will be judged and shown no mercy in hell.

B Truth Interpretation: Believers who are not merciful will not receive mercy at the Judgment Seat of Christ.

James continues his exhortations to his "brethren" (2:1) and "beloved brethren" (v. 5) with an exhortation to treat the poor among them without partiality (vv. 3-4, 9). The readers should show love (v. 8), which includes mercy extended to those who are poor (v. 13). If the readers do not show mercy, they will face God's judgment without mercy. The severity of such a judgment leads some to conclude that James is threatening the merciless with the judgment of hell, an A Truth interpretation.

The problem with making eternal salvation the issue here is not only the context addressed to believers, but the implication that salvation is earned or deserved by showing mercy to others. That these merciless believers face judgment is not questioned, but *which* judgment does James speak of? We have noted in previous discussion that there are two judgments, one for unbelievers called the Great White Throne Judgment, and one for believers called the Judgment Seat of Christ. The latter must be in view, just as it is when James mentions it again in an explicitly Christian context written to "brethren" and "teachers" in 3:1.

Since the Judgment Seat of Christ is an evaluation of believers' works, not their salvation, this fits perfectly. At the Judgment Seat of Christ, leniency will be shown to those who have been lenient (or merciful) to others, and severity will be shown to those who have been merciless with others.

All Christians should take the significance of this B Truth to heart. We must treat all of God's people equally regardless of sex, color, race, economic status, or church denomination. Furthermore, we should be willing to show mercy to those who need our help or compassion. The Lord is watching and will bring us to account for how we treat others.

Faith without works is dead. James 2:14-26

[14] *What does it profit, my brethren, if someone says he has faith but does not have works? Can faith save him?* [15] *If a brother or sister is naked and destitute of daily food,* [16] *and one of you says to them, "Depart in peace, be warmed and filled," but you do not give them the things which are needed for the body, what does it profit?* [17] *Thus also faith by itself, if it does not have works, is dead.* [18] *But someone will say, "You have faith, and I have works." Show me your faith without your works, and I will show you my faith by my works.* [19] *You believe that there is one God. You do well. Even the demons believe— and tremble!* [20] *But do you want to know, O foolish man, that faith*

without works is dead? [21] *Was not Abraham our father justified by works when he offered Isaac his son on the altar?* [22] *Do you see that faith was working together with his works, and by works faith was made perfect?* [23] *And the Scripture was fulfilled which says, "Abraham believed God, and it was accounted to him for righteousness." And he was called the friend of God.* [24] *You see then that a man is justified by works, and not by faith only.* [25] *Likewise, was not Rahab the harlot also justified by works when she received the messengers and sent them out another way?* [26] *For as the body without the spirit is dead, so faith without works is dead also.*

A Truth Interpretation: If someone says he is a Christian but has no works, he was never saved.

B Truth Interpretation: If someone says he has faith but has no works, he will not be saved from a negative judgment at the Judgment Seat of Christ.

This passage is probably one of the most misused passages in the New Testament. It has a long history of interpretation attempting to resolve the tension it seems to create with the apostle Paul's teaching about justification through faith alone. The conflict is simply this: Paul said in many places, especially in Romans and Galatians, that justification is through faith alone in Jesus Christ. Paul is unequivocal in his teaching that salvation is by grace, "not by works" (Eph. 2:8-9). He also contrasts believing with working, and grace with works (Rom. 4:4-5; 11:6). But James says that "faith by itself, if it does not have works is, dead" (2:17) and "a man is justified by works, and not by faith only" (v. 24). In short, they say, if there are not demonstrable works, a person should be judged unsaved. This traditional interpretation fits in the category of A Truth.

Of course, one of the problems with this view is that rarely, if ever, is good "works" defined. So there is a great assumption that we know what a good work is, can identify it, and can measure it to a standard of approval. As we all know, even those who are not Christians and those who contradict Christianity can do works that look good. Works can also be relative to a person's background and personality. We all progress in our growth and godliness at different rates. Another problem usually ignored is that no one ever seems to declare how many good works are necessary to prove salvation. The works that James specifically addresses in 2:14-26 involve showing mercy to those who are poor or disadvantaged, which was his previous discussion (vv. 1-13).

As much trouble as this passage has caused commentators and interpreters through the centuries, can I be so bold as to suggest the problem is resolved rather simply by observing the author's purpose and the context of his statements about faith and works? The choice between A Truth and B Truth interpretations quickly becomes apparent.

As we often should, we begin by observing who the readers of the epistle are. In the previous discussions of 1:15 and 2:12-13 above, we established that the readers are definitely Christians. This carries into our passage when James again addresses his readers as "my brethren" in 2:1 and 2:14. In 2:1, James reminds the readers that they "hold the faith of our Lord Jesus Christ, the Lord of Glory."

Another key is from the larger context. As James addresses his "beloved brethren" in 1:19-20, he intends to help his readers produce God's practical righteousness in their lives by addressing their hearing (obedience), their speaking, and their control over anger. Most have observed that these key verses give us an outline of the book. James is writing to help his Christian readers live righteous lives, and that involves obeying God's Word.

We might insert a side note here about the different approaches taken by the apostle Paul and James. Paul also writes to help his readers live righteous lives, but he argues differently from James. Paul argues from the gospel of grace and its results. With him, justification is through faith without works, but it results in a new position and power with God that allows the Christian to overcome sin. Works and righteous living for Paul are the way we can live to show our gratitude for God's grace (Rom. 12:1-2). James, however, argues from practical and eschatological motivations—who is helped, and what are the ramifications for the future judgment of the readers?

Future judgment is often overlooked in this passage, but 2:14-26 is bracketed by two bookends that speak of this judgment. We have already considered one in 2:13 and conclude that it speaks of the Judgment Seat of Christ. The other, in 3:1, warns of a "stricter judgment" for those who teach God's Word. Can this be anything other than a judgment for Christians who teach God's Word carelessly? Paul even classifies himself among these teachers with the familiar "we." What judgment does Paul speak of that could include him and others from the readers who teach God's Word? It can only be the Judgment Seat of Christ.

These observations tilt the passage strongly toward a B Truth interpretation and away from the traditional A Truth interpretation. Rather than offer a lengthy explanation of the entire passage, it will serve us well to simply make some pertinent points that reinforce the B Truth perspective.

First, the Judgment Seat of Christ looming in the background of this section helps understand the nature of the salvation James speaks of in verse 14, "Can faith save him?" Save from what? To import hell here is unnatural and fits nowhere in the argument. Some might point to the unsaved status of demons who believe (v. 19) and Abraham and Rahab's justification (vv. 21, 24-25). These will be discussed later. We know that the word *save* means to be delivered from some undesirable fate and is often used apart from the idea of eternal salvation from hell. James uses the word in 1:21, 5:15, and 5:20 for deliverance from an undesirable fate for Christians (spiritual deadness or physical death; see the discussion of Jas. 1:15). Based on the context of 2:14-26, salvation must be deliverance from an undesirable fate at the Judgment Seat of Christ. If the readers do not show mercy to those in need, there is no "profit" (v. 16)—the needy are not helped and the readers would be judged without mercy at the *bema* (2:13).

Another issue to resolve is the meaning of "dead" in verses 17 and 26. The traditional A Truth interpretation insists on the meaning *non-existent*. In other words, those who do not show mercy are not saved and never were. In their view, dead faith is no faith at all. The greater context, however, leads us to another understanding of *dead* in relation to faith. James is not concerned with the reality of his readers' faith, but the quality (1:3, 6; 2:1; 5:15) and usefulness (1:12, 26; 2:14, 16, 20) of their faith. James is not saying faith will manifest itself in works, but that without works, faith is useless or unprofitable in this life and the next. James' main concern is that his readers become "doers of the word" (1:22) which is the same as being a "doer of the work" who will "be blessed in what he does" (1:25). For example, faith that perseveres in trials earns a reward from God (1:3-12), and faith that is merciful to others receives God's mercy at the Judgment Seat of Christ (2:8-13). But faith that does not work is *useless* towards these blessings and *useless* in helping others (1:26; 2:20 use "useless" in NASB and some other versions). The word "dead" should therefore be understood as *useless* or *unprofitable* rather than *non-existent*. It is used this way in everyday speech: the battery is dead; the body is dead; the project is dead. What we mean is not that these things do not exist, but that they are not vitalized so as to be useful.

In 2:19, the faith of demons also shows the uselessness of faith without works. This verse is not about eternal salvation, because demons cannot be saved. Their fate and condemnation is sealed (Matt. 8:29; 25:41; Jude 6), which is why they tremble when they think of God. Besides, their faith is in monotheism, not Jesus Christ. The point of their mention is that since they only tremble, they do not do any good works to alleviate a fearful judgment. Their faith is useless to them, but still it exists; it is a real faith. This passage is so often misused it deserves a discussion of its own, but that cannot take place apart from the context. The A Truth interpretation of this verse is used to argue that people cannot be saved by faith alone; works have to be demonstrated. The problems with that view should now be obvious: Verse 19 speaks of demons not humans, and of faith in one God not faith in Jesus Christ.

Those who hold the A Truth view of 2:14-26 interpret James' use of justification in the same soteriological sense as the apostle Paul. However, closer examination shows that when James speaks of being "justified by works" (vv. 21, 24, 25), he is not speaking of the imputed justification which saves us eternally as Paul uses the term (Rom. 3:24; 4:5). This indeed would be a contradiction in the Bible. James is speaking of a *vindication* before others. Paul even recognizes such a use of the word *justify* in Romans 4:2, where he suggests that Abraham could be justified by works before men but not before God. There are two kinds of justification in the Bible. One concerns practical righteousness that vindicates us before people; the other concerns judicial righteousness that vindicates us before God. James obviously uses the practical sense because Abraham was judicially justified in Genesis 15:6 (2:23) before he offered Isaac in Genesis 22 (2:21).

His vindication by others is seen when they call him "the friend of God" (v. 23). Thus Abraham's faith was "made perfect" or mature by this demonstration of his faith (v. 22), as also was Rahab's (v. 25).

In 2:26, James is not saying that faith invigorates works, but that works invigorate faith. It is works which make faith useful, just as the spirit makes the body useful. The issue is not whether faith exists in a person, but how faith becomes profitable or useful to a Christian.

This passage in James is written to Christians to encourage them to do good works, which will make their faith mature and profitable to them and to others. There is no contradiction between James and Paul. In Romans 3-5, Paul is discussing how to obtain a new life in Christ. In James, James is discussing how to make that new life profitable. If this passage is taken to mean that one must demonstrate a "real" salvation through works, then works unavoidably becomes necessary for salvation—a contradiction of Ephesians 2:8-9. Also, there are no criteria mentioned for exactly what kind or how much work verifies salvation. This opens the door to subjectivism and undermines the objective basis of assurance—the promise of God's Word that all who believe in Jesus Christ and *His* work will be saved.

It is interesting how many evangelical Christians go quickly to this passage to judge the salvation of others or to pressure people into righteous behavior when the major cults like Jehovah's Witnesses and Mormons do the same. I am not implying guilt by association, but simply showing that demanding works for salvation negates the grace that distinguishes biblical Christianity from all other religions, cults, and "isms."

We cannot produce the kind of good works that honor God by pressuring people with fear or guilt about the legitimacy of their salvation. Good works must come from higher motives which are a response to the amazing undeserved grace that saves us. When we do such works, we make our faith useful to others and to our final evaluation at the Judgment Seat of Christ. James intended this B Truth to produce genuine righteousness in believers, not prove their salvation.

Lest you be condemned. James 5:9

Do not grumble against one another, brethren, lest you be condemned. Behold, the Judge is standing at the door!

A Truth Interpretation: Those who grumble against others will be condemned to hell.

B Truth Interpretation: Those who grumble against others will be judged negatively at the Judgment Seat of Christ.

The sense of this passage is similar to 2:12-13 in that James' readers are threatened with a judgment. He calls them "brethren" in 5:7 and 10, which indicates a B Truth perspective. There is an emphasis here on the immanency of this judgment because "the Judge is standing at the door."

This passage differs from 2:12-13 because the judgment is for grumbling against others, not mercilessness toward others. What may lead some to prefer an A Truth interpretation is James' threat that they could be "condemned." The word used in the Greek manuscripts behind the NKJV (*katakrinō*) means *to condemn* or *pass a negative judgment*, but this does not necessarily refer to the condemnation of hell. Another translation, "be judged," is found in the ESV, NASB, NET Bible, and NIV based on their translation of the word *krinō* used in different Greek manuscripts. With either reading, it is clear that this word is used in the context of the Judgment Seat of Christ, the only judgment that Christians face (cf. Rom. 14:10-13; 1 Cor. 4:5; Jas. 2:12).

If grumbling against others sends people to hell, then we are all in bad shape. Grumbling is a serious sin and Christians who do so face a serious judgment.

Save a life from death. James 5:19-20

[19] *Brethren, if anyone among you wanders from the truth, and someone turns him back,* [20] *let him know that he who turns a sinner from the error of his way will save a soul from death and cover a multitude of sins.*

A Truth Interpretation: Sinners who turn back to the truth will be saved from eternal death.

B Truth Interpretation: Sinning Christians who turn back to the truth will be saved from either physical death or broken fellowship with God.

One implication of the A Truth interpretation is that an unsaved person who is open to the truth of the gospel can turn away from it before he believes and be eternally condemned. Another implication of the A Truth interpretation is that a believer can "wander from the truth" (be in sin), yet reach a point where that sin condemns him to hell. Of course, this raises the question: On what point on the path of sin is salvation lost so that condemnation results? This is a problem in itself, which always accompanies the view that salvation can be lost.

The passage addresses "Brethren" about a potential problem within their ranks—"anyone among you." The fact that this person "wanders from the truth" shows that he originated in the truth. Thus, "sinner" evidently refers to one of their own who is living in disobedience in some area of life and is in danger of going deeper. The task of a concerned brother in the faith is to turn him around so that his "soul" will be saved from "death." While *death* can sometimes refer to the spiritual deadness that comes from breaking fellowship with God, the mention of "life" (a better translation for

psychē than "soul" used here; see the HCSB; the NIV uses "him.") allows for
the consequence of physical death. It is possible that James is using death
the same as in 1:15: "and sin, when it is full-grown, brings forth death" (thus
forming bookends, an inclusio). In our discussion of 1:15, we suggested
that James could be referring to sin which brings not only deadness to
the Christian's experience, but also usually involves physically dangerous
behavior that leads to the deterioration of physical life and ultimately
premature death.

Those who read eternal salvation into the word "save" in verse 20 create
a problem—salvation would be achieved on a performance basis, by not
wandering from the truth or by ceasing to sin and returning to the truth.
That is not what the Bible teaches about salvation by grace through faith.

Though the B Truth interpretation would say a sinning believer is not in
danger of hell, that does not negate the seriousness of his sin. It deadens his
fellowship with God and can lead to a premature death. One who is diverted
from that path of disobedience will live and will avoid a "multitude of sins"
that would further damage him and others.

The responsibility for "saving" a sinning Christian belongs to us who see
this person heading down a dead-end path. Certainly, the previous context
in 5:3-18 implies that prayer is an essential part of our responsibility (cf.
1 John 5:16). Finally, we should observe that James speaks about "anyone
among you" which implies that none of us is immune from this serious
error. As we keep watch over those in the body of Christ, let us also keep
watch over our own lives.

Salvation of your souls. 1 Peter 1:9

receiving the end of your faith—the salvation of your souls.

A Truth Interpretation: Only those people who persevere in faith to
the end of their lives will prove to be saved eternally.

B Truth Interpretation: Believers who persevere in their faith will
experience the richness of their blessings in Christ.

It is easy to establish the spiritual status of Peter's readers. They are
"pilgrims" (1:1), "elect" (1:2), "begotten . . . to a living hope" (1:3), and have
an inheritance "reserved in heaven" (1:4). They are "kept by the power of

God" (1:5), and in this they "greatly rejoice" (1:6). As believers, they are experiencing many trials (1:6) which is testing their faith for a future reward "at the revelation of Jesus Christ," a reference to the Judgment Seat of Christ where their faithfulness will be evaluated (1:7). They love the Lord Jesus Christ and are rejoicing in Him (1:8). Can this be interpreted in any other way than an encouragement to Christians—a B Truth?

Verse 9 then states a reality of their present experience of faithfulness— "the salvation of your souls." Given the state of the readers, it is impossible to see this phrase as an offer of justification salvation in return for their faithfulness. As noted in Chapter 4, *salvation* can be used in a variety of ways and the word "soul" (from *psychē*) is best translated "life." The phrase "salvation of [the] soul" does not refer to salvation from hell in its other uses in the New Testament (see the discussions on Matt. 10:39; 16:25-26 and Jas. 1:21 and 5:20). Peter is most likely recalling Jesus' use of the phrase (in Matt 16:25-26; cf. 10:34) when He expressed the fullness of the experience of God's life in the present as a reward for making the sacrifices of discipleship.

The salvation of which Peter speaks is a present reality and a future prospect. Future salvation is the focus of verses 3-5 where it is linked to "an inheritance incorruptible and undefiled" (v. 4). This refers to the blessings of God's rewards for faithfulness in trials which are bestowed at the "revelation of Jesus Christ" (v. 7, a reference to the Judgment Seat of Christ) and enjoyed in the kingdom. While the readers rejoice in that prospect, they can also enjoy in their present lives the richness of God's blessings ("now" in v. 8). The phrase "receiving the end of your faith" uses a verb (*komizō, to receive*) that is often used for believers who receive a reward or recompense (cf. Heb. 10:36; 2 Cor. 5:10; Col 3:25; 1 Pet. 5:4). Since ongoing faithfulness in trials is in view, "faith" is not the justifying faith of unbelievers, but the sanctifying faith of believers. Peter is not speaking of the readers' faith that saves them from hell, but their faith that saves them from failing in trials (v. 6), from a poor evaluation at the Judgment Seat of Christ (vv. 7, 17), and from an ungodly life (vv. 14-16). This meaning of their present *salvation* is reinforced in verse 22 where Peter uses the word "souls" (again, from *psychē*, or *life*) when speaking of their purity produced by the Spirit through their obedience and love for others. Putting this in its positive aspect, we would say the readers are saved to a sanctified life.

The future aspect of this salvation is in focus in verse 10 when Peter mentions that the prophets inquired about it. They saw it as "grace that would come to you." We should compare this to verse 13 which speaks of the grace that will be brought to them at "the revelation of Jesus Christ," a reference to Christ's coming in the Rapture of the church and the Judgment Seat of Christ that follows. As they live obediently, the readers will enjoy present blessings of their salvation experience; and as they live hopefully, they will enjoy richer blessings in their eternal experience (v. 13). The future blessings are referred to as "grace that would come" because the bestowal of kingdom blessings ultimately depends on God's prerogative and promise. The mention of "the sufferings of Christ and the glories that would follow" in verse 11 mirrors the present and future experiences of the readers and would be an encouragement to those who are faithfully enduring suffering in the present.

The B Truth interpretation shows us that we who have been saved (justified) need to be saved from the evil of this present world (sanctified) and ultimately be delivered into our eternal reward in the future at the Judgment Seat of Christ (glorified and rewarded). But our experience in this life and the next depends on our faithfulness in a world full of suffering and sin. As we rest our hope in our future reward, we will be motivated to live faithfully and obediently.

Baptism saves us. 1 Peter 3:21

> *There is also an antitype which now saves us—baptism (not the removal of the filth of the flesh, but the answer of a good conscience toward God), through the resurrection of Jesus Christ.*

A Truth Interpretation: Water baptism saves unbelievers from hell.

B Truth Interpretation: Spirit baptism saves believers from a guilty conscience or from the Tribulation judgments.

Second B Truth Interpretation: Water baptism saves Jewish believers from temporal judgment.

This is a notoriously difficult passage to understand. It has been used as A Truth by those who believe in baptismal regeneration. That view can be dismissed on theological grounds and the interpretive principle that unclear passages (of which this is certainly one) should be interpreted in light of clear passages. Nothing could be clearer than the New Testament teaching that salvation is by grace through faith alone, not by anything we do. Besides, the phrase "now saves us" emphasizes the present experience of the readers.

One way of interpreting this passage as B Truth sees only Spirit baptism, not water baptism. It is noted that the phrase "not the removal of filth from the flesh" and the mention that the baptism is "through the resurrection of Jesus Christ" both exclude water. The context does mention the work of the Holy Spirit in resurrecting Jesus Christ (3:18). Romans 6:3-5 teaches that Spirit baptism unites us with Christ in His resurrection. This reminds also of 1 Corinthians 12:13: "For by one Spirit we were all baptized into one body—whether Jews or Greeks, whether slaves or free—and have all been made to drink into one Spirit." United with Christ in His body, believers are safe from danger, like Noah and his family were safe in the ark (3:20). That is how baptism is the "antitype" (the fulfillment of a corresponding earlier type) for the ark.

But what danger are the readers saved from? One answer is that they are saved from a guilty conscience in the present. When believers are justified and baptized by the Spirit into the body of Christ, they are also forgiven all their sins positionally (Col. 2:13). The new position in Christ also puts them in a position to have fellowship forgiveness when they sin as Christians. By walking in forgiveness, believers maintain a clear conscience. Another interpretation of this salvation is that Peter is assuring the readers that they will be saved from the future trouble of the Tribulation. The ark saved Noah's family from God's watery wrath, so Spirit baptism that places believers safely in Christ will save them from the Tribulation coming upon the world. This would look forward to the Rapture which saves believers from the wrath of the Tribulation (1 Thess. 1:10; 5:1-11). Against this latter view is the phrase "now saves us" which indicates a present benefit, not a future one.

A second B Truth interpretation takes the baptism as water baptism and gives it the same significance as how baptism is viewed in Acts 2:38. Baptism would separate Peter's first-century Jewish readers from their evil generation and identify them instead with the new Christian community so that they would be saved from the temporal corporal judgment coming upon Israel for their terrible sin of crucifying Christ. That destruction came upon Jerusalem through the Romans in A.D. 70. They would receive forgiveness for that sin and thus a good conscience. The resurrection of Christ is mentioned as an encouragement to individual believers who might die in the coming destruction that they also will be raised.

We cannot resolve the interpretation of this passage easily. The argument seems strongest that this is a Spirit baptism that has the present benefit of saving us from a guilty conscience. One thing that is clear is that this passage does not make baptism a condition for eternal salvation. The salvation spoken of is clearly for believers, and thus clearly B Truth.

Make your call and election sure. 2 Peter 1:10-11

[10] *Therefore, brethren, be even more diligent to make your call and election sure, for if you do these things you will never stumble;* [11] *for so an entrance will be supplied to you abundantly into the everlasting kingdom of our Lord and Savior Jesus Christ.*

A Truth Interpretation: Diligent faithfulness will prove the believer's salvation that allows entrance into heaven.

B Truth Interpretation: Diligent faithfulness will confirm the believer's future and rewards in the kingdom of the Lord Jesus Christ.

This passage is a mainstay of those who claim that our eternal salvation must be proved by our works. The A Truth understanding is that we can only know or assure ourselves of our election by the fruits we produce by diligently putting on Christian virtues. Of course, the implication is that lack of fruits shows that one is not saved, or that he cannot know that he is saved. The phrase "call and election"' is interpreted as the effectual call to salvation and God's choice before time to save us.

The A Truth interpretation has a problem on the face of it. If, as some understand it, calling and election are sovereignly determined by God, then how can anything we do influence that determination in the sense of making it more sure? We can agree that our performance can give evidence of our salvation, but can we say that it proves our salvation? Added to that is the fact that the measure of fruitfulness in anyone's life is subject to various interpretations.

We begin to understand this passage when we observe that Peter is writing to Christians without any doubt on his part or theirs that they are saved. They share the same "precious faith" and "righteousness of our God and Savior Jesus Christ" (1:1). God has given the readers all they need to live a godly life (1:3), and they "may be partakers of the divine nature" (Peter could be speaking about their present position or perhaps a future privilege earned by their righteous behavior—either way it assumes their salvation;

1:4). They have also "escaped the corruption that is in the world" (1:4). After that affirming introduction, Peter exhorts the readers to add to their initial faith godly virtues (vv. 5-7) so that they will not be barren (useless, from *argos*), unfruitful, shortsighted, or blind lest they forget (or neglect to appreciate) that they were cleansed from their sins (vv. 8-9).

It should be noted that believers can be unfruitful and spiritually blind. Fruit and good works are not guaranteed in salvation. To say that they are is a theological construct coming from a deterministic view of God that omits human responsibility. Fruitfulness and godliness is the responsibility of every believer, thus Peter's exhortations. God has given believers His power to live a godly life (v. 3-4), but it is the responsibility of every believer to cooperate with God and put on godly virtues (vv. 5-7).

Peter then goes on to exhort the readers to further diligence to make their "call and election sure" (v. 10). The adjective translated "sure" (*bebaios*) means *to be certified, confirmed, validated by evidence*. But to whom is their calling and election to be confirmed? Surely it is not the reader, because Peter has repeatedly confirmed that in the preceding verses. There is no evidence that the readers were struggling with any doubts about their salvation. Peter must have in mind their visible testimony to others as their works confirm to those people their faith in Christ, which the readers claim to have (cf. Rom. 4:2, John 13:35; Jas. 2:21-25).

To what does "call and election" refer? It is assumed by many to mean the divine effectual invitation of people to salvation and God's determination to choose them for salvation before time. A problem with that view is that the word order is incorrect, for it would be "election" before "call" (Rom. 8:30). We find the order Peter gives in the words of Jesus Christ in Matthew 20:16 (in the Majority Text) and 22:14 where Jesus says, "For many are called, but few are chosen." Those words conclude two parables about the kingdom (Matt. 20:1; 22:2). In those parables, the choice to pay certain wages and the choice to allow some wedding guests into the celebratory feast follow the invitation to work or attend the wedding (the call). It is likely Peter is recalling Jesus' teachings about those who enter the kingdom and those chosen for special rewards in the kingdom (see the previous discussion of Matt. 22:1-14).

God has called all believers to His kingdom (1 Thess. 2:12), but only the faithful are chosen for special rewards (Rom. 8:17b; 2 Tim. 2:12). If that is Peter's assumption, then his words in 1:1-11, indeed the whole epistle (cf. 3:14), are designed to prepare the readers for a rewarding entrance into his kingdom. This is borne out in the words of verse 11—Peter does not speak of gaining entrance to the kingdom, but enjoying a rich entrance "supplied to you abundantly." The passive form of the verb *epichoregeō* ("will be supplied") indicates that God bestows the reward. Peter assumes that all of his readers will enter the kingdom (even the unfruitful ones), but he wants to motivate them to godliness by the prospect of an abundant welcome. He may have in mind his culture's practice of giving a victorious warrior or athlete a celebratory welcome into a city. We know from our discussion of 1 Corinthians 3:11-15 that not all Christians will enter heaven with equal rewards. That is also true of the kingdom.

The A Truth interpretation makes the issue in 1:10-11 the *fact* of entering the kingdom of God (which would be interpreted as heaven). The B Truth interpretation makes the issue the *quality* of one's entrance into God's kingdom. The first view breeds futile introspection and endless uncertainty about one's salvation. The second view motivates believers to grow in their faith and maturity on the basis of their sure salvation.

We should never treat our salvation as a static condition. God has provided all we need to grow, but it is our responsibility to avail ourselves of the things that make us mature. Our motivation is not to prove our salvation, but to honor God with the pleasure of bestowing us with a rich welcome into His eternal kingdom.

A dog returns to his vomit. 2 Peter 2:1-22

> [1] But there were also false prophets among the people, even as there will be false teachers among you, who will secretly bring in destructive heresies, even denying the Lord who bought them, and bring on themselves swift destruction. [2] And many will follow their destructive ways, because of whom the way of truth will be blasphemed. [3] By covetousness they will exploit you with deceptive words; for a long time their judgment has not been idle, and their destruction does not slumber. [4] For if God did not spare the angels who sinned, but cast them down to hell and delivered them into chains of darkness, to be reserved for judgment; [5] and did not spare the ancient world, but saved Noah, one of eight people, a preacher of righteousness, bringing in the flood on the world of the ungodly; [6] and turning the cities of Sodom and Gomorrah into ashes, condemned them to destruction, making them an example to those who afterward would live ungodly; [7] and delivered righteous Lot, who was oppressed by the

filthy conduct of the wicked [8] *(for that righteous man, dwelling among them, tormented his righteous soul from day to day by seeing and hearing their lawless deeds)—*[9] *then the Lord knows how to deliver the godly out of temptations and to reserve the unjust under punishment for the day of judgment,* [10] *and especially those who walk according to the flesh in the lust of uncleanness and despise authority. They are presumptuous, self-willed. They are not afraid to speak evil of dignitaries...* [18] *For when they speak great swelling words of emptiness, they allure through the lusts of the flesh, through lewdness, the ones who have actually escaped from those who live in error.* [19] *While they promise them liberty, they themselves are slaves of corruption; for by whom a person is overcome, by him also he is brought into bondage.* [20] *For if, after they have escaped the pollutions of the world through the knowledge of the Lord and Savior Jesus Christ, they are again entangled in them and overcome, the latter end is worse for them than the beginning.* [21] *For it would have been better for them not to have known the way of righteousness, than having known it, to turn from the holy commandment delivered to them.* [22] *But it has happened to them according to the true proverb: "A dog returns to his own vomit," and, "a sow, having washed, to her wallowing in the mire."*

A Truth Interpretation: False teachers go to hell as well as those misled by them.

B Truth Interpretation: False teachers go to hell, and those misled by them suffer a terrible fate.

It is clear that the false prophets and teachers mentioned at the beginning of this passage are unsaved and doomed to eternal destruction. The passage starts with a contrast between them and the "holy men of God" mentioned in the preceding passage (1:21). The language describing their eternal fate is explicit and unequivocal (2:3-17; cf. the parallel passage in Jude 4-6).

There seems to be a second group of people in this passage; it is those influenced by these false teachers to the point that they "follow their destructive ways" (2:2). These also appear to be unsaved. Since they are in contrast to the saved readers, a third group addressed directly ("you") in verse 3, they apparently profess to be Christians which causes the Christian way to be blasphemed when they are seduced.

This third group is the readers Peter is warning. They are referred to in a general way in verse 3 when Peter says that the false prophets "will exploit you with deceptive words." If Peter was writing to believers, as we will see he was, then he is warning about the effects that the false prophets have on those not saved (v. 2) and those to whom he writes who are saved (v. 3). After describing the doom of the false teachers and their unsaved followers, Peter directs his attention to this third group in verse 18. These believers are in danger of succumbing to the influence of the false prophets.

How do we know that the third group is comprised of saved people? They are called "ones who have actually escaped (or some translations: "barely escaped" which also implies salvation) from those who live in error" (v. 18). They have "escaped the pollution of the world through the knowledge of The Lord and Savior Jesus Christ" (v. 20). The fact that they can be "again entangled" in the world's pollution means that they had once been, but had escaped (v. 20). Peter's statement in 2:21 makes it clear that they had "known the way of righteousness." Their fate, described by the contemporary proverbs cited in verse 22, require that the dog had once left its vomit, and the pig was once washed.

So, we see a shift in Peter's address. He writes to this group of believers to warn them of the unsaved false teachers among them who will be destroyed and have led others to the same fate (vv. 1-17). The change in address is clear. After indicting the false teachers in every verse from verse 10 through 17, the indictments stop abruptly. Then in verses 18 and 19, he discusses the danger of believers who might be seduced by the false teachers.

When Peter speaks of the fate of the believing readers who could be influenced by the false teachers, he speaks in terms of possibility, not certainty. These believers would face a terrible fate, but it is not specified as destruction or hell, only that their "latter end is worse for them than the beginning" (v. 20). Whatever struggles or trials they endured as new Christians will fade in comparison to the trouble that awaits them (perhaps temporally, or at the Judgment Seat of Christ, or both). Peter says it would have been better if they had not known "the way of righteousness" than to turn from "the holy commandment delivered to them" (v. 21). Peter is not saying that it would be better if they had never gotten saved. He is saying that it would be better if they had not known the teaching about the life of righteousness, implying that because they do, they have a greater responsibility to follow it. The text indicates this life of righteousness is defined by living according to "the holy commandment delivered to them." What is this holy commandment? Apparently, it is not related to any command to believe or be saved, as that would be an unusual and unprecedented way of referring to salvation. There are a number of options that this could speak of, for example, the command to love (John 13:34) or the command to be holy (1 Pet. 1:15). But both of these are commands to Christians, B Truth commands.

It is naive to say that true Christians will not follow false doctrine. The apostle Paul was not convinced of such a notion—see Galatians and his many warnings to Christians about staying in the truth. Or, ask any pastor of tenure who has seen Christians come and go with the strangest of doctrines. It is especially sad to see and disconcerting to know that unless they repent of their error, there is a devastating fate that awaits them. It is best to avoid false teachers altogether and warn Christians about them.

Be diligent to be found blameless. 2 Peter 3:14-18

> [14] *Therefore, beloved, looking forward to these things, be diligent to be found by Him in peace, without spot and blameless;* [15] *and consider that the longsuffering of our Lord is salvation—as also our beloved brother Paul, according to the wisdom given to him, has written to you,* [16] *as also in all his epistles, speaking in them of these things, in which are some things hard to understand, which untaught and unstable people twist to their own destruction, as they do also the rest of the Scriptures.* [17] *You therefore, beloved, since you know this beforehand, beware lest you also fall from your own steadfastness, being led away with the error of the wicked;* [18] *but grow in the grace and knowledge of our Lord and Savior Jesus Christ. To Him be the glory both now and forever. Amen.*

A Truth Interpretation: Diligence in holiness results in eternal salvation.

B Truth Interpretation: Diligence in holiness prepares Christians to meet the Lord.

This passage is a good summary conclusion of the epistle and themes we have already discussed, so there is no great need to re-argue Peter's points. Verse 14 looks forward to the coming Day of the Lord as a motivation to live godly in the present. Its exhortation reminds us of 1:5-11, which speaks of diligence in adding virtues to our faith so that we can have a high quality reception into Christ's kingdom. The phrase "without spot and wrinkle" does not speak of imputed righteousness, but a blameless life which should be the readers' goal when they are presented to Jesus Christ at the Judgment Seat of Christ (cf. Eph. 5:27).

From a B Truth perspective, we would also see that it is possible for believers ("beloved") to fail in their steadfast stand in Christ and be deceived by the error of false teaching (v. 17). This does not forfeit their salvation or prove they were never saved. It proves that Christians can stop growing and even contradict the truth they know. In this way, this passage reinforces the interpretation of 2 Peter 2, which we have just discussed. Peter exhorts his readers to continue steadfastly in the truth so that they will not be led away into error.

The best preventative for error is to be diligent in growing "in the grace and knowledge of our Lord and Savior Jesus Christ" (v. 18). These are not casual words, because error usually comes first in attacks against salvation by grace alone through faith alone, and attacks upon the person and work of Christ. The more we know God's grace and God's Son, the less we are vulnerable to the error of false teaching.

The Purpose of 1 John

Before we begin a discussion of any passage in 1 John, we must know the purpose of the epistle. In essence, we must answer the question: does 1 John have an A Truth purpose or a B Truth purpose? The majority of preachers, teachers, commentators, and Christians in general interpret 1 John as A Truth. Let me explain.

When one reads 1 John, it is quickly apparent that John gives many "tests" for his Christian readers. These tests include things like walking in darkness or light, being born of God or Satan, loving or not loving others, obeying or not obeying God's commands. The common interpretation, the A Truth interpretation, is that those who pass these tests are true Christians, while those who do not are unsaved. To support the A Truth interpretation, an appeal is made to 5:11-13 as the purpose of the epistle. It is claimed that John wrote to help people know if they and others are truly saved. After all, he says plainly, "These things are written that you might know that you have eternal life" (5:13).

Indeed, it is crucial to know the purpose of the book. But 5:13 is not the only place that John says "I write these things" or "These things are written."

He says this four times throughout the book (1:4; 2:1, 26; 5:13 with the latter three referring to what John says immediately before this statement). It is significant that John says, "These things we write" at the beginning of the book in 1:4 because it would be natural for him to state his purpose at the beginning of his letter. Some may object, arguing that John states the purpose of his Gospel at the end in John 20:30-31. However, that placement makes sense because that is the only time he says, "these things are written so that . . ." He is using an inductive approach which draws his conclusion after he has presented his case. Moreover, verse 31 is simply an explanation of verse 30 that explains why John was selective in his writing.

To truly understand 1 John, we must understand what John had written previously in his Gospel in John 13-17. He taught that truth only in the presence of his disciples to enhance their fellowship with the Lord. A good way to summarize John's purposes for his Gospel and his Epistle is this: The Gospel of John is A Truth that contains some B Truth; the Epistle of 1 John is B Truth that contains some A Truth.

John's Gospel   **John's Epistle**

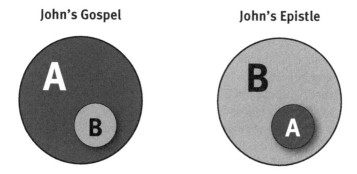

With this in mind, we consider some specific passages that can easily be misunderstood.

If we walk in darkness. 1 John 1:6, 8, 10

⁶ *If we say that we have fellowship with Him, and walk in darkness, we lie and do not practice the truth.*

⁸ *If we say that we have no sin, we deceive ourselves, and the truth is not in us.*

[10] *If we say that we have not sinned, we make Him a liar, and His word is not in us.*

A Truth Interpretation: Those who say they are saved but walk in sin or deny they have sin are not saved.

B Truth Interpretation: Those who are saved but walk in sin or deny they have sin are not in fellowship with God.

Are walking in darkness and denying sin tests of salvation or fellowship? John clearly starts this triad of statements with the theme of fellowship in verse 6. In fact, he includes himself with the first person plural "we." These are strong indications that he is giving B Truth, especially since the letter is addressed to believers.

What pushes people to an A Truth interpretation is the statement about the possibility of walking in darkness and denying sin. Can a believer walk in darkness or deny sin? Later, John says that a believer who "hates his brother, is in darkness until now" (2:9; also 2:11). However, the effect of darkness is to blind and obscure where the believer is going, not send him to hell (2:11). John is addressing the believer's "walk" or their life before God, not their doctrine or faith. In contrast, those believers who walk in openness and honesty before God walk in the light and are being cleansed with the sanctifying effect of Christ's blood (His sacrifice for sin). Those who are not living honestly before God and others will deny their sin. King David did this for about a year before he confessed his sin to the prophet Nathan and to God (1 Sam. 12:1-14; see also Ps. 51). But before his confession, his experience was spiritually dark (Ps. 32:1-5).

Believers who walk in darkness will stumble about without the clear direction that those in fellowship with God enjoy. When Christians turn their back on God who is light, they will stumble along in their own shadows. That is why the confession of 1:9 is so important.

If we confess our sins. 1 John 1:9

If we confess our sins, He is faithful and just to forgive us our sins and to cleanse us from all unrighteousness.

A Truth Interpretation: People must confess their sins to be saved and forgiven.

B Truth Interpretation: Believers must confess their sins to be restored to fellowship with God.

Once we understand that the purpose of 1 John is written to Christians about fellowship and not tests of salvation, we can understand the meaning of this verse. In light of John's declared B Truth purpose in 1:3 and the B Truth understanding of 1:6, 8, and 10, confession of sin must also be B Truth. In the immediate context of walking in light and darkness, confession is how a believer can continue to walk in the light. It shows the honesty that a believer has before God that allows him to enjoy fellowship with Him. The word "confess" (from *homologeō),* means *to agree with.* The believer who sins and confesses it to God is agreeing with God that he has indeed sinned.

It would be uniquely strange to frame one's salvation in terms of confessing sin. This language has no soteriological parallel in the New Testament. As previously discussed, *confess* is mentioned in Romans 10:9-10 as an expression of faith, but that is confession of who Jesus is, not sin.

Any relationship can only be enjoyed when both parties are open and honest with one another. On the human level, parents may always be willing to love and forgive their children, but if a child disobeys them, the enjoyment of that relationship suffers until the child "clears the air" by confessing that sin. Similarly, our position in God's family is not forfeited by sin, but our enjoyment of the relationship (fellowship) suffers when we do not confess our sins to Him.

The truth is not in him. 1 John 2:3-4, 9, 11

³ *Now by this we know that we know Him, if we keep His commandments.* ⁴ *He who says, "I know Him," and does not keep His commandments, is a liar, and the truth is not in him.*

⁹ *He who says he is in the light, and hates his brother, is in darkness until now.*

¹¹ *But he who hates his brother is in darkness and walks in darkness, and does not know where he is going, because the darkness has blinded his eyes.*

A Truth Interpretation: Those who say they are saved but do not keep God's commandments or hate others are not saved.

B Truth Interpretation: Believers who say they have fellowship with Jesus Christ but do not keep God's commandments or hate their brother do not have fellowship with Him.

The first issue to resolve is what it means to "know" God, because that is the claim disputed in the situation described. An A Truth interpretation takes this as a claim that one is saved, whereas the B Truth interpretation takes this as a claim to intimate fellowship with Jesus Christ.

That "Him" refers to Jesus Christ is evident by the context that names Jesus Christ as our Advocate and our propitiation in verses 1 and 2. Also, verse 6 says that the believer should "walk just as He walked." Jesus lived a righteous life during his earthly ministry.

One clue to the meaning of "know" is the use of the parallel term "abide" in verse 6. The difference between believing and abiding has already been discussed (see John 8:31-32). *Abide* (from *menō*) means *to adhere to, continue in, remain in*; it does not mean *believe*. These readers are already believers, as has been shown. *Abide* is a word for believers that denotes an intimate fellowship with God. Likewise, the word "know" has a range of meanings from knowing something cognitively, to knowing something experientially or intimately. In John 14:7-9, we see that though Philip knew Jesus Christ to a degree, he did not really *know* Him. Later, Jesus prayed for the saved disciples that they might know God and Jesus Christ better (John 17:3).

John is teaching that obedience to Christ's commands is the way to deeper intimacy with Christ, a reflection of the truth Jesus taught in the Upper Room Discourse (John 14:21). To obey Christ is to show an intimate love for Him (John 14:15). A believer cannot say that he knows Christ intimately if he is disobeying His commands. If he makes such a brash claim, he is lying. The chief command that Jesus left his disciples was to love one another (John 13:34). This would be a distinct testimony to others that they are His disciples (John 13:35). Love for their brothers is how believers show that they know God intimately (1 John 4:7-8), because God is love (1 John 4:16). In chapter 1, John told his believing readers about choosing to walk in either light or darkness. He now demonstrates that truth by how believers can either love or hate their brothers.

Our spirituality is not affirmed by boasting, but by obeying. Our obedience to Christ's commands, especially the command to love others, is evidence that we know Him intimately in an abiding relationship. It is crucial to understand this teaching if we are to deepen our walk with the Lord.

Whoever sins does not know God. 1 John 3:6, 9-10

> ⁶ *Whoever abides in Him does not sin. Whoever sins has neither seen Him nor known Him.*
>
> ⁹ *Whoever has been born of God does not sin, for His seed remains in him; and he cannot sin, because he has been born of God.* ¹⁰ *In this the children of God and the children of the devil are manifest: Whoever does not practice righteousness is not of God, nor is he who does not love his brother.*

A Truth Interpretation: People who continue to sin or do not love others are not saved.

B Truth Interpretation: Believers who continue to sin or do not love their brothers do not have intimate fellowship with God.

While most Christians admit that all Christians sin occasionally, there are some who use this passage to insist that Christians cannot sin continuously and still be Christians. Specifically, the lack of love for others is cited as proof that these people in question either lose their salvation or never were saved at all.

If this A Truth interpretation is correct, then these verses would contradict what John says in 1:8 and 9: "If we say that we have no sin, we deceive ourselves, and the truth is not in us. But if we confess our sins . . ." Believers sin and sin regularly, and that is why God gives us a way to deal with sins through confession.

Again, we must note that the issue is not *believing* in Christ, but *abiding* in Him. Since abiding speaks of intimate knowledge and close relationship, it is easy to see how John can say that those who abide in Christ (that is, remain in fellowship with Him) do not sin. John says that those who sin (that is, those who do not abide in Christ) "have neither seen Him or known Him." While these terms can be used for the salvation experience (as A Truth), John often uses them for the believer's experience. To *see* (from *horaō*) can refer to one's perception and experience of something (John 6:36; 12:45; 14:9; 15:24; 3 John 11), and we have already shown how *know* (from *epiginōskō*) can denote a personal acquaintance or familiarity, which we call fellowship.

Some support an A Truth interpretation by arguing from the use of the present tense in the passages. Those who claim this like to translate the verbs as "keeps on sinning" or "continues to practice sin." These translations are even reflected in many Bible versions (NIV, NET Bible, ESV, NASB). The resulting interpretation is that this describes a person who habitually or continuously sins. There are some problems with that view, however. First, if that was the meaning of the present tense, it would require additional words to clarify the sense of habitual action (much like we might clarify the statement "He is cursing" with words such as "He is cursing all the time"). Unless there are clarifying words, John's readers would not assume a habitual meaning for this present tense. It seems that the habitual interpretation is derived from a theological bias that assumes Christians will not and cannot persevere in sin. Another problem that arises from this A Truth interpretation is how to determine what qualifies as habitual sin. Would that include anger, lust, pride, and prayerlessness? And how often would it have to be committed to be considered habitual—once a day, once a week, once a month, or every year?

The key to understanding these statements about sin is what John says in 3:5 about Jesus: "in Him there is no sin." Verse 6 is simply saying that when believers abide in Jesus Christ, it is impossible to sin because there is no sin in Him. Verse 9 says they cannot sin; in other words, *fellowship with Christ never results in sin.* The Christian has a new nature from God, or as verse 9 says, we have His "seed." A sinless parent begets sinless children. This divine life in us can never express itself by sinning. Therefore, those who sin are not abiding in Christ, but are serving their old corrupt sinful desires. This struggle between our divine life and our sinful desires is described in Romans 7:14-25 and Galatians 5:16-25. In 1:8, John speaks of Christians in their general experience, while in 3:9, he speaks of Christians viewed through their new flawless life.

Real Christians sin, sometimes seriously and repeatedly. We know this from experience and from the testimony of Scripture. But God gives us a way to avoid sin—abide in Christ. When we sin, we can confess that sin and restore fellowship with God. Jesus came to take away the sin of the world. He did that provisionally when He died on the cross for all people, and we appropriate the benefit of His death when we believe in Him as Savior. But we experience the benefits of His sacrifice and avoidance of sin through fellowship when we abide in Him.

Whoever sins is of the Devil. 1 John 3:8, 10

[8] *He who sins is of the devil, for the devil has sinned from the beginning. For this purpose the Son of God was manifested, that He might destroy the works of the devil.*

[10] *In this the children of God and the children of the devil are manifest: Whoever does not practice righteousness is not of God, nor is he who does not love his brother.*

A Truth Interpretation: People who sin are of the devil and are not saved.

B Truth Interpretation: Believers who sin show that the source of their inspiration is the devil not God.

At first glance, the strong language of this passage seems to say that anyone who sins is unsaved. How can children of God be called children of the devil? However, when we compare other Scriptures, we see that such language can indeed fit Christians.

- Jesus tells Peter, "Get behind Me, Satan!" (Matt. 16:23)
- Ananias lies to the Holy Spirit because Satan filled his heart. (Acts 5:3)
- Paul writes that Christians can be taken captive by Satan to do his will. (2 Tim. 2:26)
- James says that believers can choose demonic "wisdom" over God's. (Jas. 3:15-17)

So John uses equally strong language with precedent.

If this passage teaches that those who sin are unsaved, then all professing Christians are unsaved, because all Christians sin (made clear in 1:7-10). As seen previously with 3:6 and 9, interpreting the present tense in verse 8 as "practices sins" or "continues to sin" is not a good argument because it relies on a subtlety of understanding that is not normal or apparent in the text. Christians sin, and they may sin regularly. Determining what comprises habitual sin that forfeits salvation is subjective and without Scriptural delineation.

To understand the contrast John makes between the children of God and the children of the devil, it is helpful to observe how John is fond of absolute contrasts in this epistle: He speaks of walking in darkness or light, of loving or hating one's brother, of life and death, and of Christ and antichrist. John sees two opposite sources of spiritual orientation.

In 3:8 and 10, John is distinguishing two opposite sources for Christian behavior. In 3:9, when he states that the believer in his regenerate person cannot sin because Jesus Christ cannot sin, he implies that sin must come from another source. In 3:8, he names that source as the devil who "has sinned from the beginning." The devil deceived man into sin causing him to be controlled by sin. Satan and Jesus Christ are at odds in their purposes and character, thus Jesus came to destroy the devil's works (v. 8).

When believers sin, verses 8 and 10 remind us that they are manifesting their Satan-inspired proclivity to sin, just as when believers do right, they manifest their God-given divine life (v. 9). The word "children" (*tekna*) does not imply a biological or genetic relationship, but is often used to describe those who have characteristics derived from another person in the sense of a kind or class of persons (see Matt. 11:19/Luke 7:35; Gal. 4:31; Eph. 2:3; 5:8; 1 Pet. 3:6). John is simply saying that those believers who sin show that the ultimate source of their actions is the devil, not Christ.

John goes on to use Cain murdering Abel as a physical illustration of this spiritual truth (3:12). This example is not a statement about whether Cain is saved or not, but only shows that his envious attitude and atrocious deed were inspired by Satan. In his Gospel, John recorded Jesus' declaration that the devil "was a murderer from the beginning" (John 8:44).

It is an unfortunate B Truth reality that Scripture and contemporary experience both teach that Christians can do the devil's work. Anyone who has seen Christians involved in sexual immorality, church splits, child abuse, or embezzlement of ministry money must recognize the satanic influence behind the sinner. It is too simplistic to dismiss these perpetrators as unsaved people. Why else would God direct us to practice church discipline and restorative action in the New Testament? Sin does not prove that one is not a Christian. It only shows that there are two conflicting realities competing for the believer's allegiance. As Christians we can choose to manifest our God-given divine life, or our Satan-inspired sinfulness.

Sin leading to death. 1 John 5:16

If anyone sees his brother sinning a sin which does not lead to death, he will ask, and He will give him life for those who commit sin not leading to death. There is sin leading to death. I do not say that he should pray about that.

A Truth Interpretation: Some sins will cause a believer to lose salvation and go to hell or prove that they were never really saved.

B Truth Interpretation: Some sins will lead to deadness in a believer's fellowship with God and even premature death.

This passage shows the seriousness of certain sins. John writes about a sin that does and a sin that does not lead to death. One's understanding of the death mentioned will lead one to an A Truth or a B Truth perspective on this difficult passage.

Our first observation is that the "anyone" must be a Christian since that is the audience to whom John writes concerning the reader's "brother." We also recall that there are different meanings for the word death such as spiritual death, eternal death, spiritual deadness, and physical death. But which is spoken of here?

We can begin by ruling out eternal death because John is writing to genuine Christians and a genuine brother who he assumes are saved and thus, cannot lose their salvation. For the same reason, we rule out death as spiritual separation from God. That leaves the possibilities of spiritual deadness and physical death, or perhaps both since one can lead to the other.

John spoke earlier of passing from death to life and abiding in death in 3:14. These seem to refer to the lack of spiritual vitality or spiritual deadness for those who do not love their brothers. But there is also biblical evidence of believers who sinned and died physically (Acts 5:1-11; 1 Cor. 11:27-32) for committing serious sins against the church. In 5:16, it could be that John has in mind the serious sins that the heretics were perpetrating in the church at Ephesus to which he wrote (see 1:8, 10; 2:18-19, 22-23; 3:7; 4:1-3). If the believers in Ephesus follow these teachings or refuse to show love for their brothers, it will bring them spiritual deadness *and* perhaps also physical death. All sin brings death, but it works as a progression from spiritual death to physical death. Such sin is so serious that the believer is not commanded to pray for the sinner, though he may choose to do so.

This admonition continues John's previous discussions about the importance of loving one's brother in chapters 3-5 and his immediate admonition to pray expectantly to God (5:14-15). Grievous sins bring grievous consequences. They bring separation between the believer and

God resulting in spiritual deadness, and can bring His ultimate discipline of physical death. We can pray with confidence for those committing some sins, but for others who sin more seriously, we have no assurance of answered prayer. This B Truth perspective should be a warning to us about committing serious sin, and an encouragement to pray for those who are sinning.

Whoever does evil has not seen God. 3 John 11

Beloved, do not imitate what is evil, but what is good. He who does good is of God, but he who does evil has not seen God.

A Truth Interpretation: Those who do evil are not saved.

B Truth Interpretation: Believers who do evil evidence a lack of an intimate knowledge of God.

The key to interpreting this passage is the meaning of the phrase "has not seen God." Does it refer to someone who is not saved eternally, or someone who is saved but blind to the true character of God? It would have helped us if John had used the familiar first person plural "we" that he often uses in his epistles—we could conclude that he is addressing the experience of Christians who do not "see" the true character of God. But John uses the second person "he." This makes sense in the context because John had just mentioned Diotrephes, who is acting badly (vv. 9-10), and next mentions Demetrius, who is doing good (v. 12).

John exhorts the "beloved" Christian Gaius, probably the leader of the church in Ephesus, to imitate those like Demetrius, not those like Diotrephes. Certainly, as a Christian, it is possible for Gaius to make either choice. John's exhortation is based on the fact that the one who does good is of God and the one who does evil has not seen God. As we have seen in 1 John, to be "of God" is to show that God is the source of inspiration of one's action (1 John 3:10). On the other hand, someone who "has not seen God" is walking in darkness (1 John 1:6) and is acting in spiritual blindness. All sin originates from losing sight of God (1 John 3:9). The idea of seeing God refers to one's perception and experience of something (cf. Luke 3:6; John 6:36; 12:45; 14:9; 15:24; and see the discussion of Heb. 12:14), so not seeing God is a clouded perception, a lack of an intimate knowledge of God.

Some may argue that the present participles ("He who does good/he who does evil") suggest continuous or habitual action. But as we have seen in 1 John 3:6 and 9, this is stretching the use of the present beyond its intention, which is to simply state an action (cf. John 6:33).

The important B Truth that we take from this passage is that if we take our eyes off God, we too can do evil and show a lack of familiarity with God's character and nature. When we do good however, we show that God is the source of our action. Like Gaius, we should avoid behaving like those who are spiritually blind and imitate those who show an intimate knowledge of God.

He is able to keep you from stumbling. Jude 24

Now to Him who is able to keep you from stumbling,
And to present you faultless
Before the presence of His glory with exceeding joy.

A Truth Interpretation: God will not allow true Christians to stumble finally so that they are guaranteed entrance into heaven.

B Truth Interpretation: God is able to keep Christians from stumbling so that they can have a good presentation at the Judgment Seat of Christ.

Those who interpret this passage as A Truth find support for the doctrine of Perseverance of the Saints (all true believers will continue in faith and good works until the end of their lives). They believe that God keeps every true Christian from ultimately succumbing to sin. This proves their salvation and guarantees their entrance into heaven.

However, if we note carefully the language used, the passage does not say that God "will keep you from stumbling," but that God "is able to keep you from stumbling." To say that God *is able* is different from promising that He *will* do something. The readers of Jude were warned extensively about the false teachers among them (vv. 4-16), then exhorted to take precautious actions (vv. 17-23). The implication of verse 24 is that *if* they take these actions, God is able to keep them from stumbling into error and sin.

Often, the assumption is made that the faultless and joyful presentation mentioned is entrance into heaven. We know that the believer's justification allows him to enter heaven with no more guilt and with Christ's righteousness. But that truth imposed here neglects the statement about God keeping the believer from stumbling. The status of "faultless" must mean that the believer will be kept from stumbling into the error and ways of the false teachers. This is not a condition of eternal salvation, but a condition for a good and joyful presentation before the Judgment Seat of Christ. This important B Truth should be familiar to us now: All Christians must give an account of themselves at the Judgment Seat of Christ (Rom. 14:10; 2 Cor. 5:10). We have also seen that the goal, as expressed by the apostle Paul, is to present every believer "holy, and blameless, and above reproach" (Col. 1:22) and "perfect" (or complete) at that judgment. As implied in Jude, Paul conditioned such a presentation on continuing in faith and steadfastness to the truth (Col. 1:23). Peter is helpful here too. In 2 Peter 1:10-11, he states that our spiritual growth (2 Pet. 1:5-9) will keep us from stumbling (2 Pet. 1:10) and give us an abundant entrance into the kingdom of our Lord (2 Pet. 1:11). Faithful Christians are not only given an entrance into heaven; they are given it "abundantly," which speaks of the quality of entrance.

The lesson for Christians is to rely on God and His power and truth to keep us from stumbling into the error and conduct of His enemies. If we do so, we will enjoy a high-quality presentation to the Lord Jesus at His Judgment Seat.

The Revelation

11

S EPARATING A TRUTH from B Truth in Revelation is a unique challenge because it is such a unique book. Foremost to consider is its lone position in the New Testament as apocalyptic literature, which is typically full of symbols, visions, catastrophic events, and figures of speech. Not only this, but we must interpret some of the passages from the perspective of future events.

The overcomers. Revelation chapters 2-3

"To him who overcomes . . ." or *"He who overcomes . . ." (Rev. 2:7, 11, 17, 26; 3:5, 12, 21)*

A Truth Interpretation: The overcomers are all believers who are promised an aspect of eternal life that describes entrance into heaven.

Second A Truth Interpretation: The overcomers are believers who overcome sin and persevere in faith to prove that they are genuinely saved and are promised an aspect of eternal lie that describes entrance into heaven.

B Truth Interpretation: The overcomers are believers who are faithful in temptation and are promised rewards in the kingdom and eternity.

The letters to the Seven Churches in these two chapters are structured similarly. Each begins with an address to the "angel" of the church, recalls an attribute of the Lord from chapter 1, then after any commendation, warning, and exhortation, there is a promise to the "overcomer." It is the identity of and promises to the overcomer that challenges our understanding of these promises as A Truth or B Truth. We will consider all seven as a whole rather than treat each one separately. Some especially difficult passages will be considered individually.

A couple of preliminary issues deserve a comment. It has been debated whether the seven letters to the churches represent historical churches at the time John wrote, all churches at any time, or churches of separate historical periods. We can dismiss the latter as too subjective to define. John appears to write to contemporary churches familiar to him about issues that are relevant to churches then and at all times. Another discussion is the identity of the "angel" mentioned at the beginning of each letter. Some think this is an angelic guardian of the church, but others think it refers to the pastor of the church. The word *angelos* can mean *messenger* in general or *angel* specifically. On a practical level, it seems that writing a letter to the pastor as the messenger to the church would be normal. However, the identity of the messenger does not have a bearing on the final A Truth or B Truth interpretation.

The designation of "church" applied to these local congregations assumes that these were local groups who identified with Jesus Christ. It also seems a safe assumption that for these to be addressed as churches, there were at least some saved people in each congregation. That the Lord expresses His concern through rebuke, warning, call to repentance, and exhortation shows His desire to restore negligent believers rather than call unbelievers to salvation.

Many believe that the overcomer (from *nikaō*, to *win, be victorious*, thus *victor*) in Revelation 2-3 is simply another name for one who has believed in Jesus Christ as Savior (the first A Truth interpretation). They usually refer to 1 John 5:4-5:

For whatever is born of God overcomes the world. And this is the victory that overcomes the world—our faith. Who is he who overcomes the world, but he who believes that Jesus is the Son of God?

However, John's epistle is a very different context from Revelation. In his epistle, John speaks of the final once-for-all victory that faith in Christ gives to the believer over the condemnation of this world and the victory he can continue to have by living in faith (note the present tense). In a slightly different view, the second A Truth interpretation sees the overcomers as believers who have proved their salvation by faithful obedience to the end of their lives. But in Revelation, John speaks of two groups of believers—those who have received the gift of salvation freely (Rev. 21:6) and those who receive the full privileges of inheritance and sonship by overcoming (21:7). In Revelation 2-3, overcomers live faithfully in various trials specific to each local church. The overcomer is the believer who goes through the particular trial victoriously. In 2:26, Jesus defines the overcomer as one who "keeps My works until the end."

The problem with taking the overcomer passages as A Truth becomes obvious. If *overcomer* is simply another name for a believer, then salvation would be by works, because in each context, works are either implied or explicitly involved in overcoming. Furthermore, if all believers are overcomers, then there is no room for believers who fail and even die in their sin (1 Cor. 11:30; 1 John 5:16). This is also inconsistent with our own Christian experience and our observation of other believers' experiences (unless we are willing to admit that we and they are not saved after all). The commands and warnings in the letters to the churches are empty and unnecessary if those who read them are guaranteed to be overcomers by virtue of their justification or if they are guaranteed to persevere in faithfulness because they are the true elect of God. That Jesus Christ says "I also overcame and sat down with My Father on His throne" (3:21) proves that the reference to overcoming concerns difficult circumstances, not salvation.

Although all believers overcome the world's condemnation through faith in Jesus Christ as Savior, some believers—as these in Revelation 2-3—are challenged to overcome difficult circumstances in their lives and churches. To the one who overcomes, rewards are promised:

- He will be allowed to eat from the tree of life in the paradise of God (2:7). That the overcomer is in paradise is assumed as the basis for the privilege of eating from the tree of life.

- He will not be hurt by the second death (2:11). They have a strong assurance of their eternal security.

- He will be given hidden manna to eat and a white stone with a new name on it (2:17). These are new privileges that are obviously more than entering heaven.

- He will be given power over the nations and given the morning star (2:26-28). All believers will rule with Christ, but some will have greater power and intimacy with Christ. (Matt. 25:21, 23)

- He will be clothed in white garments and his name will not be blotted out of the Book of Life but confessed before God and the angels (3:5). The garments may indicate cleansing or honor as a contrast to those in the church who soiled their garments (3:4). The promise to never blot out his name from the book of life is a comforting reaffirmation of eternal salvation (see the discussion below), and the confession before God and angels is also a way of honoring the faithful overcomer.

- He will be made a pillar in God's temple and the name of God, the New Jerusalem, and the new name of Christ will be written on him (3:12). This promise also assumes that the overcomer is in the presence of God so that he can enjoy these special privileges and intimacy with God.

- He will be granted to sit with Christ on His throne (3:21). This speaks of participation in Christ's kingdom rule, not mere presence with Christ.

In total, if these promises speak of simply entering heaven, then puzzling language is used indeed. However, if they speak of various rewards in the kingdom and eternity, then the variety and imagery makes more sense, though some imagery is difficult to understand.

At issue also is God's fairness, for if all believers are overcomers and receive all these benefits, is that fair to those who are faithful in trials when others are not? As Christians, Jesus Christ assures us that it pays to be faithful in difficult circumstances.

I will not blot out his name. Revelation 3:5

"He who overcomes shall be clothed in white garments, and I will not blot out his name from the Book of Life; but I will confess his name before My Father and before His angels."

A Truth Interpretation: The true believer will not lose his salvation, or the believer who does not remain faithful can lose his salvation.

B Truth Interpretation: The overcoming believer is assured of a secure future.

There are three promises in this verse, but the one most cited is the assurance about the Book of Life, which is taken as the register of all who are saved. Those who think all believers are overcomers say this is the Lord's promise that believers will never lose their salvation. Another interpretation found among those who think Christians can lose their salvation is that believers will not lose their salvation as long as they are faithful. This, of course, would also mean that they *can* lose their salvation if they cease to be victorious. Both of these A Truth interpretations equate the parallel promises about being clothed in white garments and having one's name confessed before the Father and His angels as simply promises of eternal salvation or events coterminous with eternal salvation.

The problems with taking these promises as only references to salvation have already been discussed, chief of which is that salvation would then depend on our performance instead of God's grace. The wearing of white garments is sometimes interpreted as believers clothed in the righteousness of Jesus Christ, an indication of their justification. But the immediate context (v. 4) speaks of those who have not defiled their garments and who are worthy to walk with the Lord in white. This clearly speaks of their works and faithfulness that makes them worthy of reward—to walk with Christ in white seems to denote a special companionship or privilege. Later in Revelation, white garments refer to righteous acts, not justification (19:8, 14). We have shown that confessing one's name before the Father (and His angels) speaks of the reward of commendation, not justification (see the discussion on Matt. 10:32-33). What would angels have to do with one's justification anyway?

What, then, does the Lord mean when He says that He will not blot out the name of the overcomer from the Book of Life? *It means exactly that.* It is an assurance that this can never happen. The Book of Life should be understood in light of Daniel 12:1 as a record of God's elect people. Jesus is using a figure of speech known as litotes, an understatement that uses a negative to emphasize a positive. It is as if someone catches a limit of fish and is asked how he did. He might say "Not bad," by which he means "Fantastic!" Or if someone invites a friend to her Thanksgiving feast and says "You won't starve!" You get the point. (Some examples of litotes in Scripture include John 6:37, Acts 20:12, 1 Cor. 10:5; Heb. 6:10; Rev. 2:11). This promise is a strong overwhelming assurance enjoyed by those who overcome difficult circumstances, that in spite of any adversity on earth (even death, 2:10), they will never ever be excluded from the company of those who are saved eternally. We should not make it imply the opposite—that Christ would ever remove the name of a believer from the Book. The intent of the promise is to commend and to comfort, not threaten. There is even a hint of special honor because one's "name" stands for one's reputation, and the parallel promise in this passage is Jesus' confession of that name before the Father and the angels. Perhaps we could say that in addition to being listed forever, the faithful overcomer gets honorable mention in both written and spoken forms.

I will not vomit you out of My mouth. Revelation 3:15-16

[15] *"I know your works, that you are neither cold nor hot. I could wish you were cold or hot.* [16] *So then, because you are lukewarm, and neither cold nor hot, I will vomit you out of My mouth."*

A Truth Interpretation: Professing Christians who are spiritually complacent will be rejected by Christ from eternal life because they are not saved.

B Truth Interpretation: Christians who are spiritually complacent are not useful to Christ and are unpleasant to Him.

We've all had the experience of looking forward to a nice hot cup of coffee (tea or hot chocolate for some) only to realize it has sat too long and is room temperature. Likewise, a cold drink that warms up in a closed car on a sunny day is just as unpleasant. We spit or pour those drinks out. Unpleasant. Repulsive. Not at all refreshing.

The context reminds us that Jesus spoke these words to a church. This assumes that He addresses at least some believers there. But it makes more sense to assume they were all identified as Christians. Jesus says He wishes they were either cold or hot. It is often assumed that "hot" refers to spiritual Christians. But if so, to whom would "cold" refer? It couldn't be unsaved people or even unfaithful believers, because Jesus said he would rather them be cold than lukewarm.

This interpretational dilemma comes from making too much of the details of an analogy instead of focusing on the main point. Jesus is simply saying that He wishes the Laodicean believers were refreshing or useful (cold or hot) instead of unpleasant and useless (lukewarm). In spite of their riches, they were so blind and self-absorbed that they were refreshing to no one, much less the Lord. The imagery of vomiting is used to make the point that the spiritually complacent and self-absorbed believers in Laodicea are useless and thus distasteful. Neither should we make too much of the significance of Jesus' threat to vomit them out. In the context, it simply speaks of unpleasantness, although it could also imply some kind of rejection (for rewards?) and punishment, though not hell.

The B Truth interpretation makes the most sense here and serves as a warning to Christians today that we should not be complacent. Those who neglect their spiritual priorities are not only useless in God's service, but are grievous and unpleasant to Him.

Knocking at the door. Revelation 3:20

> *"Behold, I stand at the door and knock. If anyone hears My voice and opens the door, I will come in to him and dine with him, and he with Me."*

A Truth Interpretation: Jesus knocks at the door of peoples' hearts seeking to enter and save them.

B Truth Interpretation: Jesus wants to be in the midst of a church and have fellowship with its believers.

"Ask Jesus into your heart" has been a standard invitation for salvation used almost everywhere. That invitation is based on this passage: "Jesus is knocking on the door of your heart—won't you let Him in?" But does this passage speak of getting saved, as an A Truth?

As noted in a previous discussion, Jesus is speaking to a church, the only church of the seven in Revelation 2-3 that He does not commend for anything. Still, it is a church, complacent though they are. His invitation is to "buy gold" and "white garments" from Him. This could not speak of the free gift of salvation Jesus offers the unsaved (22:17). We have already seen how white garments speak of the righteous acts of believers (see the discussion on Rev. 3:5). The admonition to anoint their eyes with eye salve so they may see also suits Christians who can be blind to their selfish condition and to God's will (2 Pet. 1:9). These are people who Jesus loves and chastens as His children (3:19; cf. Heb. 12:5-7), therefore, a B Truth interpretation makes the most sense. The message to these and the other disobedient believers in

Revelation chapters 2 and 3 is not to get saved, but to repent of that which displeases the Lord.

Jesus is not "knocking" on the hearts of people. He is appealing to the church to allow Him in their midst through repentance (v. 19). The command to "be zealous and repent" is then illustrated by verse 20, which shows how these believers can repent by responding to Jesus' invitation to renew fellowship with Him. Jesus has been excluded from the fellowship of the church, so He knocks seeking entrance. Since a church is made up of individuals, the invitation is to whoever in the church "hears" and "opens the door," a picture of receptivity. The promised result is that Jesus will come "in to" him. It is important to know the original language Jesus used. He did not say "into" to denote *contact with* (which would use the Greek *eis*), but he said "in to" to denote *motion toward* (using the Greek *pros*). The different emphases between the two prepositions can be seen in John 6:35: "He who comes to (*pros*) Me shall never hunger, and he who believes in (*eis*) Me shall never thirst." Jesus will come *in to* where the receptive person is (not *inside* him) to eat together with him.

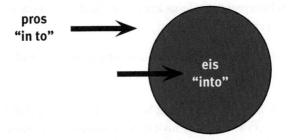

The imagery of eating together is a common biblical and cultural picture of fellowship. The reward of sitting with Jesus on His throne in verse 21 is not a result of salvation, but a reward for the conquering or victorious Christian.

In the larger context, Revelation is not a book written with the explicit purpose to tell people how to have eternal life like John's Gospel (John 20:31). The Gospel of John never uses the word *repent* but uses *believe* almost one hundred times, most often as the condition for salvation. This in itself is sufficient reason not to model our evangelistic invitation from the words of Revelation. When Revelation includes a clear invitation to salvation in 22:17, it echoes the invitations of the Gospel of John with "Come" and "take the water of life" (John 4:10; 6:37, 44, 65).

Don't tell unsaved people to ask Jesus into their heart! Tell them to believe in Jesus Christ as the one who died for their sins, arose, and guarantees them eternal salvation. But if you or your church is spiritually complacent, then repent and restore your fellowship with the Savior who loves you and wants to have close fellowship with you.

The Great White Throne Judgment. Revelation 20:11-15

[11] *Then I saw a great white throne and Him who sat on it, from whose face the earth and the heaven fled away. And there was found no place for them.* [12] *And I saw the dead, small and great, standing before God, and books were opened. And another book was opened, which is the Book of Life. And the dead were judged according to their works, by the things which were written in the books.* [13] *The sea gave up the dead who were in it, and Death and Hades delivered up the dead who were in them. And they were judged, each one according to his works.* [14] *Then Death and Hades were cast into the lake of fire. This is the second death.* [15] *And anyone not found written in the Book of Life was cast into the lake of fire.*

A Truth Interpretation: All people will face a final judgment at the Great White Throne where their works will give evidence of their salvation or not.

Second A Truth Interpretation: Only unbelievers will be finally condemned at the Great White Throne judgment where their works will determine the severity of their punishment.

One of the greatest A Truth B Truth distinctions the student of God's Word should recognize is the two different judgments of Scripture. All people face a judgment before God (Heb. 9:27), however, the judgments are different for believers and for unbelievers. Believers face the Judgment Seat of Christ where their works are evaluated and tested (Rom. 14:10-12; 1 Cor. 3:11-15; 2 Cor. 5:10). This judgment apparently happens before or at the beginning of the millennial kingdom. It is not a judgment of their salvation, because Jesus promised in John 5:24, "Most assuredly, I say to you, he who hears My word and believes in Him who sent Me has everlasting life, and shall not come into judgment, but has passed from death to life."

The judgment of Revelation 20:11-15 is different from the Judgment Seat of Christ. It is usually called the Great White Throne Judgment and takes place at the end of the millennial kingdom. It is a judgment for unbelievers only. I have designated it A Truth, but it has B truth implications, because it should comfort believers to know that they are excluded from this. All believers have been resurrected before Revelation 20:11, some at the Rapture of the church and some at the beginning of Jesus Christ's millennial rule (Rev. 20:4). Those who believe during the millennium (some of those born during the millennium) will perhaps be transformed immediately upon believing, because "flesh and blood cannot inherit the kingdom of God" (cf. 1 Cor. 15:50-54). The Scripture does not tell us when they will be judged or whether they will need to be, since they will be living transformed lives. That leaves "the rest of the dead" who will come to life at the end of the thousand-year kingdom (Rev. 20:5). These will stand before God where the record of their works will be reviewed and the absence of their name from the Book of Life will also be verified (20:12) before they are thrown into the lake of fire (20:15).

The chief observation to be made is that those judged at the Great White Throne are never given any designation or destiny as believers. They are all thrown into the lake. But before that, they are judged by their works. It is unbelief in Christ as Savior that condemns them to their fiery fate, but their past deeds evidently determine the severity of that eternal punishment, because the text says twice that they are judged "according to their works." It makes sense that a murderer rapist would experience a more severe judgment than an unbelieving family man.

Interpreting the judgment of Revelation 20:11-15 correctly is a comfort to Christians because our sins and eternal destiny have already been judged. Only unbelievers face the terrifying prospect of final judgment and sentencing to the Lake of fire. We also see how works are important in every person's life. To the Christian, they determine eternal rewards (or lack of rewards), and to the non-Christian they determine the severity of their eternal suffering. In no way should this passage be made to say that one's works will be the final proof or determination of one's salvation.

Sinners and the second death. Revelation 21:8

But the cowardly, unbelieving, abominable, murderers, sexually immoral, sorcerers, idolaters, and all liars shall have their part in the lake which burns with fire and brimstone, which is the second death.

A Truth Interpretation: Gross sinners will go to hell, including those who profess to be Christians but commit these sins or those Christians who commit these sins and lose their salvation.

B Truth Interpretation: In contrast to the believers and faithful overcoming Christians in God's presence, these unbelieving sinners will perish in the lake of fire.

There is no question about the fate of those mentioned in this passage—they are all consigned to eternal punishment in the lake of fire. We have read previously that this lake is the destiny of all unsaved people. However, this passage makes it appear that only gross sinners perish there or that their sins are the reason for their punishment. Some would also argue that believers who practice such gross sins lose their salvation and suffer the fate of the lake of fire.

An honest reading of the passage would have to admit that not all the sins listed are of the most severe kind. The list includes the "cowardly" (*deilos*, means *timid* or *fearful*) and "liars." Certainly this broadens the application to most or all Christians, so it cannot be these specific sins that prove one is unsaved or can lose his or her salvation.

The point of mentioning unbelievers and their sins in this passage is to contrast (v. 8 begins with "But") their fate with that of all believers. The text implies that there are those believers who have received the water of eternal life freely (v. 6) and that some of those believers are rewarded for their faithfulness ("overcomers," v. 7). The fates of these three groups differentiate between the importance of Jesus' free offer of eternal life to all in verse 6, the reward earned by some for serving Him in verse 7, and the consequence of rejecting Him in verse 8. The contrast between rewarded believers and unbelievers is also found in 22:11-15.

To anyone who reads these final words of Revelation, it is clear that there are only two fates for all mankind, a blessed eternity in God's presence or a horrible eternity shut out from His presence. But these final words also include the way to a blessed eternity:

And He said to me, "It is done! I am the Alpha and the Omega, the Beginning and the End. I will give of the fountain of I the water of life freely to him who thirsts." (Rev. 21:6)

And the Spirit and the bride say, "Come!" And let him who hears say,

"Come!" And let him who thirsts come. Whoever desires, let him take the water of life freely. (Rev. 22:17)

Eternal life is a free gift. Receiving it is the only way to avoid the lake of fire.

Rewards given according to one's work. Revelation 22:12

"And behold, I am coming quickly, and My reward is with Me, to give to every one according to his work."

A Truth Interpretation: At Jesus' return, He will pay back each person according to his work. By virtue of their performance, some people will go into the lake of fire, and some people will go into the New Jerusalem.

B Truth Interpretation: At Jesus' return, He will reward each believer according to his work.

The A Truth interpretation makes works the determining factor in one's eternal destiny. This must be rejected as contrary to Ephesians 2:8-9 and other clear passages that teach no one is saved by works. The passage is not teaching salvation truth.

The B Truth interpretation recognizes another strong contrast (v. 11) and a word of comfort to Christians: Jesus will reward those believers who are faithful. Those rewards are specified in verse 14 as partaking from the tree of life and entrance through the gates of the New Jerusalem. These remind us of the rewards promised to overcomers in chapters 2 and 3 (esp. 2:7; 3:12), which seem to speak of special privileges for those who are already in God's presence.

In fact, "work" is singular, not plural. As such, it serves to summarize the character of one's life. Christians will be rewarded according to the whole tenure of their lives. It is possible this verse could address unbelievers also because their fate is also mentioned in contrast to believers (v. 15). Though translated "reward," the word *mithos* can simply mean *payment*. We have seen that at the Great White Throne Judgment, unbelievers will be punished (paid back) "according to their works" (22:11-13). However, the fact that Revelation was written to churches makes the promise of reward primarily to believers (cf. John's use of "reward" in relation to believers in 2 John 8).

Jesus said He is "coming quickly," a comforting word to us who wait for the justice and rewards that make the sacrifices involved in following Him worth it all. We will all receive our reward in due time.

Whoever adds or subtracts from God's Word. 22:18-19

[18] *For I testify to everyone who hears the words of the prophecy of this book: If anyone adds to these things, God will add to him the plagues that are written in this book;* [19] *and if anyone takes away from the words of the book of this prophecy, God shall take away his part from the Book of Life, from the holy city, and from the things which are written in this book.*

A Truth Interpretation: Those who change God's Word will lose their salvation.

B Truth Interpretation: Those who change God's Word lose eternal blessings.

The severe language of verse 18 reminds of the imprecatory wishes written by the psalmists of the Old Testament. Considering the nature of the plagues mentioned in Revelation, this could not be a literal threat. The author's purpose is to amplify the seriousness of changing God's truth.

Verse 19 in the New King James Version uses the word "Book" of life, but the overwhelming manuscript evidence supports the word "tree" of life, as seen in almost all of the other English translations. With that understood, we see that verse 19 applies to those who are believers because only they have any part in the "tree of life" and the "holy city" of the New Jerusalem. Also, it would be primarily believers who read, teach, and handle the book of Revelation. The threat is not that God will take away salvation from those who tamper with these holy words, but that He will deny special privileges to the offenders.

The warning certainly does not address those who arrive at various interpretations of the Bible which may be wrong. It is more a powerful warning not to manipulate or misuse God's revelation with malfeasance. Thus, the importance of good Bible study with pure hearts.

3 Applying A Truth B Truth to Life and Ministry

PPLICATIONS HAVE BEEN made throughout the book, but this section allows us to synthesize these applications and see how distinguishing between salvation and discipleship makes a difference in our own lives, the lives of others, and in church or ministry.

Making Biblical Distinctions Count

P ERHAPS BY NOW you see the difference that a good interpretation or an erroneous interpretation can make. Differences in interpretation are not just academic or theological. Theology informs practice, and belief influences behavior. As we think, we are. Here we discuss some ways that A Truth B Truth choices can influence life and ministry.

How we view ourselves

As you now know, B Truth is about performance in the Christian life. This includes the strenuous demands of discipleship. Whenever we consider our performance under God, there is room for introspection, both healthy and unhealthy. Healthy introspection asks, "Am I living up to the demands of discipleship and godly living?" The result of self-evaluation can reveal areas of shortcomings and even failures. This gives us a basis and a motivation to better please God.

Unhealthy introspection can result in unpleasant consequences. The most severe would be that one would question his or her salvation if performance is less than the perceived standard of what God demands. Another serious consequence would be feelings of guilt, perhaps under the perception that God values us based on our performance.

Of course, those who end up doubting their salvation or doubting whether they are pleasing to God have placed themselves in a self-defeating environment for spiritual growth. *You can't grow forward if you are always looking backward.* Performance is a two-edged sword—we are always doing better than some other Christians, which can lead to pride, and we are always doing worse than some other Christians, which can lead to guilt and doubt.

Two factors address this unhealthy situation. First, our salvation does not depend on our performance; it depends on Christ's performance on our behalf. We are not and never could be acceptable to God based on our own efforts and works. Distinguishing A Truth from B Truth keeps Christian life and discipleship demands from corrupting the gospel of God's unconditional grace with works, both on the front end of the gospel and the back end of the gospel. In other words, passages that address works cannot be made a condition for initially obtaining salvation or finally proving salvation. In Christ, God sees us as having fulfilled all the righteous demands of His divine justice.

If works are left out as a condition for our righteous standing before God, that leaves us with the confidence that grace brings. Our salvation depends on God's promise, not our performance. There is the realization that we are accepted by God as a loving father accepts his own son or daughter. The basis of acceptance is not how well we behave as God's sons and daughters, but the fact that we belong to the Father in His family.

Parallel to this truth about the unconditional grace of salvation is the unconditional grace by which we are to live and relate to God. We do not fear God as a Father seeking to punish us when we mess up (unless, perhaps, we really are messing up). Instead, we are free to cry out affectionately "Abba, Father!" A famous photograph shows John Kennedy, Jr. as a small child playing under President John F. Kennedy's desk in the Oval Office. There is no fear in his father's presence, just pure delight.

Imagine a father who arrives home from work and has this interchange with his twelve-year-old son:

"Son, did you do your homework like I told you?"

"Yes, Dad."

"Great, you are a good son. Did you wash the dishes like I asked?"

"Sure did, Dad."

"That's my boy. You really are a great son! But did you clean your room like I told you to?"

"No, Dad, I didn't."

"You disobeyed me and you call yourself my son? My son would obey me. I don't think you are worthy to be called my son."

That boy is growing up in an environment of conditional acceptance based on his performance. He will live in fear of displeasing his father and losing his place in the family. That is not a healthy environment for growth and for an intimate relationship with his father. Rather, he will see his father's love as fickle, capricious, and conditional. He is valued only by what he does, not by who he is.

Keeping A Truth consistent with the gospel of grace gives us an identity that cannot be forfeited by our failures. We are unconditionally united with Jesus Christ in His death and resurrection and are placed into His spiritual body by the work of the Holy Spirit who also indwells us. On your best day, your identity is "Jesus and me," and on your worst day, it is still "Jesus and me." What B Truth does is hold us accountable for how we behave as sons with motivations of parental discipline or parental rewards.

We live in a time when many people struggle with self-image and self-worth. The A Truths of the New Testament tell us that we are loved by God, who will never cast us out of his family. We are secure because of the work that God's Son did for us, which we could never do on our own. We rest in the unconditional love of God displayed in His grace toward us.

How we present the gospel

Keeping B Truth from intruding on the A Truth of the gospel of salvation gives us not just *good news*, but *great news*. A Truths about the gospel and our salvation assure us that salvation is absolutely free. It also keeps the gospel free and clear at a time when many Christians have encumbered it with demands placed on the unbeliever. I never cease to be amazed at how many different views there are among Christians about what a person must do to be saved. As one African evangelist confessed to me after attending our conference on the gospel of grace, "I have to repent—I think I have been keeping people out of heaven by the many things I told them they have to do to be saved!" This well-intentioned evangelist was confusing B Truth with the A Truth of the Gospel. As a result, he was confusing people at their eternal peril. No wonder there are serious warnings for those who change the gospel. Galatians 1:8-9 says,

> [8] *But even if we, or an angel from heaven, preach any other gospel to you than what we have preached to you, let him be accursed.* [9] *As we have said before, so now I say again, if anyone preaches any other gospel to you than what you have received, let him be accursed.*

Whether these verses apply to outright heretics or simply to those who inadvertently confuse the gospel, it is clear that God considers changing or obfuscating the gospel a serious offense.

Unfortunately, the way so many misinterpret the gospel today by confusing A Truth with B Truth leaves us with much less than good news. Do these appeals to the unsaved sound like good news to you?

- "I can tell you how to have eternal life—if you make the commitments God demands."

- "I can tell you how to have eternal life—if you don't sin and lose it."

- "I can tell you how to have eternal life—if when you die you are still faithful and living a godly life."

Who can make all the commitments God demands, or live a life of constant victory over sin, or know that they will always remain faithful throughout life? If anything less than a one hundred percent performance report results, how can anyone have a sure hope of salvation? And who would even think that God takes our commitments and determination not to sin so seriously that He would hang our eternal destinies on them? No parent has that kind of expectation for a son or daughter. God is neither a naïve parent nor anyone's fool.

Frankly, it is deceptive to offer anything called "eternal" life under those conditions. Nothing eternal can depend on our efforts. An evangelist with such a feeble message is more foolish than bold.

On the other hand, we have great confidence when we can look an unbeliever in the eye and say, "I can tell you how to have eternal life guaranteed by God and given as a free gift that can never be lost."

Some object to such a simple message by calling it "easy believism" or "decisionism." But these are false charges. The gospel is simple, but not easy.

- It's not easy to believe that my sinfulness deserves eternal separation from God.

- It's not easy to believe that God loves me in spite of my sin.

- It's not easy to believe that God would send His Son to live and die on my behalf.

- It's not easy to believe that Jesus Christ paid the penalty for all of my sins over 2000 years ago.

- It's not easy to believe that Jesus Christ rose from the dead and now lives.

- It's not easy to believe that Jesus Christ would offer me eternal life.

- It's not easy to believe that I can receive this gift without cost but only through faith.

Simple, *not easy! Simple* means *single, without complexity. Easy* means *without difficulty.* The simple gospel means a child or a simple person can understand and believe in it.

A popular version of the gospel today is called Lordship Salvation. This view demands that a person is saved through faith, but a faith that commits and surrenders to Jesus as the Lord of all of one's life. In other words, commitment and surrender are conditions of salvation. Resulting from this starting point is the belief that a true Christian is therefore one who evidences that commitment and surrender in a life of good works. In this sad travesty of confusing A Truth with B Truth, the gospel has become difficult, costly, and one could even argue, impossible. God's grace is no longer free, faith becomes works, and the unbeliever is subject to a performance basis for acceptance with God. There is much more I could say about Lordship Salvation, but I have said it in great detail elsewhere.[14]

Let's be more careful about how we present and promote the gospel to others. A survey of gospel literature, booklets, and tracts will reveal many different gospel presentations, especially in the invitation section at the end. They cannot all be correct. We need to be discerning about how the gospel is presented in the literature we use, the missionaries we support, and the teachers we allow to influence others. One question I have used to test a person's understanding of the gospel is "If you were to die and stand before God, and He said, 'Why should I let you into My heaven?', what would you answer?" Anything other than faith in the all-sufficient work of Jesus Christ would not be a welcome answer.

---

14 Besides my book already noted, *Lordship Salvation: A Biblical Evaluation and Response,* 2nd GraceLife Edition (Burleson, TX: Xulon Press, 2014), see my chapter titled "What about Lordship Salvation?" in *Freely by His Grace: Classical Free Grace Theology,* eds. J. B. Hixon, Rick Whitmire, and Roy B. Zuck (Duluth, MN: Grace Gospel Press, 2012), pp. 97-118. More articles and short studies on topics and passages related to the Lordship view are at GraceLife.org/Resources/GraceNotes.

Our gospel presentation should be a bold declaration of the bad news that we have all sinned and deserve eternal separation from God; and the good news that God sent His Son, Jesus Christ as the One who paid the penalty for our sins on the cross, rose from the dead, and guarantees our eternal salvation if we simply and only believe Him for it. The good news of the gospel is that we can be saved by grace alone, through faith alone, in Jesus Christ alone.

How we give assurance of salvation

To know that we are eternally saved is not presumptuous, but a privilege assumed throughout the Bible.

What biblical author casts doubts on his own salvation or on the salvation of his readers? None! We have already seen that some passages used to suggest that doubts are good teach no such thing (see the discussions on Matt. 7:21-23; 24:13; 2 Cor. 13:5). We have also argued that doubt and insecurity about one's salvation is not a basis or an environment for spiritual growth.

We are told in 1 John 5:11-13,

> [11] And this is the testimony: that God has given us eternal life, and this life is in His Son. [12] He who has the Son has life; he who does not have the Son of God does not have life. [13] These things I have written to you who believe in the name of the Son of God, that you may know that you have eternal life, and that you may continue to believe in the name of the Son of God.

This passage tells us that we can know that we have eternal life, and that depends on whether we have the Son, Jesus Christ. We receive the Son when we believe His gospel. His gospel promises eternal salvation. When we believe, we are convinced that His gospel is true, including His promise. This faith in God's promise is the assurance that what God has said is true, and therefore that we are saved. It is not faith in ourselves or faith in our faith; it is faith in Jesus Christ—His person, His provision, and His promise. Because our faith rests in objective facts, not subjective feelings or performance, we can know that we are saved.

In essence, we are assured by God's Word, which promises eternal life to all who believe in Jesus Christ. Good works are important evidence, but not conclusive evidence. The testimony of the Holy Spirit is another witness, but not a conclusive witness (many rely on their subjective feelings about the Holy Spirit's presence). The only objective and final authority we can rely on is God's Word.

If we try to find assurance of salvation in the B Truths of the New Testament, our search will be futile. Truths about discipleship and the Christian life generally address the things we must do to please God—our performance. There is no final assurance in our performance.

On the other hand, A Truths focus on what Jesus Christ has done on our behalf and our singular response of faith. The performance is His, and we simply receive the benefits through faith. We can have total assurance that Jesus Christ has satisfied God's demands for justice on our behalf, therefore we know that we are saved based on His work.

Teaching B Truth as A Truth has caused many Christians to doubt their salvation. Of course it would! We need to be reminded of what Jesus Christ has done instead of constantly being probed about what we have done. Assurance of salvation is the starting point for growing in a healthy relationship with God, and an important motivation to keep growing.

How we motivate believers to godliness

Distinguishing A Truth from B Truth appeals to the highest motivations to serve God and live a godly life. Our motivations are important because they reach to the core of our spirituality. Motivating believers to outward conduct and motivating them to godliness may not be the same things. We need some insight into what are godly motivations.

Deeds alone are not a good measure of spirituality and an unreliable judge of salvation and personal holiness. The Pharisees had no shortage of outward deeds to which they could point, but they were rebuked by Jesus as hypocrites (Matt. 23:23-30). Extrinsically good deeds can come from intrinsically bad motivations. Preaching, teaching, or insisting that people do the right things can produce a Pharisee.

There are some unbiblical and unhealthy motivations to do right. One such motivation comes from a legalistic perspective on spirituality, often the result of interpreting B Truth as A Truth. In other words, the focus of such a person would be on outward acts as a way to find acceptance with God. This attitude is behind those who think they have to earn their salvation, but also infects those who have been saved. Many people believe that a "good Christian" is a busy Christian, that service is godliness. There is nothing wrong with outward good deeds, obedience to God's commands, and service, but the attitude behind it is what makes the difference. When we elevate the importance of what Christians do, we devalue the importance of what God did and does. When we focus on their works, we place them in danger of becoming proud. Legalism cannot produce godliness, because it teaches outward conformity instead of inner maturity. True maturity comes only from the grace that sets us free—free to choose to serve God or to serve selfish interests. But teaching God's unconditional free grace can be risky, even scary. Christians can and will abuse grace and cross the borders set by the legalist. But that is no reason to prejudice our interpretation of the Bible. The apostle Paul preached grace in spite of the risks and was even criticized for it (Rom. 6:1, 14).

Related to this, a Christian may serve God because of a guilty conscience. Some might think it is too easy to confess and accept God's forgiveness for free. The fleshly instinct is to do something additional to appease God's perceived anger. This is akin to the Roman Catholic concept of doing penance, or working off one's sins through prayers and good deeds. But this attitude opposes biblical grace, for grace is either given as a free gift, or it is not grace (Rom. 11:6). When we sin and then confess our sin, we rest on the finished work of Jesus Christ for our salvation, which also provides for ongoing forgiveness that allows fellowship. We should not aggravate a guilty conscience, but lead the person to enjoy the forgiveness that grace provides. A Truth presents forgiveness as a free gift based on the finished work of Christ.

Of course, there are also sinful and selfish motives behind some service. Some Christians might serve for financial gain, preeminence among others, power over others, or self-aggrandizement. Jesus exposed the hypocritical charity and praying of those who pandered to the praise of people (Matt. 6:1-6), and He condemned the Jewish scribes who feigned following God because they loved public recognition and perks (Mark 12:38-40).

So what are good biblical motivations for serving God and living godly? We would have to begin with the highest virtue of all—*love*. The first and greatest commandment is to love God and along with that, love others (Matt. 22:37-39). When we love God or others, we seek their highest good. We seek to please them. But love also expresses itself in a desire for greater intimacy. There is a definite relationship between love, obedience, and abiding. Jesus said,

"As the Father loved Me, I also have loved you; abide in My love. If you keep My commandments, you will abide in My love, just as I have kept My Father's commandments and abide in His love." (John 15:9-10; cf. 1 John 4:16)

To know Jesus Christ more intimately was the driving desire behind the apostle Paul's forward press to maturity (Phil. 3:10-14). We encourage love for God by reminding Christians that He loved us first and gave us the greatest gift of His Son (1 John 4:19). This love for God has a corresponding love for others. In a correlating and inseparable command, Jesus also says, "and love your neighbor as yourself" (Matt. 22:37-39). When Jesus says that this "second" command is like the first, He refers not to rank of importance, but logic of sequence. When someone loves another, they will care about whatever the object of their love cares about. Since God cares about people, the one who loves God will also love people, especially His children (1 John 4:21).

After love (or along with it), *gratitude* is another chief motivation for service and good works. Gratitude is a result of experiencing grace. Out of gratitude for all God's blessings mentioned in Romans chapters 1-11, Paul urges his readers to respond by offering their bodies as living sacrifices, which is their "reasonable service" (Rom. 12:1-2). To generate gratitude in people, we should remind them constantly of what God has done for them and let them respond in a reasonable manner.

Eternal significance, or the desire to fulfill God's eternal purpose, can be another significant motivation for the Christian. Salvation is not just security. It is also opportunity. What we do with our lives today matters tomorrow (in eternity). Some of the parables we have discussed teach the roles in the kingdom that await those who are faithful. But serving God faithfully also brings significance to our lives today. Christ appeals to Peter's sense of eternal significance when he calls him from a life spent merely catching fish to a life spent catching men (Luke 5:10). There is a powerful urge in most people to invest their lives in something of enduring or eternal value. Life in the present can be graced with eternal significance so that the Christian who loses his life to Christ will save or find his real life (Matt 10:38-39; 16:24-27; Mark 8:34-38; Luke 9:23-26; John 12:24-26). This refers not to eternal salvation but to the preservation of and the fulfillment of one's essential life that comes from enjoying God's eternal purpose. Since significance is conditioned upon faithfulness, obedience, and service, it motivates believers towards these virtues.

Rewards is a motivation similar to eternal significance. Many of the passages we have discussed speak of rewards both in this life and in eternity, so we will not elaborate much. You should be able to see by now that the Judgment Seat of Christ is a predominate theme in the New Testament that emerges when we correctly separate A Truth judgment from B Truth judgment. With the prospect of positive rewards at that judgment comes the prospect for a loss of rewards. If gaining rewards is a positive motivation, then losing them is a negative motivation. Believers must be reminded of both. While rewards are sometimes left unspecified, it should be enough to know that they are God-given and therefore good for both Him and His children. It may well be that the highest motivation from rewards will be the opportunity to give them back worshipfully to the Savior in the future (Rev. 4:10).

Duty is a motivation also seen in the Scriptures. Sometimes when love and gratitude for God are waning, duty might compel a person to do the right things, because they have a strong motivation to live up to their commitments and obligations. Jesus Himself was motivated by His sense of duty and purpose. When tempted to distraction from His preaching ministry, He explained He would persist "because for this purpose I have come forth" (Mark 1:38). He also died on the cross to fulfill the Father's purpose (John 12:27), so that at the end of His life, He was able to say to His Father, "I have finished the work which You have given Me to do" (John 17:4). In the same way, a believer can recognize God's calling to a certain ministry and then desire to fulfill it. The apostle Paul was so motivated by his calling to be the apostle to the Gentiles it kept him motivated to finish his ministry for the Lord (1 Tim. 1:1; 2:7; 2 Tim. 1:11; 4:7; Acts 20:24). Doing one's duty requires faithfulness. Jesus commended faithfulness in duty (Matt. 24:45; 25:23; Luke 16:10-12), as did Paul (Eph. 6:21; Col. 1:7; 4:7, 9). It is good to remind disciples of Jesus Christ that God expects certain things and that they have made commitments they should fulfill.

Fear is a final biblical motivation to godliness, though it may be the most immature of the motivations because it comes from an immature or underdeveloped love (1 John 4:18; cf. 1 Pet. 1:17). Christians can fear God's discipline in this life, and/or a negative assessment of their works and motives at the Judgment Seat of Christ. Amidst the words of encouragement and instruction and the prospect of eternal significance, we have seen that the author of Hebrews also uses warnings of dire consequences that can come upon believers who forsake the truth of Christ or neglect their spiritual growth. This is not a fear of hell (A Truth), but a fear of God's discipline (B Truth).

To summarize these motivations, you may find these illustrations useful:

- *Love*: Nine-year-old Ashley picks up her toys because she loves her parents and wants to please them.

- *Gratitude*: Ashley picks up her toys because she realizes all that her parents do for her and wants to show them her appreciation.

- *Eternal significance*: Ashley picks up her toys because she understands her significance in the family and it may bring a greater role for her in the future.

- *Rewards*: Ashley picks up her toys because her parents promise to take her for frozen yogurt after its done.

- *Fear*: Ashley picks up her toys because her parents threaten to keep her from her best friend's birthday party if she doesn't.

Obviously, some motivations are more worthy than others. But all the motivations can produce right actions.

Why do we discuss these motivations for godliness? Because when B Truth about Christian performance is interpreted as A Truth about salvation, our motivation can become to perform so that we prove we are truly believers (something that we have said is impossible). That error paves the way for doubt, fear, guilt, and legalism to be the driving forces in a Christian's life—things that will never produce true godliness. People cannot be legislated into spiritual growth, nor can they be shamed into godly service or intimidated into Christlike maturity. We should learn to inspire others to godly living and service with the highest of motivations, beginning with love and gratitude to God for all that He has done. We must constantly remind one another of all that God has freely given us by His grace. The disciplines of discipleship will fade in the believer's life without these heartfelt motives that pull one forward into maturity. These distinctions and resulting motivations come from discerning A Truth from B Truth.

How we discourage license

When we distinguish A Truth from B Truth in such a way that we teach that the gospel of grace is free from any conditions other than simple faith that guarantees the eternal security of the believer, we will inevitably be charged with encouraging sin (license). In fact, if you are not encountering this false charge, you may not be preaching the gospel of grace. The apostle Paul faced this accusation (Rom. 6:1, 15) and answered it without compromising his gospel.

Paul taught that Christians can discourage license without going back under the Old Testament law. The New Testament believer is "not under law, but under grace" (Rom. 6:14). The law was fulfilled by Jesus Christ (Rom. 10:4; Gal. 3:19-25), so we do not have to satisfy its commands in order to obtain eternal salvation or to live the Christian life. But that does not mean that we are without any laws. The New Testament speaks of a new code of conduct for Christians, the law of Christ, some of which echoes the Old Testament laws (1 Cor. 9:21; Gal. 6:2). But unlike the Old Testament law, it is a "law of liberty" (Jas. 1:25; 2:12) that is inscribed on our hearts (Heb. 8:10). The charge of lawlessness can only apply to someone who rejects all laws, those of both the Old Covenant and the New Covenant.

To discourage license in a life under grace, we teach living by faith and walking in the Holy Spirit (Gal. 5:16-25). As we walk in the Spirit, we fulfill the law of Christ and the righteous requirements of the law (Rom. 8:1-11). Love is the first fruit of walking in the Spirit (Gal. 5:22). Those who love God and others fulfill the spirit of the law, because they will do good things that please God and others (Gal. 5:14).

Keeping the gospel clear from B Truth performance also discourages license, because if we are saved only by grace and not anything we contribute, then we should feel a deeper appreciation for what God has accomplished and provided for us. Experiencing and understanding God's grace should generate a heart and life of worship and gratitude to God for His undeserved free gift (Rom. 12:1-2; Eph. 4:1). A deeply grateful heart will not want to offend God.

Another motivation to avoid license is a theme previously discussed that comes from distinguishing A Truth from B Truth: the Judgment Seat of Christ. We should teach that every believer will have to give an account of his or her life before the Judgment Seat of Christ where there will be both positive and negative consequences. After we die or after Christ returns for His church, we will each face this reckoning that has consequences into eternity (Rom. 14:10-12; 1 Cor. 3:11-15; 2 Cor. 5:10). Knowing that our behavior today has eternal consequences of rewards or denial of rewards should motivate us to live godly lives.

Still another motivation to avoid license is the temporal consequences that sin can bring. When we learn to distinguish salvation truth from

Christian life truth, we discover the biblical teaching about divine discipline. Believers who sin do not face eternal condemnation, but face God's discipline. Like a good and loving Father, God does not let His children run wild (Heb. 12:5-11). His chastisement can take innumerable forms, from things like depressed emotions, illness, or financial loss, to physical death (the sin which leads to death in Jas. 5:20 and 1 John 5:16).

Related to this is the biblical teaching of church discipline for sinning believers. In the context of the church body, sin is not ignored, but should be dealt with appropriately. This is one way that God can exercise His divine discipline. Matthew 16:15-20 teaches these truths about church discipline:

- It is a graduated process of increased confrontation with the unrepentant sinner. (vv. 15-17)

- Its goal is to restore the sinning Christian. (v. 15b)

- The church is acting on behalf of God. (vv. 18-20)

If we take an A Truth interpretation of the sinning believer, that is, he or she is not saved, then church discipline would make little sense. In that case, the church should seek to win the person to Jesus Christ for eternal life. But that is not what this passage teaches. The public pressure of a church body can be a persuasive means to bring a sinning believer to repentance.

We can also discourage license by showing a believer how a reckless lifestyle hurts others. First, it hurts God and scandalizes His glory. Second, it hurts others who might be affected by someone's sin. Third, it hurts the sinning believer, not only in the ways mentioned above, but by hindering growth and maturity.

While grace is free and results in freedom, it also teaches moral responsibility. Grace teaches us to deny ungodliness and live godly lives (Titus 2:11-14). To live under grace means we should live a righteous and holy life (Rom. 6-8; Eph. 2:8-10). All Bible teachers who understand grace should teach the moral admonitions of the Bible.

Yes, grace can be abused—that is always a risk of freedom—but those who do so invite God's discipline and other negative consequences. However, when we appreciate the high price God paid for our free gift of eternal life—His only Son—we should have a heart of worship and gratitude that leads to spiritual maturity and godly living. Of the many ways we can discourage believers from living in license, this is perhaps our purest appeal.

How we shape a church environment

It is sometimes more subtle than obvious, but a church that does not learn the biblical distinctions between A Truth and B Truth can perpetuate an unhealthy spiritual environment. The reverse is also true: learning these distinctions can create a healthy environment of freedom and growth. A grace-oriented church is able to distinguish the freeness of God's grace in salvation from the demands of discipleship and apply the implications to people's lives and to church practice.

The church environment begins with the gospel that is taught in and through the church by the leaders. If it is clear that salvation is by grace through faith plus nothing, then there is no unhealthy scrutiny of each other's works to judge if anyone is really saved. On the other hand, if commitment or works are viewed as proof of salvation, there will be judgments made, sometimes right, but sometimes tragically wrong. Assurance of salvation that comes from a grace gospel keeps the focus on Jesus Christ and His finished work rather than people's imperfect works. This assurance gives people a firm foundation for confident growth in the Lord.

Instead of constantly questioning people's salvation and causing doubts based on imperfect performance, a church that understands the difference between A Truth and B Truth will give people room to grow and change. Sin in believers will be dealt with biblically, but more importantly, unconditional acceptance of the person will give people the freedom to mature into Christlikeness. The emphasis of such a church is not what people do, but who people are in Christ, not activity, but identity. We give people something to grow into. As believers in Christ, people should be accepted for who they are. From that perspective, a church will accept differences in culture, personality, opinion, giftedness, questionable practices, and personal preferences, because God has accepted the person.

A healthy church that distinguishes the freeness of salvation from the obligations of discipleship will avoid the extremes of license and legalism. Teaching the unconditional grace of God and the accountability of the believer will keep people from licentiousness. It will also keep people from legalism. A church can exert subtle or overt pressure to conform outwardly to artificial and non-biblical standards. But a grace-oriented church holds to the Bible's clear teachings, is flexible in the unclear issues, and never allows human rules to supersede the authority of Scripture.

Since a clear understanding of God's grace frees us to love and serve Him, it also frees us to love and serve others. A grace-oriented church will balance the joyful liberty of the Christian life with a love for God and others. This means that in areas of conscience or questionable things, believers are encouraged to temper their activity by considering how it will affect others and by acting only out of love. Christians should be encouraged to use their liberty to serve others (Rom. 14; 1 Cor. 8; 10:23-33; Gal. 5:13-14).

When a church keeps the gospel clear, there should be a sincere desire to share the message of grace with the world. Those who have been freely blessed should be willing to share that blessing with others. The "God of all grace" desires all men to be saved through His provision in Christ (1 Tim 2:3-4; 1 Pet. 5:10). If a church is seeking after God's heart, they will be active in reaching the world with the gospel of grace, because that is what God's heart desires.

As already shown, a church that distinguishes A Truth from B Truth will understand how to handle those who sin. The church must understand and address the reality of sin in Christians biblically. Of course, church leaders will first want to determine if the sinning person understands and believes the gospel. If the sinning person has a clear testimony of salvation, then the next step is to lovingly confront that person with the purpose of discipline and restoration (Matt. 18:15-20; 2 Cor. 2:6-8; Gal. 6:1; 2 Thess. 3:6-15). Sinning Christians are not automatically assumed to be unsaved and therefore evangelized. The grace-oriented church reflects a healing environment rather than a critical and condemning spirit.

It is assumed that a healthy church environment is created and sustained by consistent and accurate teaching of the Scriptures. Expository preaching (treating Bible passages systematically and in context) is the best assurance that A Truth and B Truth will be distinguished properly. Not only will people gain a clearer understanding of many Scriptures, they will learn the proper way to interpret the Bible, especially difficult passages. The Bible, rightly understood, will bring life transformation.

How we view the future

Making important A Truth B Truth distinctions about the Bible's teaching on eternal salvation, future judgments, and future rewards will determine how we see our future.

Understanding the gospel of grace gives believers a firm confidence in their future. Since salvation is given by grace through faith alone without any performance criteria, we can know we are saved forever. All the promises of salvation will be realized in eternity. Here are some of the things we as believers can know and will experience forever:

- We have eternal life, which means it lasts forever. (John 3:16; 6:47)

- We are transferred into God's eternal kingdom. (Col. 1:13)

- We are forgiven all sins forever. (Col. 2:13-14)

- We will be raised to live with Christ forever. (Dan. 12:2; 1 Thess. 4:13-17)

- We are sealed by the Holy Spirit until the day of redemption, when Christ raises us. (Eph. 1:13-14; 4:30)

- We will reign with Christ in His kingdom. (Rev. 20:6)

- We will experience eternal rewards. (Rev. 22:12)

We have hope in a secure future. Hope is an important element of the Christian life. Biblical hope is not the same as a wish or desire, but is a confident expectation of future blessing. But hope can only be experienced fully by those who know they have been saved by grace apart from human merit. Hope is strongly related to the gospel of free grace (see the discussion of Col. 1:21-23).

Our hope of eternity with the Lord in heaven and the kingdom is not diminished by the prospect of being evaluated for how we lived our lives. A distinction is made between the unconditional nature of salvation and the conditional nature of our future accountability.

When someone confuses the judgment of the Great White Throne for unbelievers (A Truth) with the Judgment Seat of Christ for believers (B Truth), that person may conclude that works are necessary for eternal salvation. Such an outlook for a doubtful future undermines the confidence we should have about our salvation and the Lord's return for us.

When the Judgment Seat of Christ is correctly distinguished from the judgment of our salvation, then works find their appropriate place in the life and motivation of the believer. The quality of the Christian's future experience of God in the kingdom depends on faithfulness and the choices made in this life. A believer who lives faithfully can look forward to the future prospect of:

- Rewards and treasure in heaven and the kingdom (1 Cor. 3:11-15);

- Jesus' commendation and the Father's praise (Matt. 10:32; 25:23; 1Cor. 4:5);

- Co-ruling privileges with Christ (Rom. 8:17; 2 Tim. 2:12);
- Special crowns, blessings, and privileges (1 Cor. 9:25; 2 Tim. 4:8; Jas. 1:12; 1 Pet. 5:4; Rev. 2-3).

There is some question about the extent and duration of the negative consequences of the Judgment Seat of Christ. Some of our discussions of the parables show that there can be great regret at missing some of the blessings of the kingdom. Also, 1 John 2:28 indicates there can be shame at the coming of Christ for those who are not abiding in Christ. Certainly having one's works "go up in smoke" at the Bema cannot be a pleasant experience (1 Cor. 3:15). While negative consequences are certain, it is difficult to think that there is enduring regret, shame, or pain. In Revelation 21:4, at the creation of the new heaven and earth, we read about God's people (v. 3), that

God will wipe away every tear from their eyes; there shall be no more death, nor sorrow, nor crying. There shall be no more pain, for the former things have passed away.

I do not think there is strong evidence that indicates long-term regret or shame. Being with the Lord is overwhelmingly presented as a joyful and pleasant experience for eternity. We should also remember that God's grace covers our future as well as our past. First Peter 1:13 speaks of grace that awaits the Christian in the future: "Therefore gird up the loins of your mind, be sober, and rest your hope fully upon the grace that is to be brought to you at the revelation of Jesus Christ."

Making the distinction between the entry requirement for the kingdom (faith in Christ, A Truth) and the requirements for a rewarding experience in the kingdom (faithfulness to Christ, B Truth) will not only give Christians a firm assurance of salvation, but will also give them a motivation to live godly lives. We must teach that what we do today in this life definitely makes a difference tomorrow in eternity. It is not the threat of hell that motivates people to true godliness, but the prospect of pleasing the Lord for eternity. We should help people prepare for that great day when every believer will be presented to the Lord Jesus Christ for evaluation and reward (2 Cor. 4:14; 11:2; Eph. 5:27; 1 Thess. 5:23; Jude 24).

Distinguishing A Truth from B Truth not only gives us peace and assurance in this life; it gives us confidence in a sure future with the Lord. By God's enduring grace, we can live for tomorrow today and look forward to His return.

Eternal Security[15]

1

C AN A PERSON once saved ever lose or forfeit that salvation? The Bible answers "No," that a person who is once saved remains saved throughout eternity. This is usually called the doctrine of eternal security, and is often referred to (sometimes derogatorily) as "once saved always saved."

If we asked the question differently, it is easier to see how eternal security makes sense. For example, what if we asked, can a person eternally saved lose that eternal salvation? Or, can a person who is justified be unjustified? Or, can a person who is born spiritually be unborn? Or, can a person who is freely given the gift of eternal life lose it based on some condition?

Those who believe in eternal security are generally labeled Calvinists. Those who believe that salvation can be lost are generally labeled Arminians.

What the Bible says

The Bible teaches eternal security in many different ways.

1. The Bible speaks with certainty about the possession of a new life based solely upon faith in Christ as Savior. John 3:1-16; 5:24; 10:28; 20:31

2. The Bible refers to this life as "eternal" which means forever and implies no interruption. John 10:28; 11:25-26

3. Since salvation by grace essentially means that it is a gift, then it is an unconditional gift, which does not depend on a person's

---

15 This is adapted from Charles Bing, *GraceNotes* no. 24, "Eternal Security," at http://www.gracelife.org/resources/gracenotes/?id=24.

works, conduct or condition after salvation. Rom. 3:24; 4:5; Eph. 2:8-9

4. The Bible teaches that God's predestining purpose and initial justification result in eventual glorification without exception for every believer. Rom. 8:29-30; Eph. 1:4-5

5. The Bible presents eternal salvation as a legal and binding relationship with God that cannot be separated by anyone (including ourselves) or anything. Rom. 8:1, 31-39

6. The Bible presents eternal salvation as an irrevocable filial relationship to the Father by adoption, which results in eternal blessings. John 17:3; Rom. 8:15-17; Gal. 3:26

7. We are sealed with the Holy Spirit, Who guarantees our glorification. 2 Cor. 1:22; Eph. 1:13-14; 4:30

8. We are kept secure by the power of both the Father and the Son. John 10:28-30; 17:9-12; Jude 24

9. Since all of our sins (past, present, future) are forgiven by Jesus Christ and His eternally sufficient sacrifice, there is no sin that can cause us to lose our relationship to Him. Col. 2:13-14; Heb. 10:12-14

10. The intercessory prayers of Jesus Christ and His advocacy when we sin guarantee that our salvation will be completed eternally. John 17:9-12, 24; Heb. 7:25; 1 John 2:1

11. The Bible speaks of salvation in the passive voice, which indicates that the causality is not with us, but with God; therefore, it is based upon His work not ours. Eph. 2:5, 8; 2 Thess. 2:10; 1 Tim. 2:4

12. The Bible demonstrates by example (Abraham, David, Israel) and by precept that God is faithful to His eternal promises even when we are not. Ps. 89:30-37; Rom. 3:3-4; 4:16; 2 Tim. 2:13

Some problems with denying eternal security

Denying eternal security presents many problems, such as: How much sin or which sins forfeit salvation? How many times can a person be born again? Is there no degree of intimacy with God beyond mere acceptance or rejection by Him? Is there no consequence for a believer's sin other than Hell? If a person believes in Christ and is saved, but sins and loses that salvation, then what is left to believe that he has not already believed? A condition other than faith alone becomes necessary. It is easy to see that without eternal security, assurance becomes impossible and there is no solid foundation for Christian growth.

What about those other passages?

There are a number of Bible passages commonly cited by those who do not believe in eternal security. It would be impossible to address them all here individually. When interpreted consistently and correctly, each of these passages can be understood in a way that harmonizes with eternal security. First, they must be interpreted faithful to the context, which considers the eternal state of the readers and the purpose of the author. Second, they must be consistent with the over-arching plan of God to bless us eternally by His grace. Third, they must harmonize with the consistent teaching of justification by grace through faith alone apart from works or any other merit. Fourth, some of these passages are referring to the loss of reward, not eternal life. Fifth, some of these passages are conditions for discipleship, not eternal life.

What about providing a license to sin?

The most common objection to eternal security is that it is a convenient excuse to sin. After all, the objector would say, if a person is guaranteed eternal life, then he can do whatever he wants without fear of consequence. But this argument is weak for a number of reasons. First, an argument from a hypothetical or real (though rare) experience, does not determine the truthfulness of a doctrine. Second, while some who hold to eternal security may sin and excuse it, the same is true for those who reject eternal security. Third, the nature of salvation by grace is that it teaches the believer to deny ungodliness and to live for God (Titus 2:11-12). Fourth, new birth results in a new person with a new capacity for spiritual things. There is a new relationship with God (Rom. 6:1-5), a new freedom not to sin (Rom. 6:6-14), a new life (Rom. 6:11; Eph. 2:1), and a new perspective and orientation (2 Cor. 5:17). Fifth, the Bible teaches that there are severe consequences and loss of rewards for believers who live sinfully (1 Cor. 3:12-15; 5:5; 9:27; 2 Cor. 5:10), which is one motivation to live a godly life.

Some Implications

The eternal security of the believer (the objective reality that one possesses eternal life) is a separate issue from the assurance of the believer (the subjective realization that one possesses eternal life). However, if one does not believe in eternal security, then there will inevitably be occasions when that person loses his assurance. There are also those who may profess to know Christ as Savior, but they do not possess eternal life and therefore have no eternal security and only a false assurance. The doctrine of the eternal security of the believer in Christ ultimately rests in the character of God who is faithful to His Word, and also in the freeness of His grace.

What is "Free Grace Theology"?[16]

2

THEOLOGICAL LABELS ARE a convenient way to summarize belief systems. Many labels have become an established part of theological dialogue, like *Arminianism, Calvinism, amillennialism,* or *premillennialism*. Many who hear the label "Free Grace Theology" wonder what it means. Here is a brief summation.

1. **Free Grace teaches that the grace of salvation is absolutely free.** This is the obvious place to begin, though it should be unnecessary to say this since the word *grace* (Greek *charis*) essentially means a free and undeserved gift. However, since some speak of *costly* or *cheap* grace, it is necessary to clarify that grace is totally *free*. That does not mean it is free to the giver, who in this case is God, but it means that no payment or merit is required from those to whom it is offered, which would be all unsaved and undeserving sinners. Romans 3:24 distinguishes between the free gift to the recipient and the cost to the Giver: "having been justified freely by His grace through the redemption that is in Christ Jesus."

2. **Free Grace means that the grace of salvation can be received only through faith.** Since we as sinners can do nothing to earn God's grace, it has to be given as a gift, which can only be received through faith. By *faith* (or *believing*, which is from the same Greek word), we mean the human response of accepting something as true and trustworthy. It is a conviction, an inner persuasion. This definition precludes any other

---

16 This is adapted from Charles Bing, GraceNotes, no. 67, "What Is Free Grace Theology?" at http://www.gracelife.org/resources/gracenotes/?id=67.

conditions of works, performance, or merit (Rom. 4:4-5). Faith cannot be defined by obedience to Christian commands, baptism, surrender, commitment of one's life to God, or turning from sins. These things can and should be the results of faith, but they are distinct from faith itself, otherwise grace ceases to be grace (Rom. 11:6). Ephesians 2:8 says, "For by grace you have been saved through faith, not by works . . ." Faith is a simple response, but that does not mean that it is an easy one. Many who hold to Free Grace believe that repentance, as a change of mind or heart, can sometimes be used to describe the aspect of faith in which we come to a conviction or persuasion about something. Other Free Grace proponents do not think repentance (as turning from sins) has any role in salvation or saving faith.

3. **Free Grace believes the object of faith is the Lord Jesus Christ.** Faith must always have an object, because faith itself is not the effective cause of our salvation (We are saved "by grace"), but the instrumental means through which we are saved ("through faith"). The One who actually saves us is the Lord Jesus Christ. But it is not any Jesus, it is Jesus as the Son of God who died for our sins and rose again and guarantees eternal salvation to all who believe in Him.

4. **Free Grace holds to the finished work of Christ.** Grace is free because Jesus Christ did all the work on our behalf. His proclamation "It is finished" on the cross means that He made the final and full payment for the penalty of our sins. It also means we cannot add anything to what Jesus accomplished. We cannot do anything to earn our salvation or to keep our salvation. Free Grace therefore teaches eternal security for the believer.

5. **Free grace provides the only basis for assurance of salvation.** Any system or belief that requires our performance cannot give assurance of salvation. Human performance is subjective, variable, unpredictable, and always imperfect. Faith must rest in Jesus Christ and His promise as revealed in the Word of God. The person and work of Christ and the Word of God are objective truths that cannot change. Therefore, Free Grace offers the only basis for full assurance of salvation.

6. **Free Grace distinguishes between salvation and discipleship.** While some theological systems believe that all Christians are disciples, Free Grace understands that the condition for eternal salvation (believe) is distinct from the many conditions for discipleship (deny oneself,

take up your cross, follow Christ, abide in His Word, love Christ more than your family, etc.). Since grace is absolutely free, it cannot demand these conditions or it ceases to be grace. Free Grace believes that the commitments of discipleship should be the result of salvation, not the requirement. To make them conditions of salvation inserts works and human merit into the gospel of grace.

7. **Free Grace teaches that the Christian life is also by grace through faith.** Since we are saved by grace and kept saved by grace, we also grow by grace that is accessed through faith. Grace provides everything we don't deserve and more for anything we need. Just as in salvation, the grace to grow is available to us through faith: "through whom [the Lord Jesus Christ] also we have access by faith into this grace in which we stand . . ." (Rom. 5:2; cf. Gal. 2:20).

8. **Free Grace provides the best motivation for godly living.** If salvation is by human performance, there is no assurance, and if there is no assurance, a motivation for good conduct easily becomes to prove we are saved or to avoid hell. Guilt, fear, and doubt can produce *good* conduct, but not necessarily *godly* conduct. Godly conduct includes the inner motivations of love and gratitude. The assurance of God's grace and the finished work of Christ allow Christians to grow in an environment of freedom and unconditional love (Titus 2:11-12).

9. **Free Grace holds that the Christian is accountable.** According to Free Grace, the believer is set free from any demands of the law or works as a basis for eternal salvation. But Free Grace also teaches that Christians should live godly lives because: 1) We should be grateful for what God has done (Rom. 12:1-2); 2) God wants us to have good works (Eph. 2:10); 3) We have a new position in Christ (Rom. 6:1-14); 4) We have a new Master—Jesus (Rom. 6:15-23); and 5) We have a new power—the Holy Spirit (Rom. 8:1-11). Because of these things, Free Grace teaches that God will hold us accountable for the kind of lives we lead. God can discipline us in this life (Heb. 12:5-11), and we will face the future Judgment Seat of Christ where believers will give an account to God (Rom. 14:10-12; 1 Cor. 3:11-4:5; 2 Cor. 5:10). In this judgment, believers will be rewarded or denied rewards. In no way does Free Grace teach that Christians can sin without consequence.

10. **Free Grace is committed first to an accurate interpretation of the Bible.** This should go without saying, but is necessary because many

have forced their theological systems on their interpretations instead of letting the Bible speak for itself. The Free Grace system is the result of a literal and plain sense approach to the Bible that considers God's various ways of administering His plan for the world through the ages, and the proper contexts of any Bible passage. The Free Grace system seeks above all to be biblical. Its first commitment is not to a theological system, but to what the Bible says, even if some particulars cannot be reconciled easily to other teachings or traditional interpretations. Therefore, the Free Grace position allows for various interpretations of some biblical passages as long as they are consistent with good principles of Bible interpretation and the clear teaching of God's free grace.

Conclusion

Free Grace theology begins with the plain and clear teaching of the Bible that grace is absolutely free. From this, the Bible's teachings about salvation, faith, security, assurance, the Christian life, and discipleship are viewed consistent with the unconditional nature of grace. The free grace of God should motivate Christians to worship, serve, and live godly for the "God of all grace" (1 Pet. 5:10) who "first loved us" (1 John 4:19).

Scripture Index

Old Testament

Genesis
2:17, 40, 48
3:9-10, 40
12:3, 108
15:6, 25, 215
15:8-21, 25

Exodus
22:20-22, 197
33:20, 207

Numbers
11:1-3, 197
12:7, 200
15:22-29, 204
15:30-31, 205, 206
21:3, 167

Deuteronomy
4:24, 197, 208
6:6, 42
13:1-6, 68
18:20-22, 68
21:23, 75
30:12-14, 155
32:35-36, 206

Joshua
6:17, 167
7:12, 167
11:23, 199

Judges
1:17, 167
3:11, 199
5:31, 199

1 Samuel
2:12, 33
12:1-14, 230

2 Chronicles
7:14, 112

Psalm
7:1, 46
18:3, 46
32:1-5, 230
45:7, 199
66:12, 197
78:21, 197
79:5, 197
89:30-37, 276

Proverbs
10:27, 210
11:29, 210
Isaiah
9:19, 197
66:16, 159

Jeremiah
11:16, 197

Lamentations
2:3-4, 34, 197
4:11, 34

Ezekiel
18:4, 10
36:25-27, 118

Daniel
9:27, 97
12:1, 245

Joel
2:32, 155, 156

Amos
2:5, 34, 197

Jonah
4:3, 206

Habakkuk
2:4, 51

Zephaniah
1:18, 197

Zechariah
12:2-9, 87
12:10, 101
13:9, 159
14:11, 167

New Testament

3:22-27, 84
3:28, 85
3:28-30, 84
3:29, 84
4:2-20, 87
4:10-12, 88, 90
4:19, 89
7:1-9, 62
8:34, 74, 75
8:34-38, 265
8:35-37, 50
8:35-38, 77
8:38, 78, 79
9:33-35, 65
9:36-37, 65
9:38, 95
9:43-48, 65
10:15, 81
10:17, 82, 162
10:17-27, 80
10:21, 82, 83
10:27, 83
10:28, 83
10:30, 83
10:38, 75
11:25-26, 66, 92
12:38-40, 108, 264
13:1-2, 205
13:13, 86
14:4, 139
16:9-20, 113
16:16, 113, 114

Luke
1:29, 45
3:3-17, 111
3:6, 207, 238
3:7-14, 112
3:8, 52
3:20, 62
4:13, 89
5:1-11, 70, 71
5:10, 265
5:32, 52, 111

6:47, 128
7:35, 236
8:4-8, 87
8:9-10, 88, 90
8:11-15, 87
8:12, 88
8:14, 89
8:21, 128
9:23, 53, 74, 76, 129
9:23-26, 265
9:24-25, 50
9:24-26, 77
9:25, 77
9:26, 78, 79
10:13, 52
10:16, 128
11:32, 52
12:8-9, 78, 79
12:42, 97
12:42-48, 97
12:47-48, 98
13:3, 52
13:5, 52
13:24-30, 69
13:28, 69
14:26, 54, 71, 72, 81
14:27, 74, 75
14:33, 81
15:1-3, 111
15:4-10, 110
15:11-32, 109
15:17, 110
16:10-12, 266
16:19-31, 56
18:17, 81
18:18, 82, 162
18:18-23, 80
18:22, 82, 83
18:27, 83
18:28, 83
18:30, 83
19:10, 90
19:11-19, 191
19:11-27, 102, 104

19:16-19, 105
19:27, 105
20:46-47, 108
21:5-6, 205
21:19, 86
22:27-30, 108
22:31-32, 39
22:34, 188
22:42, 75
22:54-62, 188
24:47, 52

John
1:3-4, 24, 58
1:3-8, 66
1:4, 116
1:6, 238
1:9, 66
1:12, 116
1:18, 207
1:28, 71
1:35-42, 71
1:43, 71
1:47-49, 117
1:50-51, 117
2:3-5, 58
2:11, 71, 75, 117
2:23, 116
2:23-25, 116
2:28, 95, 98
3:1-4, 129
3:1-16, 118, 275
3:1-18, 119
3:1-21, 62
3:3, 22, 102
3:5, 25, 117, 118
3:9, 238
3:10, 238
3:15, 115, 124
3:16, 25, 87, 118, 272
3:17, 46
3:18, 116, 120
3:18-21, 121
3:20, 122

5:26, 118
5:27, 228
6:21, 266

Philippians
1:3-7, 178
1:6, 177
1:19, 35
1:27-28, 179
2:11-12, 178
2:12-13, 180
3:3-9, 193
3:10, 58
3:10-14, 265
3:11-14, 22
3:12-14, 182
3:14, 22

Colossians
1:5-6, 45
1:7, 266
1:13, 272
1:21-23, 184, 272
1:22, 240
1:23, 240
2:13, 86, 221
2:13-14, 66, 272, 276
2:14, 58
2:18, 51
3:13, 67
4:7, 266
4:9, 266

1 Thessalonians
1:3, 186
1:10, 221
2:12, 223
4:13-5, 97
4:13-17, 272
4:14, 126
4:17, 101
5:1-, 221
5:1-11, 102
5:12-13, 101

5:21, 165
5:23, 38, 185, 273

2 Thessalonians
1:3-4, 187
1:7-9, 25
1:9, 96
1:11, 187
3:6-15, 271
3:7, 53
3:9, 53

1 Timothy
1:19-20, 187
1:20, 38
2:4, 276
4:1-3, 166
4:16, 46, 188
5:8, 191
5:14-15, 188
6:12, 47
6:17-19, 108, 189
6:18-19, 41, 42
6:20-21, 188

2 Timothy
1:11, 266
1:12, 126
1:15, 166, 188
2:3, 191
2:10-13, 108, 153, 190
2:12, 103, 200, 223, 273
2:13, 188, 276
2:17-18, 166
2:18, 188
2:24-25, 13
2:24-26, 188
2:25, 52
2:26, 235
4:7, 266
4:7-8, 192
4:8, 273
4:9-10, 188

4:10, 166
4:14-16, 166, 188

Titus
2:11-12, 277, 281
2:11-14, 269
3:5, 22, 81
3:8, 126

Hebrews
2:1-4, 198
3:18-19, 197, 198
5:9, 200
5:11-13, 22
5:14, 22
6:1, 52
6:1-10, 201
6:7-8, 56
6:8, 35, 41
6:10, 245
8:10, 268
8:13, 9
9:27, 249
10:10, 38
10:12-14, 276
10:23, 165, 191
10:26-31, 203
10:27, 57
10:30, 57
11:6, 51
11:12, 49
12:1, 191
12:5-7, 56, 247
12:5-11, 25, 269, 281
12:14, 206, 238
12:15, 139
12:25-29, 208
12:29, 57
13:6, 178

James
1:2-4, 191
1:12, 191, 193
1:15, 209, 214

1:21, 50, 210, 219
1:25, 268
2:1, 92
2:10, 26
2:11, 217
2:12, 268
2:12-13, 92, 210
2:13, 92
2:14, 46
2:14-26, 211
2:17, 41
2:20, 49
2:21-25, 223
2:23, 50, 126
2:24, 40, 41
2:26, 49
3:1, 92
3:15-17, 235
5:9, 216
5:19-20, 217
5:20, 50, 210, 269

1 Peter
1:7, 159, 197
1:9, 50, 218
1:15, 227
1:17, 266
3:6, 236
3:21, 220
5:4, 193, 219, 273
5:10, 180, 271, 282

2 Peter
1:1-11, 96
1:5-9, 240
1:9, 247
1:10, 240
1:10-11, 222, 240
1:11, 240
2:1, 13
2:1-3, 68
2:1-22, 224
2:10, 68
2:12-15, 68

3:9, 52
3:14-18, 227
3:16, 139
3:18, 22

1 John
1:3-4, 24, 58
1:3-8, 66
1:6, 229, 238
1:8, 229
1:9, 154, 230
1:10, 229
2:1, 276
2:3-4, 231
2:3-5, 58
2:9, 231
2:11, 231
2:28, 95, 98, 273
3:2, 207
3:3, 102, 186
3:6, 233, 239
3:8, 235
3:9, 238
3:9-10, 233
3:10, 235, 238
3:23, 144
4:6, 128
4:7-8, 232
4:16, 232, 265
4:18, 266
4:19, 72, 168, 265, 282
4:21, 265
5:4-5, 242
5:11-13, 152, 262
5:16, 178, 218, 236, 243, 269

Revelation
2:5, 52
2:7, 241
2:11, 241, 245
2:16, 52
2:17, 241
2:26-27, 103, 191

3:3, 52
3:5, 241, 244, 247
3:12, 241
3:15-16, 246
3:18, 159
3:19, 52
3:20, 247
3:21, 191, 241
4:10, 266
7:3-8, 107
12:4-6, 97
12:17, 107
13:16-17, 106
14:1-7, 107
19:7-8, 100
19:7-8--, 94
20:4, 250
20:4-5, 106
20:4-15, 121
20:5, 250
20:6, 272
20:11, 250
20:11-15, 25, 28, 54, 56, 106, 159, 249, 250
20:12, 27
20:12-13, 108
20:14, 40, 96
20:14-15, 49
21:4, 273
21:6, 243, 251
21:8, 250
22:3-5, 191
22:12, 252, 272
22:17, 252

CPSIA information can be obtained at www.ICGtesting.com
Printed in the USA
LVOW01s0506300915

456292LV00004BA/10/P